HAND IN PAW

Nancy Schlentz

Praise for *Hand in Paw*

Hand in Paw invites us into the rich and amazing world of animal communication. An ordained Interfaith Chaplain, Nancy shares her powerful and touching journey from an intuitive longing to communicate with the non-human world to full realization of its rich chorus of voices. From her family of animals, to the world of birds, coyotes, dolphins, llamas, and animal spirit guides, to the oceans and the earth herself, Nancy shares the profound guidance and wisdom of our countless non-human companions, and what it means to love an animal, not as a pet but as friend, family member, and spirit guide.

It came as no surprise to me that I have grown closer to my own aging friend Bugsy, our eight-year-old rescue dog, who teaches me how to live cheerfully with arthritis, blindness, and too many stairs.

— **John C. Robinson**, Ph.D., D.Min., Author of *Three Secrets of Aging, Bedtime Stories for Elders,* and *What Aging Men Want*

I am touched by Nancy's ability to paint beautiful pictures with words, of the world around her, and of her spiritual experience. Nancy depicts the connection that humans can have with animals on the physical plane and in the spirit realm. You will be blessed in the reading of the special relationship and deep connection between a cat his human.

— **Rev. Jim Larkin**, Faculty of the Chaplaincy Institute and Co-Director of Tree of Life Teachings

Nancy's courageous, heartfelt journey unveils masterful gifts of wisdom that animals and the universe hold and lovingly encourage us to discover. Their teachings bring new dimensions to our life purpose and demonstrate how we are all connected.

— **Cheryl M. Ramos**, D.V.M., Jikiden Reiki Practitioner and Owner, Pets Eternal Rest

Join Chaplain Nancy Schluntz in her compelling journey, facilitated by an exceptional cat named Tyson, into the intriguing world of animal communication.

— **Marta Williams**, Biologist and author of *My Animal My Self, Learning Their Language, Beyond Words,* and *Ask Your Animal*

HAND IN PAW
A JOURNEY OF TRUST AND DISCOVERY

Nancy Schluntz

Printed by CreateSpace
Charleston, South Carolina

Tyson's and the author's poems "Ode to the Cat," "Thoughts on Leaving," and "Night Journey" were previously published in Species Link, Winter 2009.

Editor: Nancy Carleton, www.NancyCarleton.com

Cover Design: Nikki Ragsdale, www.onesourcegraphics.com

Photography: Nancy Schluntz

Author Photograph: Sean Schluntz,
    www.wanderingwolfphoto.net

Book Design & Composition:
    ©2013 BookDesignTemplates.com

Available from Amazon.com, CreateSpace.com, and other retail outlets. Also available in e-book format from Amazon.com.

A portion of the proceeds from sales of this book will be donated to animal-welfare organizations.

Hand in Paw / Nancy Schluntz

ISBN-13: 978-1499246483; ISBN-10: 149924648X

Library of Congress Control Number: 2014913278

CreateSpace Independent Publishing Platform, North Charleston, SC

I offer this book as a gift of love and gratitude to Tyson
—Poet, Pirate Cat, and Master Teacher—
who journeyed hand in paw with me
and taught me about trust
as we walked the many twists and turns of this path;
and to the animals who have been and are
part of my life.
May their words and wisdom guide you
through your own journey.

— *N.S.*

Ode to the Cat

Creature of substance,
sleek and bright,
quiet as fur-fall
deep in the night.
Primal instincts
under the skin—
not so docile,
the tiger within.

— Tyson Cat

Contents

Prologue: Transitions

Life is everlasting. It matters not the form.
Life folds in and over itself in the process of living.
Life is ever an adventure well worth the effort.
Life is a lot of fun.
                        — *Tyson Cat*

Tyson was dying. He'd made the how of his crossing clear—he wanted to do it his way, to have the fullness of the experience of dying, as he had of living. The when shifted as new things captured his interest, or he simply changed his mind. My master teacher and beloved commentator loved being a cat. He didn't like being an old cat.

The furry gray kitten who'd first come to us one June day in 1990, eighteen years earlier, had given early clues to the path we would journey together. Our daughter, Gwen, watched a semiferal tabby give birth to Tyson in the woods near her fiancé's house in the coastal mountains of Northern California. She somehow knew he would be a strong successor to Hendrix, our large male orange-and-white angora cat who'd died the previous January.

Six weeks after Tyson's birth, our family gathered on Father's Day. Soft June morning sunlight filtered through a liquid-amber tree outside the front window of our suburban Woodward, California, house. I sat on the ivory leather couch beside my husband, Gregg, with Paddy Paws, our petite black-and-white female cat, in my lap. Gwen's

1

untamed strawberry-blonde mane bounced as she came to a halt in front of her father. With an impish grin, she handed him a small towel-wrapped bundle. "Happy Father's Day, Dad!"

Gregg looked suspicious. His hands dwarfed hers as they transferred the lumpy bundle. "This isn't a cat, is it?" After Hendrix died Gregg had told us, "No more animals!"

"I knew he was special," Gwen said, ignoring Gregg's question. Gray ears and eyes poked out of the towel, followed by a fuzzy body and skinny kitten tail. Paddy Paws promptly spat at the newcomer. Her hostile reaction left no doubt about her resentment over this intrusion into her rare opportunity to be Only Cat. The kitten responded by sinking needle-sharp claws into Gregg's kneecap. The resulting howl sent two women into fits of laughter and two cats into opposite corners of the room. Paddy glared and hissed from atop the couch, engraving its slippery leather with claw marks. The kitten hid behind a potted schefflera tree, wondering what had just happened. Then the tree caught his interest, and he proceeded to climb it.

What was our daughter thinking? This kitten was so flea ridden we bathed him every day for weeks. Gregg's large hands easily held the dripping, wide-eyed kitten we named Tyson, who came to regard baths as a demonstration of affection. After that he had no fear of water. The oval bathroom sink became one of his favorite places to curl up for a nap.

Tyson was perpetually hungry, fearless, and he rose on his hind legs to box anything that moved. Gwen was right. From the beginning, he stood out as a being who knew what it meant to bc a cat and very much enjoyed it.

He came to us at a time of transition. Gwen, twenty-eight, had moved out on her own several years earlier.

Sean, our youngest child, had just graduated high school and was preparing to spread his wings at college. Gregg would soon be intrigued by new high-tech challenges offered by a small company in Boulder, Colorado. I had flowed from operating a home-based editing and technical-writing business to contract work for a nonprofit agency, presidency of a community-service group, and a brief sojourn as a real-estate loan officer—each rewarding in its way but none filling the undefined yet keenly felt need growing within me.

Perhaps the change I'd asked for three years earlier had begun. Great excitement had surrounded an event called the Harmonic Convergence on August 16–17, 1987. In his book *The Mayan Factor*, author José Argüelles wrote that on that date "the resonant frequency of the earth grid [would] shift." I'd stood on our second-floor back deck that day, looking down an unbroken slope of California native grasses, coast live oak, and eucalyptus trees to bay laurel trees that lined the creek below. I hoped for a sudden awakening, something to make everything fall into place. I had overlooked the prophecy's second part: The Harmonic Convergence marked the *beginning* of a twenty-five-year transition period culminating on winter solstice 2012. The intervening years offered an opportunity to balance the duality of our existence—light and dark, male and female, enlightenment and ignorance. I, however, wanted a shift *right now*.

Over twenty years later, I've learned that everything comes together in its own time. It's the journey that teaches us. A professor once told me, "Ninety percent of erosion occurs during storms." Storms within as well as storms without.

Storms within were familiar territory. I was born in an oil workers' town in South America, and lived in Colombia, Peru, and Argentina until my late teens. I developed an observer's view of culture and community, and had felt like an outsider for as long as I could remember—with other children in the oil town; at boarding school; as a new transplant at a high school where everyone else had known one another since junior high; even as an adult circling the periphery of any group. I was happier in or under a tree than with other people.

Teachers crossed my path who introduced me to crystals, pendulum dowsing, alternative religions, spirit guides, New Age thought, and asked good questions. I claimed Seeker as my identity. What I sought changed as I stumbled along the path. I felt a deep, intuitive connection to animals and nature, but had not yet learned what a significant role animals—especially fuzzy, gray Tyson—would play in my life.

In November 1990, when Tyson was six months old, Gregg applied for a position with a small startup computer manufacturing company in Boulder, Colorado. We were both excited by the prospect of moving to the front range of the Rocky Mountains. The following January, Gregg rented an apartment and moved there, while I stayed in Woodward to finish projects, pack our house, and help Sean move into an apartment. Our real move would come in June.

Tyson missed Gregg and searched for him, checking all the places Gregg used to sit as well as any nooks and crannies he could squeeze his kitten self into. He found treasures on these hunts—wads of paper, corks, thread spools—and delighted in them as much as in any moving prey. In one of his favorite games, he chased a six-inch strip of insulation that had worked loose from under our front door. It looked like a wiggling mouse tail when the door swung shut. He caught it time after time, and always let it go. The game was in the chasing.

One night I sat in the living room reading, while Tyson wrestled with one of his unseen foes on the upper stair landing behind me. He bumped and thumped as he rolled against the spindly railings. Then I heard a different thump. Tyson had fallen through the rails and landed on the tile entry below! He stood, shaken. I fell to my knees beside him, felt his bones, and checked his eyes. Were his pupils dilated? No. He shook his head. He groomed himself, pretending nonchalance. I watched to see if he developed symptoms of concussion. His body parts seemed to work just fine. After a minute or two, he stood, perfectly balanced, and raced upstairs to continue his game. I followed, and stretched fabric across the railing. He's such a funny kitty, I thought, and realized how much I loved him.

Paddy Paws felt differently. She remained standoffish, resenting Tyson's intrusion on her Only Cat status. Tyson stalked and teased. They growled and swiped at each other. As packed boxes grew in piles, both cats inspected the progress, and found new cubbies to nap in. One morning, Paddy Paws and Tyson refrained from growling at each other as they passed on the stairs. I sent them a mental thank-you. Even a short period of peaceful coexistence was welcome.

Watching gray Tyson and petite Paddy Paws helped me become more attuned to the natural world around me. Our second-floor back deck provided a place to watch the procession of wildlife. A pair of red-tail hawks nested nearby. They rose in easy circles on warm air currents. I now noticed deer, when they must have been there all along; Tyson in his grayness, and Paddy on a ladder, looked at me as if to say: *Look at me!* Why hadn't I noticed them?

When did I first become conscious of the teachers within Tyson and other animals? The slow movement of Project Unfolding Nancy, the beginning of the end of my years of wandering in a spiritual desert, began with uprooting. Those exposed roots, an encounter with a snapping turtle, and an early-morning adventure with Tyson helped me take the first steps on my new path.

New Beginnings

They are so big, the people.
Tall giants reaching to the sky.
Clumsy, bumping into things and walls,
needing eyes to see.
Strong. Their touch can be light as a whisker
or squeeze my breath out.
Slow to hear, they can be guided
by the loudness of my purr.
                                    — *Tyson Cat*

Moving day, June 1991. Gregg adjusted his sunglasses against the glare and settled his lanky, six-foot-four-inch frame into the driver's seat of the orange-and-white U-Haul truck. My five feet ten inches fit between bundles tucked beside and under the passenger seat. Two cat carriers nestled in the back seat. At first we faced them away from each other. A year after Tyson had arrived, he and Paddy Paws still weren't getting along well. Later in the trip we turned their carriers around. Shared misery seemed better than isolation.

Both cats wore harnesses with matching leashes. Paddy, ever the lady, seemed happy to wear the scarlet harness that accentuated her glossy, long black-and-white fur and green eyes. Tyson was an unwilling prisoner in his. I tried four different harnesses to find one that would stay on him. He rolled just so on the carpet to unbuckle the leather one. Velcro fasteners didn't last fifteen seconds. The woven harness with clips took longer, but he contorted his front legs out of it and shook it off his head with a victorious *So there!* Back to the pet-supply store I went, and returned with a leather version tight enough to hold him yet flexible enough to be comfortable. The teal color complemented his pewter-gray fur and his now green-gold eyes.

We said final goodbyes to our neighbors, and drove east to new beginnings.

The cats took turns howling and suffering in silence for a few hours, and then settled in for the long haul. Tyson chafed at confinement. The next day in the truck, we opened the cat-carrier doors. While we drove across sage-brush country and the undulating hills and valleys that stretch fingerlike from north to south across Nevada, Paddy explored briefly, and then returned to the safety of her carrier. Tyson inspected every inch of the truck's cab. I extracted him from beneath Gregg's feet. He finally settled in a little well under Gregg's seat. At every stop we went through the ritual of "Where's Tyson?" before we could open a door.

On the fourth day, my heart sang when we crested a hill and looked down into the green bowl of Boulder Valley, nestled against the Front Range of the Rockies and the landmark Flatirons Formation. Patches of snow lingered in shadows. Boulder Creek flowed out of the mountains and through town. We could see the red-tiled roofs of the University of Colorado. This place spoke to my soul in a way I hadn't heard since I was a little girl in an oil town in the jungles of Colombia, where I was born. I felt welcomed by the land.

We pulled up at the apartment Gregg had rented in the city's southwest section. The last light of day silhouetted mountains behind the buildings. The cats were our first concern. We brought their carriers inside and released them in the bedroom. They knew their long ride was over. Paddy's first order of business was a thorough grooming session.

Tyson set out to explore this new place with all the pent-up energy of a one-year-old cat. Windows in the garden-level apartment were level with outside shrubs. Sills made a perfect perch to watch outside activity. Tyson didn't just want to watch. He sat in the window, gray fur ruffled and lower jaw chattering, mewling at birds. Glass was such a frustrating barrier!

Boxes stacked in corners made platforms for Tyson to leap several feet onto other boxes, furniture, and people. Late June brought an infestation of cream-colored moths. He caught some in midair. He launched himself at windows in pursuit of his fluttery prey, snagged curtains, and rode to the hemline by a claw. In less than a week Tiger Tyson had shredded the curtains. We sighed our security deposit goodbye.

We spent three trying months in that apartment until our new house closed escrow. Paddy Paws responded to her confinement with obsessive grooming. Tyson's creativity at finding ways to escape shredded our nerves as thoroughly as the curtains.

Moving brought relief. We wanted to keep Paddy and Tyson inside for at least two weeks until they settled in and recognized our new house as theirs. Both gave us that look, conveying as clearly as if they had said: *We know where we live—we live with you.*

I told people in Woodward that the Boulder Adventure, as we came to call it, was the best thing that had happened for

Gregg in years. At first I thought the chance for him to be a vice president was an answer to an improperly formed prayer—the right job in the wrong place. As we deepened into moving, I realized the location itself was a separate gift.

Our house sat on a former meadow with a view to the Rockies, still dotted with snow in midsummer. It was a Colorado immigrant's dream: open floor plan, angles everywhere, and cedar siding. That siding attracted flicker woodpeckers, who regarded the house as an overgrown tree and treated it accordingly.

Each evening Gregg snapped his fingers as we walked around our neighborhood. Tyson followed the sound along our path, until the day a small white dog chased him up a birch tree. As Tyson grew older, he staked out territory around our house and patrolled it faithfully. Paddy was in charge inside, and the outside world was his. In Boulder, Tyson added Mr. Teeth & Claws to his collection of nicknames. He earned a red dot on his folder at the veterinarian's office, meaning "Watch out; this one draws blood!"

Frogs, turtles, and other crawly things lived in the irrigation creek that flowed beside our house in spring and summer. For Tyson, hunting expeditions made it worth getting wet. The result for us: vet bills to treat his repeated *Giardia* infections. Tyson competed with our yard's resident garter snake in hunts for mice. He found a rough-and-tumble buddy, which gave Paddy some relief.

Gregg's new job entailed setting up a computer manufacturing plant and hiring staff. Tyson had new things to investigate. Setting up a house kept me busy. A new environment for us all to explore, in a place that touched me on a deep level. Then rose a question I'd never needed to address: what would I do?

In Woodward, I'd flowed from one interest to another as opportunities arose, but lacked a long-term plan. In Boulder I had no history, no network, no support group, and no family other than Gregg. The prospect of redefining myself was exhilarating, frightening, and immobilizing. Without commitments or obligations, I could choose whatever I wanted to do. What was that? Needing to choose meant I couldn't flow from one thing to another any longer. My stomach clenched. I had no idea what I wanted, yet felt internal and external pressure to *do* something. Betrayed by my own lack of direction, I sank into a quicksand of panicky indecision.

I felt a twitch inside every time I passed the leafy campus of Naropa Institute, a Buddhist-inspired, contemplative-education university, but I didn't have the focus to enroll in graduate school. Nor did I have the courage to do nothing while sorting myself out. I applied for several jobs and discovered the competitive nature of the job market with Boulder's captive labor force, as a university town and a desirable place to live.

A magazine publisher told me that the firm had run an ad for one day, seeking an editor with some writing experience. They expected twenty resumes and received 120, so they tightened the prerequisites to require a degree in journalism and several years of hands-on experience. They reduced the offered salary. I competed with a dozen well-qualified candidates for a full-time position that paid $12,000 a year. Essentially, a successful applicant had to be retired, independently wealthy, or have a well-employed spouse. I didn't get the job.

Two insightful suggestions would come back to me years later. In Woodward, Pastor Dave at our church had been pleasantly surprised when I volunteered to serve on the board of Matthew House, a local nonprofit agency that provided shelter for homeless families. The agency was sponsored by a coalition of interdenominational churches. I admired the director's blend of efficiency and spirituality during my three years of board service. A month before we moved, Pastor Dave asked what I planned to do in Boulder. His brown eyes were warm and friendly as he said, "You should find a good nonprofit there and run it. With your background, management skills, and computer skills, you would do well."

"Me? Run a nonprofit agency? You've got to be kidding!" I laughed.

The second insightful suggestion came as a result of career counseling offered at the YWCA in Boulder. Results of a career aptitude test I'd taken in high school indicated I either was destined for clerical occupations or didn't understand the test directions. I knew I had a lot of brainpower, and felt let down by that assessment. But the judgment stuck. At the Y in Boulder, I took several batteries of tests, including my first Myers-Briggs personality inventory.

The YWCA counselor and I met in a high-ceilinged room in the old Y building. I felt comfortable in the sparsely furnished room, with its polished wooden floor, worn rug, and shelves of books lining the walls. The counselor expressed surprise that I'd tested as a strong introvert—that's not how I came across. I learned much later that having Leo as my astrological rising sign gave me the stage presence to hide my quaking interior self.

Gregg looked over my resume and said it was good, full of experience, and interesting, but he had no idea what he'd hire me for. I was overqualified for introductory levels. Higher levels required five years in a definable position with increasing responsibility, which I lacked.

The Y counselor concurred. She asked if I'd ever considered the ministry. "With your level of compassion and organizational ability," she said, "you could do well in the ministry."

"Me? A minister?" I laughed. In spite of my spiritual-seeker status, I couldn't see myself wearing a clerical collar and shepherding a congregational flock.

"The alternates," she suggested, "are librarian or Internal Revenue Service agent."

I learned that the federal portion of a real-estate license I'd earned for my brief stint doing home loans in California carried over to Colorado, and I'd only need to pass the state exam. I took this path of least resistance. Was that the right thing? I don't know. The Boulder real-estate experience taught me solid lessons about myself and other people. I wouldn't want to repeat it.

Even then, I met others on a spiritual path and marveled at the Universe's ability to bring teachers and kindred spirits together in any environment. The land itself did its work on me. I became attuned to the natural beauty and rhythms of the Colorado rocks, trees, creeks, and landscape. One day, perched at the edge of a cliff, I saw an eagle fly past below me. A cougar came to me in a dream and became my guide. (I learned later that Cougar's medicine is courage, and leadership.) I paid attention to stars and learned the constellations' movements and stories, especially the Winter Circle of Orion, Sirius, Procyon, Pollux, Castor, Capella, Aldebaran, and the pretty Pleiades. And the Front Range had real weather—seasons, four of them, sometimes all in one day.

Paddy Paws supported me with her gentle presence. She knew when I felt sad, worried, or discouraged. Tyson began his work on me in Boulder. We sat together quietly one spring day when an eight-inch snapping turtle came out of the creek to lay her eggs.

The turtle dug beside the driveway but couldn't seem to go deeper. Finally she gave up and started walking back toward the creek. Curious, I reached into the hole and extracted a round stone the size of a tennis ball. I held it up and called aloud to her, "Turtle, I've taken the cobblestone out of your hole, so you can finish digging and lay your eggs there."

The turtle paused, turned around, and came back. She backed into the hole, continued digging downward until her nose was even with the ground, and then began a slow, rhythmic rocking. She opened her jaws, snapped them closed, and swallowed. Snapping turtles shed tears when laying eggs, as do larger turtles. I sat still, grateful she would allow Tyson and me to witness as she laid her eggs. I asked the Universe for love and protection for her and her babies. She buried her leathery eggs, returned to the creek, and floated. Water flowed over her. Then she climbed up the grassy bank to rest. We watched for a long time, to protect her from lawnmowers and predators. Finally, she returned to the water, swam slowly upstream, and disappeared into the pond's muddy depth.

The snapping turtle had given me the great gift of showing that she understood my communication with her—the first time I knew that a wild animal could understand me.

That turtle reminded me of two earlier turtles who had come to me. The first had been in Peru, when I was seven or eight years old. I spotted a turtle sunning on a rock in the shallow Pariñas River; I scooped it up and carried it back to show my father. "You can keep it if you take good care of it," he said. Of course I would, I promised.

My father grew neat rows of lettuce, tomatoes, climbing beans, and jalapeños beside our house in the oil company's staff compound in Talara, Peru. The turtle lived in the garden, nibbling on vegetables and floating in furrows when my father watered. I forgot about it. Some time later, Dad reminded me about the turtle. I'd taken it away from its natural home, and if I didn't pay attention to it, the turtle had to go back to the river. I promised to pay attention to it, and for a little while I did. Then I forgot about it again. One day, my father told us, "We're all going to Pariñas to take the turtle home." I protested. We drove back to the river. He asked me, "Do you want to walk to the river with me to let the turtle go?"

I sank into the back seat, pouting, arms crossed tightly across my chest. "No." I saw it not as the right thing to do for the turtle, but as punishment for my failure. I didn't recognize the rare compassion my father showed, or the valuable lesson in responsibility he was offering.

The second turtle lived with me in the first apartment of my own, with then four-year-old Gwen. My father helped me build a cement block and board bookcase. Between books on the top shelf, waist high, I installed an aquarium for my snapping turtle.

I had temporary custody of a gray tabby cat, named Apathy by my former roommate. Apathy tended to be clumsy, and showed remarkably little curiosity for a cat—except for the turtle. She lay on top of the books, staring at it. Occasionally she tentatively reached out a paw, and withdrew it. Until one day I heard yowling and saw her racing around my apartment, swinging her front paw with something hanging onto it. She had finally swatted at the snapping turtle, and it bit back. I caught the cat, extracted the turtle, and returned it to its aquarium. Neither the cat nor the turtle was seriously harmed, but I thought it time to rename the cat.

The Boulder turtle had now given me a third chance to take Turtle into my heart, to receive her teachings. One of them is that turtles must stick their necks out to move forward.

The Boulder Adventure

What the caterpillar calls the end of the world,
the Master calls a butterfly.
— *Richard Bach*

Our sojourn in Boulder began a realignment of Gregg's and my relationship. In Woodward, after Gregg completed his graduate degree, he entered the all-consuming high-tech world. My world revolved around my home-based editing and word-processing business, the League of Women Voters, and the Matthew House board. Activities together became exceptions in what often seemed like parallel lives. The move made us come together on issues such as talking about our children's futures, and getting serious about finances. Moving halfway across the country uprooted assumptions we had let slide by every day, unspoken.

Boulder welcomed us, and we embraced it. A university town, Boulder blended Berkeley's eccentricities with the southwestern feel of Austin. I dubbed it "Berkeley in cowboy boots."

Gregg had visited several churches. Mountain View Methodist felt like a good fit, especially when a member brought home-baked chocolate-chip cookies as a welcome gift. Gregg grinned and said, "When I came home and found those cookies tied to my doorknob, there was no question about which church to join!"

The church provided a shared place from which to venture into the community. The A-frame structure, on a meadow with a view to mountains, seemed to breathe in high wind. The music was good, the pastor engaging, and it had a critical mass of people to support interest groups, including a rotating dinner group, a men's group, and a meditation group.

I signed up for a yearlong Disciple Bible study course, and found that everyone in the class also was searching in some way. Half the session we worked on history and context for the writings. The rest of the time we wrestled with "How does this apply to me today?"

Brass handbells tuned my inner self. I loved the big bells and deep notes, especially the resonant D. I needed to hold that heavy bell with two hands. With the bells, the world fell away and there was only music. We wore white cotton gloves to keep hand oils off the brass, caressed each bell with polishing cloths, and carefully tucked it into its niche in black suitcase carriers after a session. The church music director, accustomed to working with nonmusicians, highlighted our notes on sheet music. "Just keep the beat and play your notes when they come up," she said. If you lost your place, the music went on without you.

Friends invited us to square-dance. Gregg and I each had square-danced in our youth, but never together. It was fun to swirl through the steps; Gregg wore a Western shirt, and I wore a red-print full skirt (with petticoats!). Grasping work-callused hands to thread through an allemande left or promenade brought me solidly into right here, right now, just as the bells did.

After ski season, used rental equipment went on sale. We outfitted ourselves with cross-country skis, poles, and powder suits, and took lessons after first snowfall the next season. The instructor watched me and said, "You've never done much ice or roller skating, have you?"

"No," I said. "Why?"

He just said, "Keep your eyes on where you want to go, not on the ground. You'll go where you're looking." I would apply that lesson often.

I reveled in four distinct seasons, especially winter. Raised in South America and Texas, I had been in snow only a few times. For this child of the tropics, winter turned the world into a magical place. Captivating icicles dripped from houses and overhead wires. I loved to watch snow-flakes drift down from an indefinable place.

Our bemused cats observed our seasonal comings and goings around their own pursuits. Paddy made excursions into the protected yard, but didn't like the cold. She parked herself on a heating pad set to low for the duration of winter.

Fleas don't live at an altitude of over five thousand feet, which gave Paddy respite from her sensitivity both to fleas and to flea preventatives. She had been a three-quarter-sized cat to begin with, and now seemed even smaller. Her black fur had started to show reddish tints. The vet said losing pigmentation in dark fur was the feline equivalent of going gray. He surprised me by referring to twelve-year-old Paddy as a senior cat.

Tyson loved summer, his forays into the creek, and monitoring our yard's resident gopher snake. In winter, he didn't like unseen fingers of wind tickling his fur. He paced, and pestered. He would rather be outside, but not when snow was falling. He didn't mind snow on the ground, his gray a moving shadow across the whiteness. He and Gregg left together in the morning—Gregg for work and Tyson for his rounds—two sets of footprints on snow-dusted steps.

One spring we left the cats in care of a sitter and traveled through the Four Corners area, where Utah, Colorado, New Mexico, and Arizona come together. Our cat sitter stipulated that Tyson and Paddy Paws be kept inside when we went away. Tyson's attempts to escape, lying in wait to ambush the door when it opened, won him the sitter's watchful respect and the nicknames Tyson the Terrible and Attila the Tyson.

In Boulder, Gregg and I had fun, and remembered why we had come together. Our business pursuits weren't as much fun as the social ones. Those three years of frontline real estate gave me valuable training and experience. I enjoyed the challenge of legal and financial intricacies—pieces of a puzzle to assemble for each transaction. When I went door-to-door prospecting for listings, I often met people who "used to do real estate." It didn't take long to learn why there were so many former Realtors. The profession requires thick skin and the ability to sell yourself as the best person for the job.

I asked my broker if it would ever stop hurting when I lost a listing or a buyer to another agent. She half smiled and said, "Only when you have so many that losing one doesn't matter."

After one discouraging week, Paddy and I sat under a tree by the little pond close to our house, watching late-afternoon light play on flowing water. Tyson hunted minnows, splashing in the creek like a miniature bear hunting salmon. I wrestled with questions. "What is my purpose?" When I compared myself to others, I came out at the lesser end. I wondered where I'd gotten these blazing insecurities. I was more than willing to accept other people as they were, why not myself?

I sank into feeling unproductive, unsuccessful, and not worthwhile. Outwardly, I appeared competent and confident. Inwardly, I felt uncertain and a failure. At times I felt like my outer and inner selves were two distinct people with little connection between them.

I kept these thoughts to my journal. Gregg was deep in his own problems with work. There was no one else I felt comfortable enough with to talk this through.

The path for Gregg had turned from initial excitement into a bumpy ride. The company's major customer kept altering product specifications, yet was unwilling to adapt the timeline or cost to accommodate changes. Gregg began to suspect another agenda at play.

During a trip to Steamboat Springs in the autumn of our third year in Colorado, Gregg studied the mountain landscape from our rental condo's balcony, hands on hips in his characteristic stance. "The writing's on the wall," he said. "I expect the company to close by year's end." The parent company had tightened the purse strings, and the major customer had backed away. He felt like a pawn in a game where the rules had changed.

We drove home to Boulder the long way, through Rocky Mountain National Park, cherishing every sight: the delicate black legs of a red fox, the unmistakable nose of a bull moose, the surprising cream-colored rump of an elk cow, marmots scampering over rocks and among alpine flowers. We had entered a period of uncertainty.

What would our next steps be? If we left Boulder, where would we go? Wherever, I would again face the question of what I would do.

I lay on the grass in front of Gregg's company building one unseasonably warm October afternoon, waiting for him to gather personal things from his office. Another company employee came out of the building. He'd cleaned his office of "nonessentials—possibly also self." He apologized for sounding bitter. "I'm not just sad," he said, looking down at the cardboard box in his arms. "I'm feeling a sense of loss."

I asked Gregg if he felt a sense of grief or loss. He said, "No, just disappointment." He'd seen it coming. Some spring had gone out of his step, though. He said, "I keep trying to figure out why things didn't turn out the way I wanted them to and worked so hard for."

By November the company issued its notice of closure. Gregg helped his team members secure other positions. He wasn't as concerned for himself as for the people he'd hired. He had access to the company's computer system for a few weeks after his last official day, and logged many hours finishing documentation his team hadn't had time to do: "I want to leave it neat."

One day, his log-on was denied. Perhaps that was what made it real. His hands dropped from the computer keyboard into his lap and he said, "I really do no longer work there."

He sent out a series of resumes, and called to follow up. They didn't remember him. "I'm a nobody now," he said, "without title or position."

Gregg talked of returning to California, but we both liked Boulder. I thought: I'll do whatever's necessary to stay in Boulder. Immediately, my inner voice questioned: "What if prospecting for listings three hours every day is what's necessary?" I hesitated.

We realized that one gift of the Boulder experience was for Gregg and me to get to know each other by ourselves. When we'd married twenty years earlier, we'd each been married before and had a four-year-old child. My daughter, Gwen, lived with us until she branched out on her own. Gregg's son, Jeff, lived with his mother but visited often. Together, we gave birth to Sean. This time in Boulder was the first in our married life when we'd been alone together. Leaving, we'd lose friends, bike rides along the creek, the place itself. Church programs, especially the handbells, had been together activities. At least we wouldn't have to start over with each other again.

Small beauties took on more significance. We drove into the mountains in search of aspens, and found a forest of gold—leaves on trees and on the ground, shimmering. Even the dappled tree trunks had a pale-gold cast. We marveled that aspens were all related, connected by common roots, holding hands under ground. The photo I took of Gregg, leaning against an aspen tree in his red coat, is such a perfect scene it looks as if he'd posed against an artificial backdrop.

The holidays approached, promising to be different this year. On our first Christmas in Boulder two years before, our son Sean had joined us from California. He and a friend had explored snow country during a break from college. Gregg's son, Jeff, and his longtime girlfriend, Karen, had married at Thanksgiving. Early the following January, my mother had come from Texas, and we'd flown to California for Gwen and Allen's wedding.

The second Christmas, Gregg and I were alone, but decorated a little tree. We drove up to historic Leadville to spend a few days exploring the old Carnegie library, trying to breathe at 10,430 feet, and going on a snowmobile excursion. When we stepped out of the hotel dining room after dinner at night, the cold sucked the breath out of us.

I wanted this Christmas to be a party. My mother, Gwen and Allen, and Sean and his girlfriend, Rachel, were coming to visit. Sean had grown so much in the three years since we'd moved here. I'd heard his growing maturity in our phone calls, and seen a new solidity about him during his visits. Now came a major shift. Sean had called earlier in the fall to tell us we were going to be grandparents the following summer. At Christmas, we would meet the young woman of his choice, and the mother of our first grandchild. My baby was going to have a baby.

I bought an eight-foot-tall fluffy fir tree and put every decoration we had on it.

Gregg decided to rebuild the master bathroom.

What turned out to be our last Christmas in Boulder provided a musical high note too. Our visiting family sat in the congregation on Christmas Eve while Gregg and I, with the bell choir, played the "Carol of the Bells." Bells still rang in my ears when we walked out into the clear, starry night. The Winter Circle of Orion and friends glistened above, and crystal snow crackled on the ground. I held that moment deep in the cells of my body.

Furrows over the Rockies

Prowling in the deepening night,
wide-eyed, staring intently,
trying to make her hear my words.
— Tyson Cat

On January 6, my birthday, I wandered into the kitchen bundled in my housecoat and fluffy slippers. Gregg asked, "Aren't you going to work today?"

"I'd rather stay home. It's my birthday."

"I know it's your birthday, but you need to go to work!"

I figured he was up to something, so I dressed and went to work, disgruntled. A surprise party awaited me there. Cake, ice cream, and party plates! They knew I'd turned fifty, the older end of the spectrum in this group. The number was hard for me to comprehend. The mental shift from forty-nine to fifty was greater than the year it took.

Another party waited at home that evening. Gregg had cooked a Tex-Mex feast from favorite recipes: refried beans, enchiladas, tostadas. He'd gathered people who were significant in our Boulder lives. In this group, nearly everyone was the same age or older. I felt tender gratitude for Gregg and for those friends who welcomed me into a new age group.

A few days later, stopped at a red light at the crossroad of Foothill and Baseline Road, the major north-south and east-west arteries through Boulder, my body temperature suddenly spiked. Beads of sweat broke out on my forehead and upper lip. Unmistakable. My first menopausal hot flash. I didn't miss the metaphor. Here I sat at a major crossroads in Boulder, in my life, and now in my body. That night I studied my reflection in the bathroom mirror, and noticed the highlights of pretty silver threads in my wavy, dark-brown hair.

Gregg began traveling back to the San Francisco Bay Area. "I get invigorated whenever I go back there. The Bay Area is so rich in diversity it makes Boulder look bland."

From an ethnic perspective he was right, but I felt differently about the place. Boulder called to my soul in a way the Bay Area never had. The prospect of moving back to California filled Gregg with excitement, and me with sadness. Going back might be another chance for me to start over, this time with more skills, but I felt vulnerable and uncertain. The single bright spot for me was the approaching birth of our first grandchild, Sean and Rachel's baby.

In early spring a women's group formed, facilitated by Sue Thoele, who had published several women's books. Near my age, Sue had an unassuming manner over a core of confidence. I felt comfortable on the pillowed couches around a coffee table turned altar. We called ourselves the Pathfinders.

Home after the first meeting, I sat outside to watch stars emerge. In my journal I mused why, now that we were leaving, was I being introduced to a women's group while entering a new level of internal work? A revelation in itself, I realized that I often had subtle insights that served as directional correctors like steering thrusters on a spaceship. My writing was messy; Paddy delicately scratched her nose on the end of my pen while I wrote.

Tyson sensed approaching change, and with warmer weather began staying out at night. One night I couldn't sleep, and took a cup of herbal tea outside. Bright Jupiter hung above with starry companions, clouds, and distant lightning. Purring Tyson came up to me. He seemed glad for me to share his outside world at unusual times. Lines of a poem came to me:

> *Tyson, Tyson, gray as night,*
> *eyes of tiger, golden bright.*

Another voice said: *Lion.*

"What?" Startled, I looked at Tyson. He stared back, intent.

Lion, I heard again. I understood, and changed the poem:

> *Tyson, Tyson, gray as night,*
> *eyes of lion, golden bright.*

I looked at Tyson. Statue-still, he let his eyelids lower in the slow blink cats use to convey acknowledgment. The moment held, and then broke. Tyson turned to pounce on a movement in the grass. A door had cracked open, giving me a glimpse of what was to come.

Gregg's trips shifted from living in Boulder and visiting California to living in California and visiting Boulder. Friends in the Bay Area offered their guest room as long as he needed it. In early April, he drove away in the blue Bronco he'd bought to come here, towing a tightly packed, overloaded U-Haul trailer. He admitted later that he lost brakes and had trouble controlling it descending the mountains between Wyoming and Utah. He described his descent as stomach-clenched, white-knuckled determination. He'd pulled off at the first coffee shop when the road leveled out to "Let the brakes cool and my blood pressure return to a semblance of normal." Gregg tried to stay optimistic about his job search, which produced inquiries and interviews, but no offers. Concerned about cash flow, he told me, "We need you to sell a couple of more houses."

I lost several listings and buyers to other agents. At the next staff meeting I announced we were leaving, and our home would be listed for sale soon. I left after the meeting, consumed by a pervasive sense of loss. I began dispassionate closet cleaning. Piles grew—donate, sell, throw out, recycle, keep. I didn't want to haul back everything we'd brought with us.

Both cats were antsy, moving from place to place. I hoped it would be better for all of us when the disarray cleared, but for a time piles and upheaval ruled.

In mid-April, large, fluffy flakes of snow fell uniformly, softly straight down. I thought about the futile persistence of late-spring snow, flakes destined to melt when they hit the ground. How like my wish to stay in Boulder they were! Later the snow became an icy rain that fell *peck*, *peck*, on the hood of my parka. Change happens. Could I be like the snowflakes and turn as easily into ice or water, and continue to grow internally whether in Colorado or California?

My office mate from work took me to dinner one night. Over chicken caesar salads, she asked a simple question: "Do you feel more at peace now that the decision has been made?"

"I want to get on with it," I said. "I've been strung between here and there for months. I'm just not sure how to best use this time, waiting to move."

"You have an excellent opportunity," she counseled, "to let yourself—give yourself permission to—enjoy the things you've wanted to do here, but haven't. Be a tourist. Explore."

I wanted to hug her. I would have explored and felt guilty about it, and then regretted not doing more after we moved. Now I considered myself on assignment to visit the llamas pastured north of town, take long drives in the Front Range mountains, walk beside tumbling creeks. I could spend my last weeks in Boulder saying goodbye to the place.

I came home that night to a wet family room. The bottom had dropped out of the water heater. I took a sponge bath with water heated in a kettle on the stove. The next morning I called a plumber and a carpet cleaner. An inconvenient reminder that life goes on.

My task for the day was to list our house for sale. With every surface cleaned and polished, the house now felt like no one lived there—at least not us.

On Mother's Day I came home from work to find a pretty arrangement of spring flowers by the front door—cream, yellow, gold, pink. The card read: "From your family." One by one, Gregg, Gwen, and Sean called, and I felt such overwhelming love it was hard to speak. As much as I crave solitude, I enjoy it most in parallel with shared time.

The next day I spruced up the house for a showing and mowed the lawn. It was fun using an electric mower until I ran over the power cord and blew fuses to several circuits in our house.

Gregg called. I heard panic in his voice. He'd come in second on one interview after another. Discouraged, he suspected he was being used as a standard against which to measure younger candidates with less experience. The vice-president title that had seemed like such a good career move when we came to Boulder now hung like an albatross on his resume. An executive-search firm approached him to sign up for their expensive services, using words like "still looking," and questioning my faith in him with phrases like "for now."

I told him, "If there's one thing I've learned from real estate, it's what you're going through. It's hard to sell yourself. Give it time."

He asked, "What do you think you'll do back here?"

"Not frontline real estate, but it's a big industry. There'll be a place for me somewhere." My prayer became, "Help me find the occupation that's best and right for me."

Time seemed to slow during the months between Gregg's move back to California and our actual move, as it had during our similar transition from Woodward to Boulder three years earlier. One rainy day, I reflected on moving back to California. Did the hawk still roost in trees behind our house there? Did the spirit of Hendrix, Tyson's predecessor, still visit? During a break in the weather I went outside and found Tyson watching our garter snake, which had returned with warmer weather. I hoped the next people to live in our house would honor the snake as we did—a graceful dragon with no wings.

Evenings grew soft and inviting. I spread my sleeping bag on a flat place of lawn close to our slatted wooden fence, arranged my pillow, and climbed in. The ground isn't getting any softer, I noted. Waking throughout the night, even without my glasses I could see the Big Dipper's main stars overhead. It swings clockwise! I felt happy.

On an exploration into the mountains, I saw a vertical formation of majestically weathered sandstone striped in shades of pinkish red, climbed over quartzite crystal-embedded rocks, and sat in warm sun, enjoying the breeze and azure blue sky. Clouds ranged from fleecy white to tumbled gray. Lizards, wild turkeys, a couple of mule deer does and a young buck in velvet passed by. Crossing a ditch meant balancing on a pair of pipes, but I kept repeating the ski instructor's directions: "Look where you want to

go." I took pleasure in adventuring this way by myself—
another indicator that something had shifted in me.

Chosen isolation is different from loneliness, yet it can
be an easy way out. Relationship requires opening up. After
a Pathfinders gathering, Sue suggested that in meditation I
go back to the little girl who learned to put up walls, and let
her know she's loved. That a five-year-old child deep inside
me could affect my current actions was a concept I'd heard
others talk about, but hadn't applied to myself. When others
had spoken of tending to their inner child, I had given a
mental eye roll at their self-indulgence. How much I had yet
to learn!

I pulled myself together to consider why we'd had little
interest in the house. It had been on the market three
weeks, with few showings and no offers. Intuitively, I knew I
was reluctant to let it go. That evening I made a ritual of
releasing the house. I lit a candle, carried it into each room,
and said aloud, "Thank you for our life in you, for shelter-
ing us. Please say goodbye to our family, and gather energies to attract a family who will appreciate you as you
deserve."

There were two showings the next day, and a purchase
contract by week's end. The offer was acceptable, and for
cash. Two weeks to closing and moving!

I hoped Paddy and Tyson would make the move well.
Paddy seemed to grow frailer, but the vet said there was
nothing wrong with her: "She's in remarkable condition for
a cat her age." I talked to the cats about our approaching
move, and felt they understood. Tyson would miss the
creek. I hoped the waving grasses behind our Woodward
house would make up for it

I needed to let go of Boulder too. A friend gave me three envelopes that contained a parting exercise. I drove to Boulder Creek, took off my shoes, rolled up my pant legs, and held my journal high to wade out to a large boulder mid-river. Cold water splashed on me as it tumbled over and slid by rocks. Sun filtered through tree branches felt hot on my back. My journal ready, I opened the first envelope. On a yellow piece of paper within was written:

> *Listen. Listen.*
> *Listen, listen, listen,*
> *to my heart song.*
> *I will never forsake you,*
> *I will never forget you.*
> *Listen, listen, listen,*
> *to my heart song.*

I wrote: "What does me inside myself want to do when I get to Woodward? Spirit indicates that growth continues. I want to do something that is from my heart and sharing. At Pathfinders, Sue said to ask, 'What does the wise woman inside myself want to do?' Well?" I crumpled the first paper into a small ball, gave thanks, and tossed it into Boulder Creek. It bobbled away downstream.

The second envelope contained a pink piece of paper:

> *Look back with the willingness to forgive yourself*
> *and others. Forgiveness is the key to happiness.*
> *I will awaken from the dream that I am mortal, falli*
> *ble, and full of fear and know that I am the perfect*
> *daughter of God.*

I wrote: "I feel deep pleasure in the simplicity of sitting on a rock, feet splashing in water. At this moment I feel full. I can go forward and know there is infinitely more beyond." I crumpled the second paper, gave thanks, and tossed it into the river to follow the first.

The third envelope held a blue paper: *"Write your worries in the sand and see how long they last."*

There was only coarse-grained dirt, so I wrote on the paper. I listed my worries about Sean, Gwen, Gregg, and myself. My strongest fear: "I don't know what I want to do!" I watched the river and thought: The river keeps flowing. It's hard to imagine where the water comes from and where it goes. Does one part of the riverbed know what's up-stream or downstream? How does it relate to millions of drops that flow by? Does it relate at all? The river just is. I gave the paper with my worries written on it to the river, and watched it float downstream.

Three hours after wading out to sit on a rock in the middle of the river, I gave thanks to the rock, balanced against the strong current to make my way back to shore, and stood on another rock to dry my feet. That rock felt deliciously warm!

The next morning I flew to California. Sean and Rachel's baby daughter, Katherine Gwen, was born two days later. Rachel said, "I've made Sean a father, Gregg a grandfather, and Gregg's father Ken a great-grandfather, all on Father's Day!" Sean was commended for being such a good labor coach, and the most composed nonmedical person around that day.

I had mixed feelings about going back to Colorado after Katy Gwen was born. Gregg and I had been trimming the hedge at our Woodward house when a call came: "Things are starting to happen." Gregg asked if I wanted to drop everything and go, but I let his desire to finish trimming and my indecision get in the way. By the time we arrived at the hospital, the baby had been taken to the nursery. I was upset with myself for missing the chance to hold her. I hadn't realized it was so important to me, which mystified

Gregg since I'm not usually a baby person, but I felt a strong connection to this child.

Back in Boulder, I continued letting go. A succession of friends and neighbors came over to help pack or to bring food. "This isn't a time for you to be thinking about cooking," one said. I was grateful for friends who helped in this way, and with little things that Gregg had done.

My last night with the Pathfinders, everyone was letting go in some way. I cried as much as I ever had in one night. Sue asked us how we were on scale of zero to ten. I felt I was about an eight. She asked, "Is that eight from the head or from the heart?" It was from the head.

"Why this group now?" I asked. "On the verge of leaving, to find all these kindred souls?" It didn't seem fair. Yet as soon as I said that, I knew it was to show me what was possible, to give me a boost when I needed it most.

Sue led us on a visualization to see our subpersonalities and qualities they represent. In guided meditation we each went into a dark theater and waited for characters to come onstage. My first character appeared, a big orange with arms, legs, and head. It changed into traditional black-and-white jester garb. I recognized my self-deprecating humor and mastery of the one-liner joke. Then came the duke. Reserved and regal, dressed in dark-velvet doublet and tights, he looked like a character from an Elizabethan play. Then a lady in white came on stage—a lithe young woman with fair skin, wearing a long white-satin slip dress. She was so pretty! I asked if she would talk with me.

She said, *But of course, dear, I'm a part of you.*

Tears stung behind my closed eyelids at the thought that this beautiful woman could be within me. I later chose to call her Grace. I asked, "What do you need from me?"

For you to recognize that I'm within you, she answered. Her voice was as gentle as her appearance. *You're doing fine opening up. Continue as you're now doing.*

I recognized this being as my feminine self, asking me to acknowledge her. I didn't share this conversation with the group. I'd shed enough tears already.

Sue led us in a parting ceremony for my last meeting. Each person signed a sand-dollar shell and told what they appreciated about me: kind, generous, and caring; loving leadership; strength; wisdom. I felt subdued and hopeful. Each woman had qualities I treasured and would like to see within myself. Their thinking highly of me, together with my conversation with the woman in white in the meditation, cracked open my denial of my own worth. I began to consider that there might be value in who I was, after all.

Our last three days in Boulder, I rented a big U-Haul truck and hired students to pack it. Gregg flew in to help.

Tyson was more willing to wear his harness as a four-year-old than he had been as a one-year-old. The commotion was too much for our senior furry lady, and Paddy Paws disappeared. Gregg found her hiding behind the house. She was happy to be placed in her secure carrier.

At noon on July 1, Gregg's fifty-third birthday, we left Boulder. Gregg was excited about his "birthday gift of going home." I leaned against the truck's cool window glass, bit my lip, and held back my tears. I would later say that those deep furrows across the Rockies were left by my heels as I was dragged back to California.

Return of the Sojourners

Acceptance is different from settling,
or ceasing to pursue that which is beyond our reach
at a particular moment—for it is not.
— Tyson Cat

Packing boxes lined the hallway of our Woodward house. The empty U-Haul truck idled by the curb in front. Gregg and I looked at each other. "We're back." Our Colorado adventure was over.

Tyson and Paddy Paws remained confined while we unloaded. Paddy sat out the commotion contentedly in the safety of her carrier. Tyson was anxious to be released. He knew another place to explore beckoned.

Gregg left to deliver the truck. I unlatched the cat-carrier gates. A gray streak bounded out. Paddy stretched and reached out a delicate white-tipped paw. Gregg came back—he'd forgotten the rental paperwork.

"Watch out for the cats!" I called out.

"Oops." Gregg snatched the envelope of papers and turned to go out the door again. Tyson headed his way.

As the paneled door swung closed, Tyson pounced on a trailing strip of insulation. *Aha! I know this house!* I heard a joyous connection click. Tyson remembered that mouse-tail strip. He had loved to play with it as a kitten and now, three years later, it was still there for him. Tyson knew he was home.

Paddy found a spot where late-afternoon sun warmed the carpet. Her black fur shone henna in the sunlight. She attended to her first priority—thorough grooming from nose to tail.

Another time of transition unfolded, this one felt more strongly by the humans than by the cats. The high-tech world had changed since the 1970s when Gregg first entered it. Now in his fifties, Gregg had an impressive resume, but his age, experience, and manufacturing operations moving overseas combined to make his job search much longer than he'd anticipated. "It's a good thing we weren't able to sell this house," he said. "We needed it to come back to." Selling our house in Boulder gave us a few months of financial cushion.

We slipped back into our roles at church as if we'd never left. I wasn't sure about returning to the same church, and pleaded with Gregg when he moved back ahead of me, "Please, don't volunteer for anything until I get there."

The new pastor at First Methodist was more persuasive. On Gregg's first Sunday back, he walked into church and heard "Ah, our treasurer has returned from Colorado" announced from the pulpit. All eyes turned toward him. The interim treasurer happily handed over the accounting books and church keys.

On my first Sunday back in church, relief showed on the interim Matthew House board member's face. "I kept the seat warm for you," he said, and thrust a three-inch-thick black binder into my hands.

At least it helped me focus. I would have liked to simply contemplate the world, yet I also felt one of us needed to be employed. I didn't want to continue in real estate, and was drawn to work in nonprofits. I halfheartedly perused want ads and went on a few interviews.

A temporary job turned up with my friend Gail, who'd been elected to public office during our absence. She was "drowning in paper." Stacks of documents covered furniture and floor, with narrow paths from one place to another. I culled, recycled, and brought order to the paper flow. The pay brought a little ease to our concerns about dwindling cash reserves.

I'd met Gail years earlier through the League of Women Voters. She had the incessant drive of one who knows what the community needs and had adopted that as a life goal. Alison, Gail's chief of staff, was also a longtime friend and League member. Alison had a quick, discerning mind and an unfailing sense of fairness. She often asked me questions I found difficult to answer. I enjoyed working with these women again, as I had on contract projects when they managed a small local nonprofit agency. Alison modeled how to say what I meant ("Should I turn off the computer?" instead of "Will you be using the computer?"). Gail showed insight and sensitivity to how others felt and thought. Together, they demonstrated nuances and shades of gray—a different experience for me, in that I tended to draw straight lines from one place to another.

I came home one day to the welcome sight of two hawks circling in flight, and sat on our back steps to watch them and listen to their calls. Paddy climbed into my lap, having forgiven or forgotten my getting upset with her earlier that day for stealing cheese. A hawk glided directly over the house and yard, wings spread and air brakes on, and landed in a eucalyptus tree. The natural world continued to exert its steady pull on me.

Part of that natural world was a sturdy brown-and-black dog with a saucy curled tail and a wrinkled forehead. It came up out of the canyon and seemed to watch us and the neighborhood. It wore a collar. It visited regularly, cutting through our unfenced backyard on its rounds and often sleeping behind our house or on a neighbor's porch. The dog stayed well out of reach, but left behind a strong odor.

Mid-August, six weeks back from Boulder, Gregg was happy to be back. Paddy and Tyson had settled in. I wasn't settling or adjusting. Everything seemed harsh, hazy. Woodward didn't make my soul sparkle the way Boulder did. Part of it was change and the natural process of grieving. I didn't talk to Gregg about my feelings. He had plenty to worry about with his slumping self-confidence, but I was pretty sure he knew how I felt. I'll find a niche, I told myself. Numbness spread inside me.

Spots of beauty gladdened my heart, such as sneaking up to our local park at night to lie on a grassy hill and watch the Perseid meteor showers. We saw several bright ones with tails that lasted two to three seconds. It reminded me of spending a night in our yard in Boulder, watching the Big Dipper swing around the North Star. Other beauties appeared when I paused to see them: Gray Tyson regally surveyed his kingdom from a rock, then stalked and pounced on a critter, tail swishing, while a feral cat watched with detached curiosity. The sun slid behind green-gray eucalyptus trees, splashed red gold on grass and backlit leaves, emphasizing the steep hill slope down to bay trees below.

Ten months between positions for Gregg. I journaled: "He's being so hard on himself, doubting himself. How we define ourselves by our work!" Unfortunately, other measures of self-worth wouldn't staunch the flow of red tide on our financial balance sheet.

I applied for a position as director of a small local non-profit agency, even though I was uncertain whether to take the job if it were offered. Low pay and no benefits. I questioned if this were the direction I'd been preparing for. Another application to a larger nonprofit agency in Oakland, where I overpresented myself for what turned out to be a clerical job. I came in second for the first position, and was deemed overqualified for the other.

One of my complaints about the Bay Area was the lack of real weather—the seasonal and daily shifts I loved in Colorado. Yet a day came that brought bright strong winds out of the southwest, spots of sun between clouds and rain. Hawks called. Tyson, curled at foot of our bed, snored and purred at the same time. Thunder, then rain, and the skyline appeared and disappeared behind gray clouds. Stalks of pampas grass bent heavy, wet plumes to the ground.

The next morning peach streaked a nearly turquoise sky. Two delicate does stood statue still at the sound of my deck door siding open. Tyson and a couple of feral cats went about their morning rounds. Crisp, cold air, so good to breathe deep! My heart swelled with joy to see and hear the hawks. The weather turned dramatic as the rainy season started. Clouds in shades of gray scudded across the sky. Gusting winds rattled screens and shook trees. I wondered about the dog. Did it have a home? Where did it go when it rained like this?

Gregg secured a contract position as manager of the weekend shift in a disk-drive manufacturing plant. He needed to be up and out by 4:00 a.m., four days a week. I was glad he'd landed this position, even though the hours were unusual. He felt better to be working, and taking some financial pressure off. Half-waking after he left, I watched the sky change colors and felt the distinctive weights of two cats. Tyson stretched at my feet, and lighter Paddy curled beside me. Nice, I said to myself.

The November 1994 Matthew House board meeting, my third since returning to the board of directors, took place in the fellowship hall of our church. A table of refreshments— coffee, cookies, fruit, breads—stood to one side. I expected this to be another regular meeting as I found my way back into the agency. It wasn't. The director submitted her resignation effective December. The agency had financial problems, and she recommended merging with a larger nonprofit. The worn-out board president also resigned. Silence followed. I felt a pause.

The board decided to form an interim transition team to run the agency. Even with my faltering sense of worth, I volunteered to be board president and work with the outgoing director to better understand agency operations. I had admired her blend of efficient yet spiritual management, and saw shadowing her as an unpaid internship that might lead to employment with another agency. Or to finding out this also wasn't right for me.

I soon felt that I was in over my head. The volume on my inner turmoil turned to high. There was so much to do and learn. Could I rise to that level? I remembered thinking that if I'd picked anything ten or twenty years earlier and stuck with it, I'd have a sense of who I was to build on. Instead, I had a pattern of continual reinvention of self. Was this to be another cycle in that pattern? Or was I now holding myself to a higher standard? I noted ruefully that I was quite good at criticizing myself.

The Matthew House transition team soon determined that an interim executive director was needed. Again, I was the logical person. A founding board member had recently retired, and offered to step in as board president if I became interim director.

In December, an attractive job opened as grant writer for another local agency. I held that agency and its director in high regard. I applied. My initial interview was promising.

Which way to go? I couldn't do justice to both. The grant-writer position had potential to be long-term, would expand my skills, and offered mentoring by someone I trusted and respected. The interim executive-director position was a short-term, project-specific rescue.

I talked over my quandary with Gail and Alison, separately. Each gave eloquent reasons for taking the opposite approach. Alison asked which course provided the best benefit to everyone, the more logical path. She suggested I examine my motivations and asked, "For you, is it a career or a ministry [why did she use the word *ministry*?], and is fixing a crisis you didn't create the kind of experience you want?"

Gail's advice was to go with my gut feelings and be where I was needed. Gail said, "Matthew House needs you."

I asked myself, "I didn't create this mess, so why do I feel an obligation to help fix it?" My motivations clarified. I wanted to take on an important project and accomplish it well, merging Matthew House with grace and dignity into the umbrella of a larger organization. I needed to do it for me, to show myself I could measure up and follow through.

The next morning I woke rested and with a sense of calm sureness and direction. That evening, after another meeting, I knew it would be difficult but felt confident that I was doing the right thing. Time would tell. Gregg, Gail, and Alison all understood and supported my choice. It was a good feeling.

In January 1995, I became interim executive director of Matthew House. I had a six-month contract with a mandate to keep the agency operating, and to merge it with another nonprofit human service agency.

So began a thirteen-year run that would call on everything I had ever learned, and would frame one of the most significant periods of self-development in my life.

Decisions, and a Dog

Given that All is what we are,
then All That Is is all we are.
To be more or to be less is of our own doing.
— Tyson Cat

My first days at the Matthew House office were sub-merged in massaging budget numbers and trying to make sense of the remaining funder contracts. It wasn't until late on my birthday that I thought to compare this year's birthday with the last one. At fifty the year before, I was on the threshold of something. I didn't know what that something was, and had only questions. One year later, I was defending a funding proposal written by my predecessor to a hostile group of commissioners who initially recommended no funding. Matthew House was awarded only half of what our proposal requested, but it was something.

At home in the evening, I watched a lone turkey vulture roost in the eucalyptus trees behind our house, its wings closed against the drizzle and cold. Great, blustery winds danced rain against the windows. Tyson wanted to go out, but not in weather like that. The drought that plagued Northern California for several years had come to an end. I couldn't remember ever seeing such an extended period of hard-driving rain and strong winds. Real weather, I thought, even here. Flooding closed parts of freeways. Mud from denuded embankments blocked storm sewers.

The creek that flowed through town, constrained to its concrete channel, changed from a trickle to a raging brown torrent. The rain seemed to wash everything clean.

The transition team at Matthew House identified two potential partner agencies. Our program director, Mary, guided me through site visits by representatives of each agency. A licensed therapist, Mary had a gently insightful way of coaching me on how to be a director, even though she had her own job as program director and counselor. We were both overwhelmed.

I rose to a new level of responsibility and commitment: the how of a merger, and day-to-day agency operation. A major issue had been the board's overreliance on the former director; I started decentralizing administration. "I can do this with your help," I told the board. "Matthew House needs you to step up." And they did. We reminded churches that the agency was a product of their mandate to serve the poor and homeless—a covenant relationship, not just another charity with its hand out. We assured them that services for homeless families would continue regardless of the structure that resulted from a merger.

By February, Mary, board members, and I had made presentations at half the coalition churches. A wait-and-see attitude prevailed. Most churches and funders were reluctant to commit resources until they knew what would happen with the agency, yet neither potential merger partner wanted a stepchild that wasn't fully funded. A classic Catch-22. I was slowly learning to be an executive director, but still felt I'd stepped in over my head.

At home, Tyson seemed to know I needed extra kitty time and was unusually affectionate, with purr volume turned way up. After Tyson vacated my lap, Paddy took his place. We sat in our darkened living room and listened to the rising wind. I worried about the stray dog. She seemed to chew on herself a lot, and had bared a large spot on her left flank.

Then Gregg called to tell me he'd received a formal job offer, and it was good. He sounded excited and relieved. He said, "Now we can get on with our lives." It had been a year and a half without a solid full-time position for him, a period of soul-searching for both of us. I bought him a celebratory bouquet of balloons.

Gregg's celebration balloons still held air the next afternoon, when Sean and Katy came to our house. Baby Katy loved them. She sat surrounded by the balloons, pushing them and giggling when they reached the end of their strings and came back to her. She loved Paddy. I spent precious time with her while Gregg and Sean went for a job-celebration beer and to move office furniture for me. I wanted my office at Matthew House to be more open, rather than having the desk a barrier between me and others.

Later, Sean and I shared mugs of hot tea. I watched his strong hands grasp the mug, his reddish hair shining in the overhead light. I could sense him turning more inside himself. Quietly, he admitted that things weren't going well between him and Rachel. I admired how he had adjusted to his role as husband and father, and felt his feelings running deep. I told him, "We love you a lot and will always be here for you."

Gregg and I came home one day to find a complaint attached to our front door from County Animal Control: Our dog was being allowed to run loose. Our dog? I decided to make friends with her, and find her a home. Her rounds followed a regular schedule. We put water and dry dog food on our back porch. I waited on our upper deck until she appeared, and sang to her while she ate so she would become accustomed to my voice.

One morning, I saw her stare at our back door with an alert air of expectation. Then her stance sagged. She turned. Our eyes met. The sadness in her eyes flowed into my heart. What was her story? What had happened to her family? Who would abandon such a magnificent dog? I hadn't met an Akita before. This one appeared to be a purebred tricolor with a powerful front end, a thick neck, and characteristic triangular ears. Her brow furrowed between small dark eyes. The white tip of her full-curl tail bounced when she walked. Her presence was striking.

Gradually she came to trust me. I stood by the sliding-glass door while she ate, but when I opened it, she left. One day, when she had almost finished eating, I slid the door open. She started to leave, paused, and came back to finish her bowl of dog food. After a week of letting me stand nearby while she ate, she let me touch her. Eventually I was able to cut off the too-tight collar and replace it with a larger one. The name on her tooled leather collar, Boogie, didn't suit her dignity. We renamed her Buki.

Finding her a home proved a challenge. Our veterinarian estimated her age at four years old. With her age and breed, she probably would be euthanized at a shelter. The Akita rescue organizations had no room. The phone number on her tag was disconnected. People at the address of record for her dog license said she wasn't theirs. We visited potential homes with no success—partly because she smelled awful. She was patient with all these efforts, and didn't mind a leash or trips in the car.

It finally became clear that this dog was cooperating, with the understanding that she would live with us. The vet's diagnosis of Buki's smelly skin condition revealed that, after living on the street and eating garbage and food left out for feral cats, she had developed an allergic reaction. Gregg administered her allergy shots. She put up with the course of treatment, but after that was suspicious of him whenever he came near her with something slender in his hand.

Paddy was too frail to be concerned about the dog; Tyson was wary and kept his distance. He had earned his reputation with neighborhood cats and monitored his turf with resolve. A dog moving into his territory was something new.

I continued my spiritual pursuit, with several unsuccessful attempts to meet my power animal. This time, assisted by a tape of drumming, I envisioned myself at the rock in Boulder Creek where I'd done my leaving ritual. I sank below the water, came out in a cave, stepped out of the river, and was dry. A tropical jungle clearing waited outside the cave. The air felt warm, but not hot, under a clear blue sky. I met a cougar with deep gold fur. It blended into me. I could feel our paws on the ground and our tail swishing. Then, Cougar and I separated, and sat facing each other. It let me stroke it. Cougar purred. I asked, "Are you my power animal?"

Cougar blinked. *Of course.*

"What is my task?"

You will know when you are ready. Think first, and then speak from your heart.

When it was time to come back, I asked Cougar to come with me. Cougar nestled into me. We flicked our tail, stretched, and then swam back up the river. Cougar complained about that. Grace, from the meditation on my last night with the Pathfinders in Boulder, waited on the bank in her white dress. Cougar was happy to see her, and rubbed purring circles around her legs. She sprinkled sparkles over him with a sweep of her hand, and blended into him as he had into me. I recognized it as parts of myself coming together. Cougar, Grace, and I returned to my rocking chair beside the window overlooking our back deck. I said a prayer of thanks, felt warm afternoon sun and the light pressure of Paddy in my lap, and heard Tyson purring from our bed a few feet away.

I held those moments with tenderness in my heart. Paddy had always been there for me, supporting me with her gentle presence. Less than two months later, on the anniversary of our departure from Boulder, Paddy would take her last breath in my arms.

The Mantle Passes

For one species to mourn the death of another is a
noble thing.

— Aldo Leopold

If anyone thinks animals don't have plans of their own,
let's put that misconception to rest. Animals are for the
most part confident in their knowledge of who they are.
With each of our succession of cats, our relationship
deepened. Each shared special gifts, and worked steadily
on our education in his or her particular idiosyncratic way.

Paddy taught me compassion.

She came to us in 1979. We'd been without a cat for several
years, and eight-year-old Sean had started asking for a pet.

Gregg had said, "No more animals!" He didn't like the
pain of losing them. But Sean persisted, and Gregg finally
said he could have a pet—just not a cat or dog.

Sean and I went to a pet-supply store to look at guinea
pigs and hamsters. Sean couldn't pick out one he liked.

I asked him, "Would you like to take a walk and think
about it?" We left the old, wood-floored store and walked
down the street, past stores at the older end of town.

"What's up, Sean?" I asked.

"Mom," he said, "I really want a cat."

"Okay," I said, "let's go back and look at cats." The store
had a small play area with a litter of free kittens. Sean

picked out a tiny black-and-white female kitten with a black nose, green eyes, and long fur. We bought cat food, litter, and a litterbox, and headed out to our car.

"Maybe you should put her in your backpack, Sean. She may get frightened out on the street."

He placed the fluffy kitten into his red backpack. She squeezed her head through a torn seam on its side. "She looks good in red," Sean said.

We introduced the kitten to Gregg, who grumbled, "I knew you were going to bring home a cat." As he feared, Gregg quickly succumbed to the kitten's feminine charms.

Paddy Paws earned her name. She prowled the hallway outside Sean's bedroom at night, her sharp kitten claws snagging the green shag carpet. "Pad, pad, pad on your little paws," Sean chanted. Paddy Paws used those sharp claws to climb the burlap-textured wallpaper in his room. She mewed for help after she walked out the top of his open bedroom door to its edge, and then couldn't get down again.

She never grew large. We called her our three-quarter-sized cat. She was an Only Cat until we acquired Hendrix from friends who couldn't keep him any longer.

Hendrix, a large orange-and-white angora male with gold eyes, was so laid-back that Paddy could ignore him and pretend she was still an Only Cat. A brief period with a third cat changed that. The third cat, an assertive tabby female, picked fights with Paddy. Hendrix came to Paddy's defense. We found another home for the tabby, and Paddy then accepted Hendrix. It was Hendrix's death that created the void filled by young, gray Tyson.

Paddy was sensitive, and always knew when I needed comforting. Her healing purr worked magic, its vibration seeping into me. She was Sean's cat, but put in her time with Gregg and me too. When Gregg and I moved to Colorado, and Sean moved out on his own, we all agreed it would be best for Paddy to come with us.

When we returned to California, sixteen-year-old Paddy was in her decline. I was shocked each time I noticed—really noticed—that she was now an old cat. A prim, fussy little old lady. She had always been fastidious about grooming, which with her long fur led to a reputation for Olympic hairball ejection. One of her hairballs—so tightly packed it survived being laundered—still sits on my altar.

Although Paddy's black fur faded to henna, her green eyes remained bright. She began to lose bowel control and strength in her hind legs. It took me a while to understand what was happening. I asked her forgiveness for my bad reaction to finding piles of cat feces on the carpet. Fleas were the worst part of her decline. Weakened, she couldn't fight them off, nor did we want to risk putting flea repellents on her. Bay leaves and other herbal remedies were our only hope. Each night, I carefully flea-combed her long fur. Water in the bathroom sink swam with black dots of fleas.

Two days before Gregg's birthday, I let Paddy outside to enjoy the early summer sun for a couple of hours while I went to a meeting at work. When I returned home, the neighbor who fed feral cats came running over. "Are you missing a cat?"

Paddy had gone to their house, moved the feral cats aside, eaten two bowls of red-meat tuna, drank a bowl of milk, and started on a third bowl of tuna. I picked her up and brought her home, expecting her to throw up all that rich food after being on a bland diet. But she had chosen something with strong flavor for her last meal.

The next morning Gregg said, "Paddy isn't doing well. She's under your desk." She had attempted to disgorge in a couple of places and was unable to stand. Weak, she meowed miserably. I picked her up and held her for an hour or so, and tried to give her some water with an eyedropper. She seemed to feel better just being held. I made her comfortable in her bed, put some water and diluted baby food nearby, and papered the area around her with newspapers.

"Paddy, I have to go to work for a little while. Don't die while I'm gone, please."

I came home to find Paddy still in her bed. She had disgorged more and defecated. I picked her up and cleaned her, trying to handle her gently. She was almost completely limp. She meowed steadily. I gave her water with an eyedropper, wrapped her in her favorite baby blanket, and softly stroked her. She seemed happy then, and tried to purr. After that she meowed infrequently, when she was passing more feces. I cleaned it off as soon as the movement stopped. I didn't think ladylike Paddy was pleased to lose bowel control at the last.

We sat that way for a long time. I talked to her, and thanked her for being part of our lives and being so sweet with Sean and baby Katy, for putting up with our bringing interlopers into her house, and for often not understanding what she was trying to tell us. I thanked her for being such a loving companion. She always managed to get me out of myself through concern for her.

Gregg made dinner that night and fed the dog so I could continue to hold Paddy. He said, "She's given us a lot of years. We can give her these last hours."

We stayed in the kitchen. I talked to her, stroked her, and checked periodically to see if she was breathing. She didn't move. Her strong heart kept beating, and her breathing was shallow but steady. Gregg called Sean to let him know Paddy was dying and wouldn't last the night. Around 10:20 Paddy gave a deep, ragged breath. Her brave heart stopped beating.

Petite Paddy Paws, with her pretty green eyes and little black nose. I felt blessed to accept and share her passing, rather than making a stressful, useless dash to the vet, or not being around at all. She gave me the great gift of passing away in my arms. For those hours, Paddy was finally our Only Cat.

I made a coffin for her from one of Gregg's shoeboxes, for she wouldn't like being put directly on dirt. One of Sean's old Star Trek pillowcases served as a shroud, wrapped around her but leaving her head uncovered as if she were resting. Her eyes wouldn't close.

When Sean came the next day, he and Gregg dug a grave on the slope below our house, near Hendrix's grave. Gwen and her husband, Allen, arrived just as we were carrying Paddy outside. We all had private thoughts, and words to share. Sean put her box in the grave. I put a rose on top of it and said, "Thank you, Paddy." Sean filled in the grave, and put a large stone on top of the mound of earth.

Tyson had gone out with us, his grayness blending with shadows of creosote bushes. He remained by Paddy, watching over her. Sean went back to Paddy's grave later that evening. He said, "There's a ring of white dandelion puffballs like a necklace all around her gravestone."

I wondered if Tyson would miss her, and whether Katy would remember her. One-year-old Katy had looked for the kitty when she first arrived.

After sweet Paddy died, I moved under a veil of sadness and sought solitude. Afternoon sun and a gentle breeze from the canyon helped lift my spirits. A young deer sat at rest under bushes in back. A calico cat sat on a sentinel rock. I thought, am I being greeted more often by other solitary creatures? I'm surrounded by love and family and Gregg and friends, but feel like I'm working out something internal and cherish my solitude. As if to emphasize that thought, a lone red-shouldered hawk landed in a eucalyptus tree behind our house.

Gray Tyson became senior and Only Cat, a strong young male in his prime. Buki became a member of our family. Buki chose to spend most of her time outdoors, and was patient with our absence during the day. Tyson ruled the upstairs and front yard, while Buki watched downstairs and the back.

Buki and Tyson developed a respectful partnership, with its entertaining moments. Sometimes Buki would pretend to be asleep near the foot of the hallway stairs, and jump *Boo!* as an unsuspecting Tyson came down, sending him racing back upstairs. We could almost hear Buki chuckle. Tyson always felt safe with Buki, though.

Tyson and Buki learned to deal with the increasing number of our grandchildren, teaching them how to behave around animals. Together, Tyson and Buki maintained the energy balance in the house when their human companions had hectic schedules. We needed that in years to come.

A dozen years later, I would learn that Paddy, having seen to our education as far as she could, had called another teacher for us. That call was answered by the wolf-bear shaman spirit squeezed into an Akita body we'd named Buki.

Twists and Turns

I purr to heal, I purr to comfort, I purr in love,
I purr in happiness, I purr because.
She doesn't hear the tonal differences,
the resonances, but she knows.
— Tyson Cat

What a year our first back in California had been, with Buki Akita adopting us, my starting work at Matthew House, the death of Paddy Paws, and all that happened in between! I found myself wondering what the coming year would bring.

It didn't take long to find out.

Matthew House progressed down the aisle to the altar of merger. The board's transition committee selected Social Charities as the partner agency. Churches and volunteers seemed supportive. Then I talked to grant funders about the match.

"You know, of course," a funder said, "that we only award one grant to each agency. If we already fund the larger agency, Matthew House would no longer be eligible."

Key volunteers began to drop hints. "When Matthew House becomes an arm of the octopus, you won't need us anymore." That applied to their donations and their time.

The closer our M Date came, the more I felt this was not the best course either for the agency or the families we served. I called Mary, our program director. "We need to talk. Can we meet away from the agency for lunch?"

"I was going to call you too," she said. "How about the Japanese Garden?"

We arrived at the Japanese Garden gates at the same time, sandwiches in hand. Wordlessly, we walked to a covered overlook by the creek and sat on a wooden bench, our backs against the railing. Sun fell between slats of the arbor overhead. Alternating stripes of sun and shade, warm and cool. The garden's silence was broken only by birdsong, the trickling creek, and occasional traffic sounds.

"This merger isn't feeling right," I told Mary.

Her blue eyes reflected back my own. "Why not?"

"Nothing will change but ownership," I answered. I took a deep breath, held it, and released it slowly. "We'll still need to raise money for our programs. We'll lose a lot of grant funding. The board will have responsibility but no authority. Word on the street is that Social Charities is having its own internal and funding problems."

"I was having similar thoughts," Mary admitted. "They came for a site visit. It was as if they were taking inventory. They were more interested in the facility and furnishings than in the programs or families we serve. It seemed that we'd be a poor stepchild among their other programs. I had no sense that they would continue to operate Matthew House as a shelter for families, but perhaps for some other population of homeless."

We looked at each other, sharing surprise and recognition. We had taken different paths to arrive at the same conclusion.

We called a transition team meeting to outline our reasons for recommending discontinuation of merger talks: "Matthew House has a good reputation in this community.

We hit a bump. We can make it on our own if we all work at it." The board concurred.

Mary and I went with a delegation from the board to Social Charities' home office. Their representatives lined one side of a long walnut conference table. The Matthew House delegation sat across from them. We looked like a United Nations meeting, or maybe a Spanish Inquisition tribunal. Their director announced, "I have wonderful news! Our board met last night and agreed that Matthew House will have a dedicated seat on our board!"

I thanked her for her effort, and then dropped the bombshell. "Thank you, all, for your willingness to work with us during this critical time. After much thought, prayer, and discussion, though, we've decided that merger isn't in the best interests of Matthew House, our programs, or the families we serve. We apologize for any inconvenience these talks have caused for Social Charities; we hope that we can go forward as partners in service to our constituencies."

Silence. Stunned silence. It was as if the air had been sucked out of the room.

Their navy blue-suited board president recovered first. "Thank you," he said with formality, "for your openness and honesty. We wish you well, and look forward to working with you as colleagues in service." The rest of their representatives nodded.

"Thank you," our board president said. Our delegation rose in unison. Formality carried us out the door. Outside in the warm summer sun, everyone took a deep breath and released it in a chorus of whooshes. "We're committed. We can do this." Heads nodded. A terrible weight had been lifted. I was elated as we drove back to Woodward.

There was fallout. Some board members resigned, not wanting to be part of the folly. New members came on, bringing fresh ideas and energy. We knew what we had to do—save this agency and our programs. I was invigorated. I felt up to this challenge.

At home, things weren't as clear. I complained to my journal: "My soul still does not feel glory in California. I have occasional days and moments, not overall. But Gregg is happy."

Three months later, the world tilted again. Gregg's employer wanted to consolidate operations on the East Coast. Would we be willing to move to South Carolina?

I surprised myself by telling Gregg I was reluctant to leave, now that I was hitting my stride at Matthew House. Nor did I want to move away from our children and grandbaby.

We continued the conversation over several days, sorting out our feelings about work, moving, children and grandchildren, and ourselves. Gregg wasn't enthusiastic about moving to the East Coast either. I almost gave way to tears when he said, "Nothing should ever happen to you. I need you, even when you're peevish."

"I love you, too, dear."

The prospect of moving became moot. Gregg submitted a proposal for reorganization of the West Coast facility. He was invited to South Carolina to discuss it. The company president didn't like Gregg's plan or the questions he raised. He came home to a termination notice.

We learned over the next months that we'd made the right choice in honoring our reluctance to move. All of the company's California employees either left or were fired within a year, even those who'd moved to the East Coast.

Gregg set out again on the job-search path. Buki kept him company during the day, her furrowed brow matching his. Gregg needed a project, and began building her a doghouse. Buki preferred to stay outside, where it was cooler and closer to nature. Gregg measured her height, calculated dimensions, and constructed the doghouse out of marine plywood. He sealed it against the weather, with ventilation spaces under the roof overhang. He installed the sturdy doghouse on a corner of our back porch where Buki often slept. She sniffed it, walked in, and curled up. She found it acceptable. Gregg was pleased.

Tyson checked out the doghouse and gave his seal of approval by lying down next to it. Some agreement had been reached between Gregg and me, and between Buki and Tyson.

In the sanctity of early quiet at home, I sat by our front window and sipped my coffee. I watched the liquid-amber tree in front of our house change colors, felt the weight of Tyson in my lap and the vibration of his purr, and heard Buki's toenails click on the tile floor in our kitchen. I quieted into meditation, and later emerged, enjoying the lingering breath of a conversation with God. I realized how much I enjoyed slipping gently into morning.

Many Sundays I visited Matthew House's coalition churches, telling stories about the families we served. I became familiar with the different ways denominations worshipped and operated. Some were conservative, literal, and Bible based, others more liberal with an expansive view of faith. In some a cloak of ritual wrapped around me, while others seemed so unstructured that I felt disconnected during the service. I was intrigued by how all these splinters had formed from a single cross, and how many had confined God in a box of their church walls.

In one such visit, a sermon on the Beatitudes helped me understand how much of our Puritan heritage is based on getting a reward later for good behavior. The Sermon on the

Mount, though, starts with a blessing, and emphasizes that what you do for a living is not as important as how you live your life, and these cannot be mutually exclusive.

Between these visits I read Marion Zimmer Bradley's *The Mists of Avalon*. Its narrative of conflict between the old gods and goddess and the Nazarene fed my shifting perceptions on faith and religion. A wry notation in my journal says: "It seems that God and faith persist in spite of priests and churches."

My appreciation for cycles of nature and the outside world grew. I found subtle answers to many questions: Each flower blooms, brings joy, and fades. Does a flower feel failure if no one sees it? No; it has done what it intended to do. The answers are often simple, but we sometimes have a hard time believing it in our search for the complicated.

I watched a turkey vulture rest on a tree branch, silhouetted in the fog. It had become a friend to be admired in flight. A red-tail hawk flew a double circle above eucalyptus trees before flying off into the distance. I noted that vultures need to flap only two or three times to soar, but hawks need to *flap, flap, flap, flap*, and work for altitude. A reminder that we all have skills that come easily, and others that require more work.

I didn't remember my dreams, but knew when I woke that I'd been to school. One morning I woke feeling completely rested, thoroughly peaceful, and filled with immense love and overwhelming gratitude. I understood why God sends messengers and teaches in dreams, for its own brightness would be too much for us to handle—like plugging a toaster into 220V and frying its circuits.

I deepened in understanding that this world and all in it, from God to a rock and everything in between, are bits and pieces of the same Oneness—all connected, apart or a part. There is no separation from the Oneness; it's our awareness of it that shrinks and expands. I wondered how to reconcile the duality I often felt with the Oneness. Was bringing the parts together the real work of a lifetime?

Sean brought news that tore my heart. He and Rachel were breaking up. Baby Katy would stay with him. He was called to step up to a new level in finding himself and in becoming a single parent. My heart went out to him. I admired how he'd grown, yet worried about this new level of responsibility. I knew how hard it could be as a single parent of a young child. I'd done it myself. Sean was strong and proud. He wouldn't ask for help; Gregg and I needed to find ways to offer it. Rachel's decision took courage too. I held them all in my heart, praying that each of them would find his or her true path, with strength and courage.

In January, Haley Marie was born to elder son Jeff and his wife, Karen. Grandchild number two! Haley would fall in love with the stuffed penguin I brought back from Argentina many years before, and penguins became a theme of our gifts for several years.

In July, we greeted Gwen's baby boy, Max. I felt honored to be her labor coach. After several hours in labor, Gwen looked at me and said, "Mom, you're wearing purple eye shadow!" We both laughed. Among what would turn out to be seven grandchildren, Max is the only one I was able to watch being born. In the delivery room, I was moved to tears of overwhelming awe as a new life entered the world.

Gregg's frustration with his shifting work situation and his irritation at my "incomplete cycles" at home came together. "No one's in charge here," he complained about the house.

He disliked coming home to a house empty of people, yet I had meetings several nights a week.

I noted the irony of the situation. Gregg was between positions, with his self-confidence eroding, while I'd stepped into power mode. Everything I'd ever done had come together in this time and place, with work the arena where it played out. I felt a new ability and confidence, although glaring insecurities still erupted regularly.

Lessons from Matthew House led me to be more decisive and to drive the current project to completion, regardless of the setting. Impatient with people operating at other speeds and dancing around an issue rather than addressing it directly, I was slow to accept that others approach decisions in different ways. I hoped I'd live long enough to learn true patience. I read that some Native American traditions say a woman matures at fifty-two. I said to myself, Here we go again—feeling like I'm coming into my own on one hand, and like an unworthy aspirant on the other. Is this just a reminder that there's more? That question cracked open another door. Buki emphasized it later at night. She howled—primal, wild. She scared the fur off Tyson!

In December, almost a year after starting at Matthew House, I felt unsettled. I'd begun this emergency job thinking it would be for six months, with a specific focus. That focus changed, and a year had passed. It was hard for me to believe I was running a nonprofit agency. I had long forgotten Pastor Dave's comment before we moved to Colorado: "You should find a good nonprofit and run it." At the time I'd just laughed at the suggestion. And yet here I stood.

Changes happened all around. Tyson became more affectionate, and I felt he needed reassurance. I discovered an abscess at the base of his tail. The vet said it meant he'd turned away from a fight. He'd been spiked in the back by another cat landing the last blow.

Buki's energy spread throughout the house and yard, claiming ownership and being protective. She surprised us one night with a baritone bark. We had never heard her bark and at first didn't realize who it was. She was warning us that someone was breaking into Gregg's car to steal the radio. After that, whenever she barked we jumped up to investigate.

Buki answered the call of the wild by taking walkabouts that lasted a few days. I worried, knowing her confidence led her to believe cars would stop for her. There were tales of coyotes and mountain lions in the creek area too. Tyson seemed to grow larger when Buki was away.

Buki and Tyson taught our grandchildren how to treat and be around animals, how to play, how to be gentle, and in some cases how to walk. One of Katy's earliest memories is sitting on the carpeted floor, running her stubby fingers through Buki's fur. Buki stood slowly, pulling Katy to her feet. As Buki carefully moved forward, Katy took her first steps, her pudgy hand holding onto a fistful of fur. They made it several feet before Katy realized what was happening.

She let go of Buki's fur and plopped back down to the floor on her diapered bottom. I saw a little smile on Buki's face as she walked on down the hallway.

In due time Sean introduced us to a delightful young woman, Elizabeth. She was a teacher and part of a close-knit family. When Sean said he'd read her his poems, I knew it was more than a casual friendship.

Gregg had been having bouts of nostalgia, and read that it's a desire to go back to simpler times and relationships that maybe didn't exist. I saw loving Sean, Gwen, and Jeff as a series of things we could have done much better when rearing them. In many ways neither of us was there for them enough or in the right ways, although I think they know we're here for them now.

Scattered, feeling nonproductive and ill at ease, I drove into Berkeley to look for a rock outcropping friends had described. I found the park tucked into a corner of a hill-side residential area: solid granite rocks, shade from bay laurel and eucalyptus trees planted to replace old-growth redwoods chopped down years ago, and a view of the South Bay. A tree welcomed me beneath it. I picked up a small rock. I asked Spirit, "What's wrong with me?" I received a picture of myself scattered far and wide, and asked for help in rejoining my pieces and parts into a centered whole. I could feel the rejoining take place, then a completion. I lingered, and asked if I could take the rock I held. I understood *No*, so put it back where I'd found it, with my thanks. The sense of peace and well-being persisted after I left the park.

At home, Buki was still on her walkabout. Tyson explored outside. Crickets chorused. I felt acutely aware of the blessings in my life. I'd come a long way, and had a long way yet to go. The problem was, I couldn't see *where* I was going.

Changing Landscape

We Are.
How much of All we are is our life's journey.
It takes us into the unknown places,
carried on the breath of Light,
and teaches us things we thought unknowable.
Willingness grows with remembering.
                                        — Tyson Cat

"How is Nancy?" My friend Alison and I had intersected at a street corner across from the library in downtown Woodward. The sun shone warm and the breeze blew dry as we stood in the welcome shade of trees alive with birds and squirrels. I'd been with Matthew House three and a half years as Alison asked one of her penetrating questions.

I recited a litany of the latest developments at work and with my family. Alison paused, a smile growing around her eyes. "Thank you," she said, "for the update about your world. Now, somewhere in there is Nancy, and I want to know how she is."

I couldn't answer.

Later, I wrote in my journal: "Footnote for future: Alison said I'm defining myself by what I do, which tends to be a masculine trait." She was right. I was defining myself by my work, my self-concept built on productivity and acknowledgment. Now that I'd finally found rewarding work, the question remained, how (and who) is Nancy? I still couldn't answer.

The years between 1995, when I started at Matthew House, and the summer of 1998 had been full and fast paced. Gregg secured a series of shorter-term positions, and then a long-term position in computer manufacturing and new product introduction that would last until his retirement. Invigorated by renewed confidence and challenges to conquer, he was sucked back into the pressures and stresses of the high-tech world.

Buki continued her quiet training of us. Through her we met many neighbors and dog people we might not otherwise have known. Among them was Nikki, whose Irish wolfhound, Finn, became Buki's best dog friend. Nikki's open spirituality provided a ray of light in my work-focused world. She always wore black with Native American or Celtic jewelry or both, and taught her dog commands in Irish. Buki and Finn took us for walks on the trails and canyons, her bouncing tail and his loping gait side by side.

Tyson matured into a handsome gentle warrior who kept his territory intact, and worked steadily to show me how to just *be*, while my world increasingly focused on *do*.

Running a midsized nonprofit agency called on my every skill, talent, and experience. I learned many lessons, made my share of mistakes, raised a lot of money, and with help from the board and community brought the agency from the brink of merger into a growth period. Matthew House and the nonprofit world were an all-consuming occupation and life.

That too was soon to change.

On Midsummer Day Buki and I met Nikki and Finn to hike a trail above the park. The dogs investigated scents and furtive movements in the madrone, redwoods, and scrub beside the steep dirt trail. At the top, a fog bank obscured all but the tip of Mt. Tamalpais. We stood on dry grass and watched the sun set behind that mountain, turning the sky and fog bright rose. We wished one another blessings of the summer solstice. I told Nikki about my growing acceptance of place here. Even though it wasn't home to my soul, "After so long as a seeker, I'm where I'm supposed to be at this time, and doing what I'm supposed to be doing."

Nikki told me about a book she'd read, Penelope Smith's *Animal Talk*. I'd never heard of animal communication, and was intrigued. Nikki said she was thinking of calling for a consultation. "I want to know what Finn has to say," she said. "I'll let you know what happens."

That conversation clung to me. I bought Penelope's book and began reading about a vibrant world, new yet somehow familiar. The key made another turn in the lock of my self.

December and January were my busiest months, with Matthew House's holiday programs and reports due to funders. In the middle of it my sister, Linda, called to tell me our mother had had an incident with her medication and wound up in the hospital. Mother pulled through and returned to her apartment in a senior housing complex. We talked about Mother's resiliency. I admired Mother's ability to keep bouncing back, but wished she enjoyed her life more. Her world had shrunk by stages until it was barely larger than the walls of her apartment.

With thoughts of Mother's diminished world in the back of our minds, Gregg and I talked about balance and "getting a life." The Bay Area has rich opportunities for exploration, yet we did little. So on New Year's Eve day, we took Buki for her first visit to the beach. She didn't care for the drive to San Gregorio Beach on the Pacific Coast, but was happy to investigate sand and new sniffs when we arrived. A creek flows from the Santa Cruz Mountains to empty into the surf. Buki played in the creek, chased shorebirds, and socialized with other dogs, but didn't like the surf or salt water. She found a dead sea lion to roll in. Back into the creek to rinse off some of the smell. Buki was relaxed on the drive home—not all car trips wind up at the vet!

That evening Tyson joined us as we enjoyed our traditional dinner of shrimp and crab. Then Gregg and I took Buki for a late walk to the park. We found Nikki and Finn there. The pure joyousness of dogs at play made us all laugh. Ever since Colorado I'd been especially attuned to the winter sky. All is right with the world when Orion is up there with his friends of the Winter Circle. The night was clear and cold. A bright full moon cast shadows like daylight and dimmed the stars. The new year felt like it was off to a good start.

Labyrinths had meandered into my awareness over recent months, and one of the finest was across the bay. I told Gregg I wanted to walk the labyrinths at Grace Cathedral in San Francisco for my birthday. The specially woven carpet indoor labyrinth in the main cathedral, and an outdoor one of terrazzo and marble, were copies of the eleven-circuit labyrinth at Chartres Cathedral in France. I was glad the growing labyrinth movement gave people ways, outside the walls of a church, to participate in spiritual activity.

Walking a labyrinth is a moving meditation, and can be a metaphor for the spiritual journey. Inside the cathedral, descriptive signs gave the labyrinth's history. The instructions are simple: Walk the path to the center, stay there for a while, then retrace the path back out. I took off my shoes, paused at the entry, and took my first step onto a labyrinth. I began completely in my head, trying to stay on the path, wondering how fast or slow to go, and what to think about or not think about. I moved out of the way of people coming out, then gradually settled into my walk and felt it start to flow. Somewhere on the way out I had a distinct sensation of letting go, and acceptance of just following the path, letting it take me where it went.

The environment around the outdoor labyrinth was different, with ambient noise from the surrounding city, but I sank into my walk more quickly outside. At some point I lost awareness of whether I was going in or out. I just walked the path.

Getting a life also meant spending time with grandchildren. I picked up Katy from elementary school and kept her overnight a couple of days a month. We made a lot of cookies, and she enjoyed snuggling with a surprisingly compliant Tyson. She was such a sensitive little girl, I asked Spirit how best to support her, and understood to just spend time together.

Gwen, her son Max, and her new baby boy, Sam, came by one day. While Gwen nursed Sam, I enjoyed time with two-year-old Max. We sat in our backyard swing and conversed on his level. He wanted to take Buki for a walk. The two of them wandered behind our house, into deep grass almost as tall as Max. I could barely see his straw-blonde hair. Buki didn't move more than two feet away from him.

I resumed taking time to sit on the backyard swing to watch the world. Birds chattered. Buki and Tyson stayed close, paying attention when I talked to them about what was in my heart. When the wind blew, the brass Soleri bell we'd bought on a trip through Arizona rang its clear, deep notes. Sometimes it developed harmonics and a multitonal rhythm.

In April 1999, Matthew House's four-unit transitional housing opened. It was my first major construction project—the culmination of four years as director. It felt as if I'd birthed another child! The agency could have rested on its laurels, but momentum was strong and community need was great. Soon I would be deep in planning and raising funds for another facility.

Two months later, our family gathered on a hillside above the athletic field at California State University to watch Gwen receive her bachelor's diploma. I was so proud of her! I had taken fifteen years to complete my own bachelor's, working my way through school, raising a family, and taking many detours. I'd graduated from Cal State a few days before Gwen's high school graduation. Now she'd reached the same culmination after walking much the same path. I saw her take a victory leap from the stage, bypassing steps altogether, before I left the stands to find a quiet place with a tree to lean against. Baby Sam had fallen asleep on my shoulder.

A few nights later, Gregg's son, Jeff, and his family came to visit. I took three-year-old Haley outside to show her Jupiter. "That bright star is a planet like earth is a planet. It's called Jupiter, and it's the biggest one." Then I pointed out Saturn right below it. She said Saturn was dimmer because it needed new batteries.

In late October Tyson didn't eat one Saturday morning, and disappeared. I trusted he was inside, but both Gregg and I searched and couldn't find him. No sign of him Saturday night or Sunday. He hadn't eaten or used his litterbox. Buki stayed close, her steadiness letting me know it would be okay. Sunday night, a weak Tyson turned up on our bed. Not well, but at least he was eating again. The vet revealed he was fighting off the first of what would be three viral infections. Now ten years old, as the irascible side of his personality emerged, Tyson wasn't a good sport about taking pills three times a day for a week. The following Friday I let him outside. He stood in the sunlight, stunned. It had been six days since he'd been out.

These subtle and not-so-subtle changes wove through my days and awareness, the beginning of the beginning of change. It reminded me of when I've laid out pieces of a pattern on a length of uncut cloth, getting ready to sew a new garment.

Completions

When one door closes another one opens;
but we so often look so long and so regretfully upon
the closed door, that we do not see the ones which
open for us.
— *Alexander Graham Bell*

The distinctive sound of a willow switch whipping through the air. The sting of it landing on my legs. My concern, even then, for how the willow tree felt about its slender branches being put to such a use. Remembrance of these sensations rose from deep within.

I'd come to Texas to visit my mother, and have a getting-on-the-same-page conversation with my sister, Linda. The first day, Linda and I sat side by side on her creaking wooden porch swing. Bright-red cardinals flitted among trees in the garden sanctuary she'd created. Linda's slender hands gestured as we talked about Mother, who operated at diminished physical capacity even though her mind was bridge-player sharp. Her lack of exercise and unwillingness to engage in new social activity reinforced her isolation. Mother stubbornly refused to discuss giving up her apartment. Linda and I felt it would take a major incident for her to consider it. That had been the case with giving up her car. It was just a matter of time.

I spent the rest of my stay at Mother's apartment. Her daily routine never varied. She organized the day's medications in a neat row on her kitchen counter, and checked off each pill on a handwritten list when she took it. Once a week she went to the beauty parlor and grocery store. At one time she'd written long chatty letters to friends, but few were left. "It's hard to outlive all your friends," she said. She'd already outlived my father by seventeen years.

We lunched at Mother's favorite cafeteria a couple of times. Her plate filled with the Central Texas cafeteria version of Chinese food—oily noodles, vegetables stir-fried almost beyond recognition, sweet-and-sour soup thick with cornstarch. She meticulously ate each item before moving on to the next, always leaving room for dessert. I tried to find a deeper understanding of her. Watching Mother and Linda, I felt they danced around unacknowledged hurts that needed to be aired before either could heal.

From time to time Mother let me do the dishes or cook supper, but always followed behind me to make adjustments. She sewed, her stitches precise, her fingers deft with a needle in spite of their knobbed knuckles. Mother's creativity found an outlet through fabric and her 1932 black Singer sewing machine. She'd taken pride in making many of our clothes when we were young. She still did occasional alteration work for acquaintances, for a small fee.

I asked Mother to tell me about her family. Her childhood must have been hard. Her mother died when Mother was eight years old; then she and her brother lived with a succession of relatives. With someone listening, the stories flowed.

Gregg had suggested I bring a laptop computer. I had work projects pending, and he may have thought there'd be another reason to have it along. There was. When Mother lay down for her nap, I sat at the dining table and typed the stories she told me.

During supper, I asked clarifying questions: "Say, Mom, what happened to that trunk of your mother's things?" Mother fingered the ruffled edge of the orange-flowered placemat; sometimes her mauve-painted fingernails tapped the mat for emphasis. She said she talked more during my weeklong visit than she had since her bridge-playing days. After she went to bed, always by eight p.m., I typed stories before falling into the hide-a-bed couch with its permanent indentations where the mattress folded. By the end of my visit I'd compiled two dozen pages of stories, and gathered some photos. I later asked my sister to add to it; then I gave copies to Sean and Gwen so they'd know more about my family.

The stories of how my mother was raised—essentially an orphan—helped me understand her need to control and her unwillingness to engage in dialogue about decisions. When she made up her mind, that was it. No discussion. For Mother, "What will people think?" reigned paramount. She'd given me birth and now said she loved and was proud of me, but during my childhood she'd only seemed to care about my tendency to embarrass her. In many ways I had been a difficult daughter who moved unpredictably from reticent to inquisitive, said things that made her uncomfortable, and sometimes acted on impulse.

Mother was candid concerning her feelings about living in South America. After our father's contract in Colombia finished, she'd thought they would move back to the States. She wasn't in favor of his taking a contract to work in Peru— especially when she learned we would spend the first year in the dusty, windblown coastal hamlet of Negritos. She'd initially agreed to the South American tour thinking it would be for two to four years. It turned into nearly thirty. The life she lived wasn't the one she thought she'd signed up for.

Mother's inability to express her emotions led to an underlying rage that erupted unpredictably at the nearest target, usually my sister or me. Linda and I stayed semi-guarded, never quite knowing when some trigger would unleash Mother's anger.

Linda adopted a defiant "I'm not going to cry" stance, which angered Mother even more. I turned invisible, an observer, noticing people's interactions, and tucking them away in my mental filing cabinet. I spent hours alone in my room, reading or sitting quietly. I never felt alone in the stillness of my room, for there I was in the company of a presence that was greater than I, greater than the family to which I felt I didn't belong. That presence assured me I was a loved part of a larger body. Sometimes that presence had a voice, although I quickly learned to not repeat what it told me. Many years later, I came to understand how this guarded childhood silence influenced my adult hesitancy to speak out. I had learned to avoid confrontation at any cost. I lived with the perpetual hope that if I ignored it, a problem would go away. It never did.

Linda reminded me of an incident when Mother punished her for lying. We'd cleaned up our room by shoving toys under our beds. Mother knew that Linda, two and a half years my elder, was the instigator. She ushered us into the white-tiled bathroom, making me watch so I too would "learn a lesson." Mother held Linda by the wrist with her left hand while the willow switch in her other hand whipped through the air, landing on Linda's arms and legs in sharp, stinging streaks. I cowered in the corner, crying and screaming "Stop it! Stop it!" Each stroke of the switch left its mark on Linda's body, and inside my five-year-old self. The first switch broke; without breaking her motion Mother continued with a second. When the second switch broke, Mother reached for a third. At that point our father, who'd kept his distance, spoke quietly. "That's enough, Dot. That's enough." His even voice reached through to her and she stopped, panting. She dropped Linda's wrist, but still held the switch.

Mother made Linda wear a dress to school so the purple welts and black-and-yellow bruises on her arms and legs would show. She wanted Linda to be shamed. It didn't work that way. When Mother asked Linda what everyone had said, Linda reported, "Nothing."

"Nothing?" Mother asked.

"Nothing" Linda repeated. She told me, though, that other students had been quiet around her and kept their distance, and that teachers were nicer to her that day. No one could see the welts and bruises on my heart. My legs would feel the sting of switches and wear welts and bruises too. The surface bruises healed quickly; the internal ones did not.

Mother said she didn't remember ever doing that, but "If I ever did anything like that to hurt you, I'm sorry." Denial and apology in the same breath. I felt that I'd mostly come to terms with it, but knew Linda still carried hurt and resentment about that and similar incidents.

Did this framework affect how I had parented? Looking back on incidents in my upbringing and with my own children, I saw that communication could be a minefield of potential devastation. Some hurts were inflicted deliberately, but many resulted from lack of understanding, impatience, fear, or poor choice of words or actions, and were therefore innocent if misguided. I wondered how hard is it for us to slow down and think through what we're about to say or do. Pretty challenging in the moment, especially if we're feeling insecure ourselves.

I wished I could go back and do parenting over! My attention to my children suffered while I flopped between attempts at self-discovery and retreating behind unnamed fear, between emotional absence and smothering. I learned so much from the young women in the Matthew House office—all of whom had teenagers—that I wished I'd known when my children were young. Somehow Gwen and Sean grew into remarkable people and good parents. I hoped I could apply what I learned from my children's generation to my relationship with my grandchildren.

Before I left Texas, I asked Mother to do something for me: reach out to Linda and her children. Mother didn't call them unless she needed something, but wanted them to call her.

She asked, "What should I say?"

"It doesn't matter, Mom. What matters is making the call. You're the mother, and Linda has a lot of baggage to air and get rid of."

Mother's mouth pursed. She began with her characteristic "Well . . ." and let the sentence trail off. I hoped for the best.

On the flight back home, changing planes in Denver, I saw familiar mountains with patches of snow through the terminal windows. My flight took off and flew north over Boulder, then turned west. I could see the red-tiled roofs of the university below. I felt a physical pull, and imagined myself climbing out the airplane's window and drifting, spread-eagled, to the ground below. Then the continental divide slid underneath the airplane and clouds obscured the landscape. I knew that Boulder would always call to me. But I didn't live in Colorado, or Texas, or South America anymore. I straightened in my seat and faced forward. My life now was in California, and I had an agency to run and a construction project to finish.

It was good to get back home, even though I sensed change coming.

New Cycles

Blue jays screech.
Roses and bougainvillea bloom riotous color,
all because it's what they do.
I am a grateful witness.
— N.S.

Winter solstice 1999 fell on an alignment of moon, earth, and sun that happens only every 133 years. Another cycle of life began, and the music to the dance grew ever faster. Gregg had left for a walk with Buki by the time I came home from work. I changed into comfy sweatpants and tennis shoes, and set out to meet them. We must have passed in the dark, for I never saw them, and they were back when I returned. Things often turn out the way they need to.

Walking to the park by myself, I felt utterly alone, squat and dense. I lay on cool grass on the hilltop, and looked up at the full moon and stars in an indigo sky. I prayed for everyone and gave thanks for all I could think of.

I saw a clear connection between how much energy I focused on Gregg's and my relationship and our home, and how smoothly they flowed. He's not easy to live with, given his need to collect piles of data and his engineering-logical view of things I needed to feel my way through. He knew that, although he was mellowing. He pointed out I wasn't all that easy to live with either, with my reluctance to speak up and my tendency to move on to something else before finishing what I'd started. He chafed at the way I could walk through our kitchen and leave every cabinet door standing open in my wake. Confidence gained at Matthew House helped me grow more resilient in our relationship. I don't mean to sell Gregg short. He just has a strong personality and approaches things differently than I do. He's vocal, extroverted, and driven. He filled voids where he saw them, and my marshmallow, unboundaried self invited it.

My home-and-relationship self and my work self seemed like two different people inhabiting the same body. Yet I knew a large part of my success at work was due to Gregg's tutelage on basic management. I took many problems to him, and invariably received back a workable suggestion in the form of "Have you thought of . . . ?"

I lay on the grassy hilltop for a long time. The full moon shone like a softer daylight. Even so, it was achingly beautiful to greet stars of the Winter Circle as old friends. I floated in gratitude to be part of it all. When it seemed time to leave, I felt taller and full of light again, and alone but in a good way. Walking home, I gave the big tree at a curve in the road a hug. There's so much beauty and love in this world it almost hurt even to think about it. I wondered what would happen if I were to experience a full dose.

In the closing days of the century-turning year, we welcomed Jeff and Karen's second daughter, Helen Ann, into the flock. Our extended family gathered at our house for the holidays. I alternated between watching the flow of activity, and finding ways to have a one-on-one with each child. Katy and Haley, the two older girls and distinct opposites, shared and taught each other. Quiet Katy got Haley to sit still long enough to watch a snail extend its eyestalks and crawl down a board. Then Haley showed Katy how to bounce on beds!

Children remember only snatches of their lives during their formative years before about age six. I wondered how many of the special moments we shared each child would remember. When a child forgets those early years, is that the slow transition into this life when they lose their memory of the other side and their ability to hear God?

New Year's Day 2000 began without the feared crashes of computer and financial systems. Instead, clocks turned from numbers beginning with 1000 to numbers beginning with 2000 as smoothly as a car's odometer. A subdued way to start a new century. Weather contributed, opening the year cloudy and cold. Turkey vultures soared. Two bay chestnut horses next door grazed among passing deer, with no concept that this day was different from any other. Was it? Only to us calendar-driven people. Our Soleri brass bell and the wooden yak bell beside it sounded rhythms.

Bare branches of the liquid-amber tree in front of our house thrashed in the wind. Buki twitched in her sleep. Tyson curled beside me, warm on the living-room couch. I read and dozed. I'd started reading Anne Lamott's *Traveling Mercies*. Her life had been different from mine, but her search or not-search for God was much the same. I was pleased to find that she included my favorite scripture in her book: Micah 6:8: "What does God want of you but to seek justice, love mercy, and walk humbly with your God."

A nice resting day, perhaps preparing for hectic days to come. Gregg and I, without talking about it directly, arranged time to be together—both trying to put priority on our relationship in the swirl of everything else. One of the great things about a lifelong partner is remembering when you both were younger, and that as you grow older together you can become more gentle with each other's lapses. Daughter Gwen said Gregg and I are so busy by choice. She said I've been *busy* for as long as she can remember. She's right.

Buki and Tyson helped us keep perspective. Buki and I were skunked during one of our winter-evening excursions. The acrid smell lingered in pockets around our house and yard for days. While Buki assumed the forefront of our attention, cajoling us into long walks, Tyson stabilized the home front. He rubbed and purred, a gray furry rug in which I could wrap myself and know I was held and loved unconditionally. He was biding his time, waiting for me to cross into the next phase he knew was coming.

The world began to change in 2001. I did too, but didn't know it yet.

My beliefs were reshaping. I began to realize that many people weren't aligned with the catholicized version of Christianity, which had only been modified by Protestants. I grew less comfortable with the structured church, but kept silent. My evolving beliefs were still in their infancy; I didn't have the words to express, much less defend, them. Matthew House was sponsored by a coalition of churches. I visited them regularly, comfortably stood in the pulpit, and quoted Bible and New Testament verses in appeals for support for the agency. Privately, I sometimes questioned if I were even Christian—a baseline assumption from childhood.

I found solace in the outside world—a necessity, not an option. One morning in early February, I stepped onto our back deck and saw an eight-point buck standing in a clearing beyond the creosote bushes. Then a red-tail hawk swooped low and landed in eucalyptus trees above him. Buki returned from her morning rounds. Would she see the buck? Would it run and she chase it? I watched. Buki saw the buck. She stood at attention. The buck didn't move.

Buki watched and didn't move. The hawk watched and didn't move. Minutes passed. Silence resounded. The frozen diorama could have been behind glass in a nature museum. Then Buki's white-tipped curled tail relaxed down. She walked the length of our fence, and peed on the grass. Then she came back to our gate, entered the yard, and lay down by her doghouse. The buck never moved, nor did the hawk. After another minute the buck began its stately, stiff-legged march down the slope. The hawk sat until the buck was out of sight, then flew away. The tableau over, the bushes once again flitted with life and the small brown birds who had grown silent during the exchange. Some message, some agreement, had passed among those three—the buck, the hawk, and Buki. I didn't know what it was, but felt privileged to have witnessed it.

One Sunday in January I had to confront the passage of time, change, and people growing older. The previous week I'd stopped being *busy* long enough to sit for half an hour after church with Gladys Kelly. Feisty Gladys was well into her nineties, still driving and active in community organizations. Her untamed, frizzy gray hair had thinned, but her pale blue eyes held sharp. She didn't mince words. "I'm a lone wolf," she told me. "Life is great, kid, if you don't weaken." Gladys dropped dead on the sidewalk outside her home the following Thursday. I questioned: What am I doing that's so important I don't take time for people?

A week later, I found a letter on my desk chair at work from Mary, the program director who had guided me so helpfully since I'd begun as executive director. She had hinted, and I had avoided believing, that her retirement was drawing near. The letter gave two months' notice. For the first time since starting work at Matthew House, I closed my office door. Disbelief gave way to sadness. Mary had been a daily friend, colleague, and teacher who'd helped me learn this job, and a great deal about people and ministry. Everything had to change now. I finally would have to grow up and be alone at the top.

After Mary told the shelter staff about her retirement, I went to see LeRoy. Officially the house manager, LeRoy was the shelter's de facto dad—that dedicated, caring African-American man so many of our residents longed to have in their lives. He treated the shelter as his own home, nurturing it through idiosyncratic creaks and repairs to keep its 1916 self intact under heavy usage. LeRoy's black curls and mahogany skin framed brown eyes that reflected his heart. We stood on the shelter's front steps in companionable silence, sharing our feeling of loss. He asked me, "You're not going to leave too, are you?"

"Not anytime soon," I assured him. "I have another project to finish." After the housing project opened, Mary and I had reviewed our programs. Again we arrived at the same place by different paths. A former convalescent home provided the ideal mixture of private and community space for a new cohousing program. That project neared completion. Mary had been instrumental in its conception and gestation. Her successor would see its birth and operation.

The next weekend I gave presentations for six masses at one of Matthew House's sponsoring Catholic churches. The mantle of ritual wrapped around me. In his homily, the priest said the season of Lent should not be a self-centered battle of wills to give up something, but an opportunity to expand our time for contemplation, prayer, and doing something good. I resolved to set aside time to listen to other people, and to myself.

As if on schedule, opportunities began to crop up. A man I'd regarded as a community icon came by my office. Did I have time to talk over a tenant problem? Of course. He had the weathered face of one who'd spent many years in building construction. He did most of the talking. I sensed it helped for someone to listen. He outlined his tenant issue, and I offered some suggestions. He went on to tell me about his Jewish family living in Poland in the 1930s at the beginning of World War II, how he and his brothers survived the Holocaust, and how he met and married his wife. She'd survived breast cancer, and they'd just celebrated their fiftieth wedding anniversary. I was struck by his story's depth, and by my depth of interest in it.

The next day I visited one of our board members in the hospital. He sat up in bed, wearing a hospital gown. A smile spread across his stubble of beard. He said he was going to be fine. He didn't tell me it was terminal prostate cancer, but I could sense his time was short. I sat by his bed, holding his hand, and listened to him talk about his service in the merchant marine during World War II. I felt deep gratitude listening to this humble man share part of his life story.

At home, I found joy in the activity behind our house. Birdsong brought me into nature, especially the three-note descending call of little brown, gold-crowned sparrows. They flew freely through holes in our chain-link fence, while larger gray-and-blue scrub jays, brown wrens, and robins flew over it or flitted through our open gate. In midsummer, birdsong serenaded us all day, and at night a mockingbird recited its litany of remembered songs and then started over again. Two young red-shouldered hawks flew in and out of the trees. Four big-eared mule deer nibbled their way across the meadow below our house—a doe, her new spotted fawn, and her buck and doe yearlings. One antler of the yearling bucks always seemed to grow at an odd angle. I breathed in all that life and its cycles and said to myself, "Love one another. Love is all there is." The Beatles were on to something.

As the year reached its halfway point, and babies grew inside daughter Gwen and Elizabeth, Sean's wife, thoughts of change gestated in me. I knew a time would come when someone with greater skills would need to lead Matthew House to its next level. I felt a definite ending-beginning shift. Yet I loved what I was doing, and felt a tremendous sense of validation and accomplishment. At the same time, I was intrigued by Oakland Mayor Jerry Brown's success in bringing a branch of Boulder's Naropa Institute and Matthew Fox's University of Creation Spirituality to Oakland, a rapid transit ride away. I thought of taking courses on world cultures and religions there while Matthew Fox was still around to teach them.

Change coalesced toward the end of 2001. Two more grandsons joined the family: Gwen and Allen's third son, Greggy as we came to call him, was born at the end of July. Sean and Elizabeth's baby, Logan, was born at the end of August. Sean commented that he'd provided the bookends for the set of seven grandchildren: Katy the eldest, and Logan the youngest.

Twelve days after Logan's birth, fully fueled airplanes flew into New York City's World Trade Center, reducing landmark buildings to rubble and killing thousands of people in a few minutes. The world paused and watched televised replays of those moments over and over. Gregg called to warn me what was happening. I was stunned, shocked into frozen suspension.

I went to work, one of millions of people who felt helpless and also had to pay attention to daily business. I mechanically prepared for a presentation at a City Council meeting that night, while questioning how business could continue as usual when the world had just shifted on its axis. The Council held its meeting, despite calls from local pastors and others to cancel it. An impromptu silent memorial gathered outside City Hall. I joined them after my presentation.

The generous financial contributions for relief of victims of the tragedy spurred an undercurrent of concern. A reporter called me. "Has the outpouring of donations for New York affected contributions for Matthew House?"

I answered, "People are digging deep to make over-and-above contributions to help victims of this tragedy, and also will continue helping us provide year-round services for local people in need." That was partly wishful thinking. The effect would come, just not immediately.

By the next year, 2002, impacts of the declining economy and another major tragedy—the Indian Ocean tsunami—started to be felt locally. Community contributions shrank. Some donors lost jobs; some even became clients. We struggled to raise funds for the agency's expanded programs and services. The rules had changed, and the gradient had stiffened.

That was just the beginning.

Is It Time to Move On?

Locked in a meeting,
I heard a hawk calling, calling to me.
Then came silence and I knew
the hawk had flown, the moment passed.
I wonder now, what was the right thing for me to do?
— N.S.

"Dance, dance, wherever you may be . . ." rang through my brain as I gritted my teeth and marched determinedly forward on a path I couldn't seem to change.

"How do you do it all?" people asked.

Smiling, I'd always reply, "It's the duck syndrome—calm and collected on the surface, paddling hard underneath." I wasn't kidding.

I began to feel pulled in another, unseen direction. I just didn't know how, or when, or what. Matthew House had grown under my leadership, and was no longer the close-knit agency I'd joined six years earlier. Programs were more complex. I didn't know some of the new staff—an unfortunate part of decentralization and delegation. I'd reached a plateau. Was I willing, and able, to continue devoting myself nearly exclusively to the agency? When is it time to move on?

In my acceptance remarks for a local community service award, I told assembled youth: "When you're a leader, you can lead people down any number of paths. It's your responsibility to choose the right one." Had I chosen the right one for Matthew House?

The last year had been extraordinarily hard. We were denied a key federal shelter grant for the first time in Matthew House's history. When I read "realigned funding priorities," I gasped for breath through the pain in my chest. My stomach pulled in on itself. Nausea crept up the back of my throat. I swallowed hard. Other, similar letters followed. How would we manage? I'd always felt we'd make it through somehow, but now I couldn't just write a few more grant proposals and pull us out of a hole. The agency was being forced to a new level, where politics had priority over services to clients, and funding grew ever tighter.

I was pulling back emotionally, as well. Was it because we learn when we're little kids not to keep putting our hands on a hot stove? I didn't know how to cut loose pieces and parts without feeling like I was cutting loose pieces and parts of myself. I didn't want to put the agency at risk.

When I started thinking along those lines, all sorts of information popped up. Two workshops—"How to Prepare Your Agency for Transition" and "Should I Stay or Should I Go?"—gave me a framework and vocabulary. Both stressed the importance of a well-handled transition process. One suggestion was to identify tasks you imagined you couldn't ask of a successor, and delegate them. I remembered that a real-estate coach in Boulder had said: "Never quit when you're down—you'll always feel like a failure. Get back up, make yourself successful, and then quit if you still want to." That sounded like a Catch-22 then, but now it made sense.

These resources helped me focus on strengthening the agency's infrastructure, putting positions in place that we'd been doing without. Making the list was easy. Funding was another matter. And from the moment I said anything about departing, I'd be a lame duck, a manager but no longer a leader. Agencies are vulnerable in transition. Matthew House had been there before.

Then there was the difficulty of letting go. My coworkers had become my second family. Much of my self-concept was tied up in Matthew House. This was the longest I'd worked anywhere, the place I'd been most successful. Was there a Nancy separate from the agency? Could I realize that no one is irreplaceable, including myself? In my observer stance, I could see these conflicting feelings roiling around in my head, heart, and gut.

Hints of a possible life after Matthew House appeared. A local church sponsored a daylong retreat, "Everyday Spirituality/Reinventing Work," with Matthew Fox, former Dominican monk and founder of the University of Creation Spirituality (UCS). I attended, inspired to be in the room with him. He was funny and approachable. I considered taking courses at UCS, which by that time was affiliated with Naropa University's West Coast branch. The prospect of delving deeply into world religions and mystical traditions washed me with joy.

Labyrinths provided another beacon of light. Gregg and I had walked Grace Cathedral's two labyrinths a couple of years earlier. I learned that Sibley Volcanic Regional Park, in the hills above Oakland, held unofficial labyrinths. Visitors had constructed them in the abandoned quarries. A makeshift altar had accumulated in the center of one, with crystals, messages scrawled on bits of paper, candles, and other offerings. I added a glistening rock to the pile.

A local church installed an outdoor modified Chartres labyrinth, burgundy painted on concrete. Open to the public, yet surrounded by protective trees and bushes, it offered privacy. When no one else was around, I could walk it undisturbed. One day I took eight-year-old Katy with me. I told her, "The labyrinth is like the path of life. It has many twists and turns, but if you stay on the path eventually you get to the center."

Katy put on her serious face and walked it. We stood in the center, enjoying the late afternoon breeze from the bay. She asked, "Could I just walk across to the playground?"

"Sure," I told her.

She started across the painted pathways, then stopped and came back. "You can't take shortcuts in life," she said, and followed the meandering pathway back to its beginning.

I offered prayers of gratitude for her insight.

Looming Crossroads

I hear the red-tail calling. It is distant yet.
Crows closer, songbirds.
Leaves glide in brief downward flights.
I am here, and now. Bless'd, blessing, I am.
　　　　　　　　　　　　— N.S.

Animal communication danced before me. My friend Nikki had told me about reading *Animal Talk*, the book on animal communication by Penelope Smith, a pioneer in the field. I'd been intrigued if dubious—until I read the book, and others on the topic.

Penelope had focused on teaching and no longer took individual clients, but referred Nikki to Cathy Currea, one of her advanced students. Nikki had a consultation, and found it deeply insightful. Cathy had told Nikki things about her Irish wolfhound, Finn, that Cathy could not have known except through communicating with Finn himself. Nikki wanted to discern the best treatment for the bone cancer in Finn's leg. Finn wasn't ready to leave this life, so his leg was amputated. He learned how to maneuver as a tripod.

A few months later, cancer had spread to his other leg. The day Finn died, I took Buki to sniff his empty bed. She knew. The next day Buki had a spring to her step, as if she'd been bearing part of her good friend's pain and now could let it go.

Nikki asked friends to write remembrances of Finn. He was Buki's best dog friend. They had played, body-blocked, and trotted side by side on many walks. I sat in quiet and asked, "What would Buki want to say about Finn?" I felt as if I were inside Buki, or she were inside me. Words came. It wasn't until I read them out loud through a tear-choked voice at Finn's wake that I realized the words were in first person—Buki's words, from her point of view.

I wondered if Buki and Tyson would want to talk with me this way. Nikki said, "Cathy told me that when animals are asked if they want to talk, they almost always say yes."

I called for a reading, and felt deep validation as so many of the feelings I felt and things I knew were verified by someone else—such as how much Tyson liked sitting in high places, and that the words I'd read at Finn's wake did come from Buki.

Cathy suggested that I set the intention to open to animals in my meditations, invite them to talk with me, and listen to them. Little by little, in addition to sensing what Tyson and Buki felt, I could sometimes hear their words. I re-membered that night in Boulder, when young Tyson had corrected my poem from *tiger* to *lion*. Chirps of gold-crowned sparrows hinted at meaning. Understanding whis-pered at the edge of my mind. Was this real? I began voracious reading of the books Cathy recommended, and began keeping a separate journal to record impressions and snatches of words I received. Where did they come from?

Opening to communication on a new level with Tyson and Buki deepened our connection, just as we needed it to find our way through medical issues for both of them.

One August night, Gregg was long asleep when I crawled into bed after working late on a funding proposal. I had just fallen asleep when I was suddenly wide-awake. Buki paced the yard below our bedroom window, whimpering. Buki wasn't one to whimper. Something was wrong. I pulled on a housecoat and ran down to check on her. She seemed uncomfortable. I ran my hands over her body. "Oh, Buki!" was all I could say when I felt her terribly distended belly.

It was bloat—a health risk of larger, deep-chested dogs. The stomach literally turns over, sealing off intake and output channels like the twist tie of an inflated balloon. It's fatal if not handled immediately. A painful way to die.

No time to waste. I made a quick call to the emergency veterinary clinic and ran back upstairs to throw on some clothes. I considered waking Gregg, but what could he do? I let him sleep—he was exhausted and had to get up early the next morning. Within ten minutes I'd helped Buki into my car and we were headed down the freeway to the clinic. Within half an hour she was being examined. Even in such pain, Buki was the soul of patience. She stood there quietly while the vet staff checked her over. She knew that they were trying to help her.

I tried to call Cathy. No answer. I was on my own. While the vet staff conducted tests, I reached out to Buki mentally. I felt calm reassurance from her, and the certainty that it was not her time to die. She had called out to me, and I had heard. I authorized the procedures, and sat huddled in the cold waiting room while my beloved dog underwent emergency surgery. I stayed in mental contact with her, assuring her she would be okay. Around three a.m. the doctor came out to tell me the surgery had been successful, and Buki was sleeping peacefully. The doctor said I could go home, but would need to return by 7:45 to transfer Buki to our regular vet, where she would be monitored for the day.

After a couple hours' sleep, I woke when Gregg's alarm went off, and related the story to him. He was dismayed that he'd slept through the whole thing. I assured him, "It's okay; you're on sleep deprivation already and need to go to work. I can come home early to take a nap."

I returned to the emergency clinic on time to pick up Buki, and took her straight to our regular vet, where she spent the day. And back every day for over a week. I asked for a frequent-flier discount. They didn't even laugh, just said no.

After her stomach and incisions healed, we needed to deal with Buki's spinal arthritis. She was already beyond the average Akita life expectancy of ten to twelve years, and it was starting to show. Calcification and bone spurs had fused two pair of vertebrae, putting pressure on the nerves and keeping her back legs from working well. On a younger dog surgery might have made sense, but not on an older dog. We admired her stoic presence when the pain was bad, and her front-end determination to keep going when her back end lagged behind. Her heart and spirit were so strong, it was painful to see her limited by her body. Her front legs tired from doing all the work, so we bought a support harness to help her. Her physical condition didn't keep her from going through one of her modified heat cycles (our vet later told us that the stub of her uterus, left behind when she was spayed, still released hormones). She responded to the call of the wild, getting even more stubborn and headstrong than usual. She howled at night. I sensed she was getting in touch with her primal self.

Buki wanted both Gregg and me along on her walks. She entered a period of greater dignity, savoring her time on this earth. I felt we'd been granted an extension of her life, and spent more time with her, sometime just sitting outside together. In a consultation with Cathy, Buki told her: *I want to live every moment I can until it becomes too hard.*

Buki's gracious teaching extended to the rest of our family. One day when Sean, Gwen, and their families gathered at our house for cousin time, the three youngest went missing. We found Sam, Greggy, and Logan in a semicircle around the opening of Buki's doghouse. Sitting sphinxlike, with her head and front paws outside her doghouse, Buki seemed to be sharing ancient wisdom, teaching them, even letting them touch her. She seemed uplifted and brightened by these little people and their obvious respect for her.

Even though I felt I could understand what Tyson and Buki were communicating to me, I turned to Cathy for confirmation and details. In our phone sessions I asked questions, and Cathy relayed answers she received intuitively. Sometimes her information matched what I had intuited. This method helped us discern the best treatment when Tyson developed glaucoma in his right eye. He had willingly moved to the attention back burner during Buki's emergency and healing, but had health issues of his own.

I had noticed that Tyson's right eye seemed a little larger than his left, and was a shade greener. The vet confirmed glaucoma. Tyson was not pleased with the many half-hour car trips to a more distant eye specialist, or with the handling, measuring of tension in his eyeball, and eye drops. He wanted to choose when and how he was shown attention, and didn't like being messed with! After several months of treatment, Tyson didn't seem to have any vision in that eye. I felt it was causing him pain. The vet said, "Humans with glaucoma often say it's like having a constant migraine, or a knife stabbing behind the eye."

Tyson told Cathy that the pressure was *really bad*, affecting his sinuses. He complained of nausea and a decreased sense of smell and taste. Finally, he said: *Just take it out.* He warned us to tell the vet to go light on anesthetic; he was sensitive to it.

I sat quietly on the small couch by our living-room window, with Tyson in my lap, and made the mental connection with him. I asked which veterinarian he wanted to perform his surgery. I heard him say: *The big man* (meaning Dr. Hackler). He liked Dr. Hackler's straightforward manner. *His mind is steady and focused.*

After the surgery, Tyson demonstrated his ability to disappear—I called it going interdimensional—for a full day. Without an Elizabethan collar to restrict his movement, he disappeared somewhere in our house. He reappeared when he began to feel better and recover from the anesthetic, stately if a bit wobbly.

The fur over his closed eye grew in a different pattern. It looked like an eye patch, earning Tyson the new name of Pirate Cat—a name he enjoyed for capturing another element of his personality. His intensity now focused through one gold eye.

Not long after Tyson's eye healed, my mother had another episode that put her in the hospital. At ninety-three, she was diagnosed with congestive heart failure. Somehow I didn't feel that either Buki or Mother would last past spring. Tyson would probably be around longer. Gregg and I decided to fly to Texas to visit Mother and enjoy a gathering of our extended family at Thanksgiving. Even though Mother and I had our difficulties, and she had not been a big part of my life for many years, she was still my mother. Neither Buki nor Tyson was happy about our going, but both understood its importance. I wanted to see Mother again while she was still alive.

After we came back from Texas, Tyson and Buki redoubled their efforts to bring Gregg and especially me along the path of spiritual development and deepening. When I read books about animal communication and practiced on them and the deer and birds that passed behind our house, Tyson and Buki were a furry cheering squad. Both listened as I talked over the changes I was going through, sat nearby as I filled page after page in my journals, and purred or breathed calmly when I cried into their fur. Or they sometimes walked away with a twitch of the tail that clearly said: *Pull yourself together!* They had no patience with my feeling sorry for myself.

Triple Whammy

This is love: to fly toward a secret sky,
To cause a hundred veils to fall each moment.
First to let go of life.
Finally, to take a step without feet.
— Rumi

The crossroads beckoned. I wavered, feeling the push of new energies, the pull of a new direction I couldn't yet identify, and the growing sense it was time to make a major shift. Yet I hesitated. Too many questions, too little detail. The answer—*just trust*—wasn't strong enough to move me off dead center.

Then the phone rang. Noon on Christmas Day. Gwen slipped into our home office to answer it.

Our family had gathered for Christmas. The house resounded with multiple conversations punctuated by the din of children's games. We'd rearranged our living room to make room for a fragrant pine tree, now covered with homemade and memento ornaments. Children circled like young vultures, peering at wrapped presents crowded under the tree. The office, though, strewn with papers and things tucked in there to protect them, was off-limits to kids. With the blinds closed and lights off, it felt comfortably dark.

I sensed what the call was about and followed Gwen into the office. She had a stricken look on her face as she handed me the phone. "It's about Grandma," she said.

It was the nursing home in Texas. "Is this Nancy, Mrs. Warner's daughter?"

"Yes," I said, my senses tingling. "What's happening?"

"We're sorry to have to call to tell you, but we couldn't reach your sister. Your mother passed away this morning."

I felt the world shift. Now I understood the pervasive sadness I'd felt the day before when Gregg and I had visited Union Square in San Francisco on our annual trek to see the decorated windows. Watching the lighting of a twenty-foot-high menorah filled my need for ritual, but the sadness had haunted me. Guarded and controlled as our mother was, she loved my sister and me as well as she could. She had given us great gifts—artistic creativity and writing. Having a mother, even if we're not close, means there's someone to go to with questions—a higher authority, someone to ask for advice even if that advice is not followed. She represents history, connection to a family line, answers and hints of truth, even if filtered, and much more.

I put the phone down and turned to Gwen. "She's gone, dear. I'm sorry, I know how close you were."

I wrapped my arms around my daughter, and held her while she cried. Gwen's strawberry-blonde curls moved as I breathed through them. My throat clamped down and tears flowed, although I couldn't tell if these were my feelings or Gwen's. She was close to my mother. Gwen was the first grandchild, and she and I had lived with my parents for a time when she was little. Mother opened her heart to Gwen. They talked often, and Gwen had been so proud when she'd flown from California back to Texas to introduce Max, her first child, to his great-grandmother.

We stood in the darkened office for several minutes, and then became aware of an increased noise level from the living room. Kids clamored for adults to gather for the ritual gift opening.

"We should go out," I said.

"Okay."

We detoured by the bathroom to wash our faces, and then rejoined the gathering. Gregg gave me a questioning look from across the room. I nodded. He understood. We shared the news of my mother's death. The older children had some understanding, but to the younger ones the concept of death wasn't real. The morning's gift exchange was bittersweet. Our celebration of a birth and coming together of family for the holidays was underscored by a feeling of loss. I thought of past Christmases with my parents, the fragile nature of life, the ever-expanding ripples of relationships, and how important people are to one another. In the midst of shredded wrapping paper and opened boxes, I knew Christmas would never be the same.

Later, Gregg and I retreated to our office for a quiet moment. Calls came from my sister and the nursing home. I made flight reservations. Sean would fly with me. Gwen would come separately, as she needed an extra day to arrange childcare. Gregg would stay home and take care of the dog and cat, both of whom needed medication and special diets.

I formed the heart-and-mind connection with Buki and Tyson, and asked them to take care of themselves and Gregg. I promised to check in with them while I was gone. I felt a sense of knowing from each of them: *You're needed there. We'll be okay.* They'd said that at Thanksgiving too, when Gregg and I had journeyed to Texas to spend time with Mother.

During that Thanksgiving visit to Texas, I'd reconnected with my mother on a new level. When Gregg and I took her back to her retirement home the last day of our visit, she'd looked so small standing in her room, fingering fringe on the white chenille bedspread. I gave her a hug.

"I love you, Mom."

"I love you too, dear."

We just looked at each other, knowing it might be the last time.

The week in Texas for Mother's funeral was filled with notifying family and Mother's friends, making funeral arrangements, and trading stories. Sean and Gwen spent time with their Texas cousins, and learned they had many things in common. The light from the stove highlighted my sister's long fingers as they moved over food trays, creating edible artistry. I circulated, talking with guests and the officiating pastor. Gwen and I were grateful for Sean's grounding presence.

In our long talks, I assured my sister that she had done everything she could. Linda had arranged for someone to be with Mother around the clock, except for that two-hour period on Christmas morning. Linda felt she'd failed Mother by leaving her to die alone. I knew Mother had needed to be alone to die. She loved an audience, and wouldn't die when she had company.

After we returned home, when people offered condolences, I didn't seem to feel the depth of loss they assumed I'd feel. Things felt different, yes, but day-to-day life hadn't changed.

Two weeks after Mother died, I turned sixty—a signifi-cant passage age. Frosting on the cake of my cronedom, mirrored in my long gray mane, its tips fringed with the brown that was a distant memory. As a child growing up in South America, January 6 was celebrated with parades, music, and gift giving. Epiphany is the day the magi were said to have arrived at Bethlehem with their gifts of gold, frankincense, and myrrh for the baby Jesus. All of this joyousness on my birthday had made me feel special, even after I learned the celebrations weren't for me. Mother had kept some of it alive through her unfailing practice of sending birthday cards. I felt a pang when the mail came without the traditional card from her. There was one from my sister, though, and she called later. We spent an hour on the phone, in one of the many conversations we would have about "growing up with Mother."

Perhaps prophetically, Matthew House's program director, Michael, gave me the gift of a kit to take an impression of a pet's footprint: "I know how much Buki means to you."

Three weeks later, on January 29, after sharing more of her wisdom and giving us the great gift of allowing us to attend her during her final days, Buki crossed into spirit.

My worlds collided while I sat with Buki on her last day. Gregg answered the phone. "It's a reporter," he said, handing me the handset. I hesitated, and then took the call. I don't remember the reporter's exact words. He'd called to congratulate me on "winning the award," and to ask a few questions. I didn't understand. He explained again. "Have you heard of the Alameda County Women's Hall of Fame? Did you know you'd been nominated?"

"Yes, I have, and, no, I didn't."

The reporter told me I'd been chosen for this annual countywide award. I hadn't yet received the notification letter. I was stunned. There I sat with my dying dog, deep in the grief of losing my cherished companion, while I learned I'd received an award that was, for me, a pinnacle of recognition. The 2004 award in the business category also was significant in that a nonprofit agency was recognized as a business. Despair, elation, and confusion jumbled within me. I stumbled out thanks to the reporter. The awards ceremony would be in March. In my acceptance speech I would talk about leadership in the face of over-whelming community need. I was steeped in gratitude, if still wrapped in a feeling of unreality.

Buki's last week was one of clear decline. All of the young cousins came to our house over the weekend, and Buki took what would be her last long, slow walk up to the park with Gregg and granddaughter Haley. By Sunday she'd stopped eating. I tried to give her some chicken broth, but she retreated into her doghouse. The vet reported infec-tion of her uterine stub, with not much remedy except sur-gery or heavy medication. We watched and worried, and encouraged her to at least drink water. I talked with Cathy, who relayed that Buki was trying to fight it. Buki agreed to drink some water, and said she wanted to see our friend Nikki again.

Buki was clearly happy when Nikki arrived, and came out of her doghouse to lie down on the back porch, where she'd slept so often when she first came to us. Nikki brought Buki part of a bay-tree branch that had fallen on the trail we walked together. While she was there, Buki stood and took a couple of steps to her water bowl. Gregg called to me: "Buki's standing! Bring the putty!"

I hastily massaged the glob of putty from the footprint kit to soften it, flattened it into a small pancake, and rushed to our back porch. Buki, still standing, let us lift her paw and place it on the putty to get a paw print. She spent that night in our house, one of the few times she'd done so. The next day I came home at noon to sit with her. Buki was so present, so alert, Gregg felt we should try everything to fight for her. "Maybe some subcutaneous fluids and more antibiotics," he said. He wanted another vet conference.

Gregg and our vet carried Buki into the examination room. Dr. Hackler spent a long time with us, his strong hands and straightforward manner comforting. He described the infection for Gregg, whose graduate years as a medical laboratory technician gave him better understanding of it than I had been able to grasp. The two men determined that the best thing for Buki was to help her go. "It'll only get worse for her as her systems shut down," Dr. Hackler said.

A technician shaved a spot on Buki's left foreleg, put a catheter in, and secured it in place with white surgical tape. I sat on the floor with Buki during this procedure, tears streaming down my face, unable to speak. Dr. Hackler gave Gregg a syringe and the medication.

At home, I called Cathy and asked her to tell Buki what was happening. Even Gregg talked with Cathy, although he wasn't sure about this animal-communication business. The next day Gregg and I stayed home, cherishing every moment with Buki. She alternated between being alert and present with us, and drawing within herself, preparing to transition into spirit.

I started writing remembrances of our adventures with her, such as the little toy bear she'd carried in her mouth and her gentle way of removing stuffed toys from the children's grasp. The list was long: walking with her in the park at night, trusting our feet on the path, seeing only her white forelegs and tip of her tail in the moonlight; the cave she'd dug under the house; how she disliked being photographed. We remembered laughing at Finn's birthday party when Buki stole his dry-food bowl and buried it under the bathmat. She was famous for her excited R2-D2 dance, and for her locked-leg stubborn stance when we differed on which way to go. I remembered the night her tail drooped and she refused to enter the trail down the canyon (we heard later there had been reports of mountain lions), and the way she sprinted after a deer and trotted back with a smile on her face. Gregg and I loved Buki's expressive, triangular ears that no one could touch until she allowed Sean to do so. We'd always remember her curiosity, her kind, small chocolate brown eyes and the love in them, and the time she'd quietly pulled my walking coat off the stair newel post where I'd tossed it, and chewed a hole in the pocket to get a bag of treats. The list would continue to grow.

We hoped for sun in the afternoon, but the day remained shrouded in the fog we all felt. In midafternoon, I asked Buki if she was ready. She said: *Yes, close.*

Gregg and I made a sling from a blanket and carried her down the slope to the middle of a grove of trees behind our house. We laid her on the earth. We sat together, listening, feeling, enjoying those last moments. Buki lifted her head, sniffed the breeze, and lowered it again.

Gregg said, "I have to do it now, or I won't be able to." I held Buki's head while he administered the dose. It took a lot of love and courage for him to do that. Gregg and I both told Buki "We love you" over and over, as the medication took hold and her body went limp. Just like that, Buki's spirit slid from her body and she was dead. While Gregg wept, I raised a broken howl to let the spirits know a great spirit was joining them.

I held Buki while Gregg dug a grave behind the house. It was the longest I'd ever been able to hold her. The grave was deep. We lowered her into it and arranged her so she looked comfortable. We included her toys and the bay branch Nikki had brought. I helped fill in the grave. We covered it with rocks and planted wildflowers on it.

The sky cried too.

With Buki's loss I felt crushing grief. She was my companion and teacher. Buki found a place in my heart that I hadn't known existed, and filled it with great love. I remain deeply grateful that she came to us, loved us, and took us for all those walks.

Buki's death created a palpable gap. Neither Gregg nor I had been aware of what a big part of our lives she had become. I missed little things like juggling fixing her special diet with cooking my oatmeal in the morning. I'd been making boiled chicken and rice for her since her surgery for bloat. Now the rice spoiled in the cooker; Gregg and I didn't eat it fast enough. Four chickens lay in the freezer. Whenever I boned a chicken, I would think of Buki. I missed her happy warble when I pulled into the driveway after work, each day the silence reminding me she wasn't alive any longer. I felt numb. Life without her seemed empty. Being with Buki was like being with Jesus in fur and four feet.

Tyson mourned in his own way, visiting the places Buki had lain. I saw him sitting on her grave, looking out over the sloped hillside. He didn't try to fill the gap she left.

I realized I hadn't heard a hawk call since we buried Buki. The other birds were quiet too.

A couple of weeks later I heard birds singing as the sun came out from behind the grayness that had cocooned us for weeks. That night I heard an owl hooting from trees above where Buki had died. Venus shone bright as the evening star. I could see Mars receding, Saturn at the edge of Gemini, and Jupiter shining brighter than Venus. A full moon rose. This reconnection with the night sky lifted some of the cloud that rested on my soul.

Buki gave me another gift. The next full moon after her crossing, the night felt different, special, with an otherworldly electric quality. It was crisp and cold, a Buki-walkabout kind of night. The bright moon shone like daylight on grass and trees. I fell asleep almost instantly, and didn't dream. Around four a.m. I woke, knowing I had been somewhere and that I was back. A consultation with Cathy confirmed that Buki in spirit had taken me on a shamanic journey, and I would remember it when the time was right.

The next day Buki came to me as I sat in my rocking chair in meditation. She surprised us both by leaping into my heart and curling up there. She will remain in my heart always, a source of love, comfort, and guidance.

I felt an intense aloneness, and wondered if the world would ever seem real or normal or right again. I regretted not spending enough time with Buki, not understanding as her body began to fail, not being a good enough student of all she was willing to teach. When she was in pain and discomfort, Gregg and I administered the medication to help her die. We questioned that action. Did we wait too long? Did we do it too soon? Was she ready?

I learned that outside my immediate family and closest friends, few understood this depth of grief over loss of a companion animal. At work, at church, in the community, well-meaning condolences were offered for the loss of my mother, but someone's suggestion regarding the dog was that we could get another one. Others questioned if my grief over Buki's death was misplaced grief for my mother. Since then I've talked with and counseled many others with similar experiences. Beloved companion animals are with us each day, and love us unconditionally. Their deaths can feel like a greater loss than the death of a family member with whom we may have unresolved issues. The bonding is different.

I stopped talking about my grief except to Gregg and Tyson. They grew accustomed to me shedding tears at odd times. Gregg also suffered Buki's loss. He added to our still-growing list of remembrances about her. Sometimes we just stood and held each other, not talking, each letting the other know we understood and felt it too.

In the weeks and months after Buki's death I wore an insulating shroud of sadness, under, over, and through all else. On one hand I thought I should snap out of it; on the other, I felt I hadn't let myself grieve as intensely as I needed, only in fragmented bouts. Buki had helped me keep internal balance with an increasingly difficult struggle at work. She helped me form a bridge of connection to the natural world and to the intuitive world of animal communication. Now I needed to form that connection on my own, with gray Tyson's and Gregg's help.

Friends and people at work treated me gently, tentatively, even after queries of "How are you doing?" stopped. As time passed, tears didn't come as often, but the sadness persisted. And I faced stepping aside and letting go of Matthew House as well. "This is hard," I journaled. "I know it's time, but the attachment is strong, so much a part of who I am. I fear the loss of my friends there, my coworkers, and even the board. I don't know what's to come next."

But this triple whammy—Mother's death, my turning sixty, and Buki's crossing into spirit—ended my wavering at the crossroads and propelled me onto my new path.

Thresholds of New Doorways

When we learn to say a deep, passionate Yes
to the things that really matter . . .
then peace begins to settle onto our lives
like golden sunlight sifting to a forest floor.
— *Thomas Kinkade*

Is it okay for me to be here? My characteristic reluctance to try anything new yammered in my head. Yet I felt both pushed and called.

A white sawhorse bore the sign "Labyrinth Walk Tonight." I parked on a graveled turnout. Strains of melody floated toward me. Except for soft lantern lights from below, the night was black. A glow behind hills and trees to the east hinted where the full moon would rise.

Two women had just entered a vine-covered arch that marked the entrance. I paused, letting distance between us widen. I asked permission of the space to enter, with the intention to gain clarity. Then I stepped across the grassy threshold onto the Chartres-pattern labyrinth.

By this time I'd walked numerous labyrinths, but never a garden labyrinth. The uneven path wound up and down the hillside. Steps led up steeper portions. Some plants felt soft and fuzzy as I passed; others prickled. The perfume of flowers grazed my senses. In the center, a stone bench invited walkers to sit. I sat. Listened to the melody that wove through the labyrinth's circuits. Breathed. Felt the safe welcoming of this space.

An answer to my beginning question—*Walk the path*—came from somewhere.

I made my way out of the labyrinth, reluctant to leave the peace it had brought me. Three women and a man gathered around a picnic table on the driveway, near a small table that held cups, a thermos of hot water, and a selection of herbal teas. Peppermint tea in hand, I eased toward the group like a dog circling an established pack, seeking an invitation to join.

A round-faced man turned and held out his thick hand. "Hi. I'm Chuck. Welcome." His genuine openness washed away my trepidation, and I joined the circle. Chuck asked what I knew about labyrinths. I recited a brief history of labyrinths as a metaphor for the pilgrim's journey.

"Have you tried a finger labyrinth?" He gestured toward several models on the table.

The carved wooden labyrinth, polished to a deep shine, glowed in the light. I traced the pattern with my index finger. In, and back out, feeling wood slide beneath my finger and the slight pressure of carved grooves. Another tabletop labyrinth was carved in the three-thousand-year-old Cretan pattern, back and forth, like whorls in the brain. A third, handheld version was pewter, with paths so narrow I traced them with a jewel-topped pointer.

By the time I'd finished all three tabletop labyrinths, Chuck's wife, Dori, had joined us. I sank into her open friendliness like a drowning person into the bottom of a lifeboat. After we'd talked a bit, she ran back to the house and returned with her book, *The Healing Room.*

"I need to pay you for this," I protested.

"No, you just need to read it." It was the story of their daughter CJ's illness and death, and the origin of their full-moon labyrinth walks.

In the swirl of those moments, I don't remember who brought up the subject of Matthew Fox's University of Creation Spirituality, but there it hung in the circle that also included Dori's houseguests. All were students at UCS, staying with Dori during the current module.

"I've wanted to go there," I ventured. "I took a workshop on spirituality in the workplace with Matthew Fox, and I'd like to study with him while he's still there."

"I was in that workshop too," Dori said.

I told her that I had the equivalent of a master's degree in a couple of areas, but not the degree itself. I wanted to apply directly for the doctorate of ministry. Dori introduced me to one of the other UCS students, who'd written a petition for master's equivalency that had been accepted. Dori offered to review my petition if I decided to write one.

The full moon rose, big, bright, illuminating the earth and casting shadows like a gentle version of daylight. My request at the threshold of the labyrinth had been granted. I understood why I'd needed to come here this night. I could scarcely contain myself!

At home over the next couple of days I wrote a petition for UCS, detailing why my life and work experience were equivalent to a master's degree in business or public administration. For the first time, I put into words what had been growing within me:

Reestablishing communication and intentional relationships with animals is part of the path I envision. During our dog's illness, I began practicing intuitive animal communication. I am embarking on further training. Along with the disease of the soul that we as part of a so-called civilized society suffer (as described by Matthew Fox in Creation Spirituality), is our disconnection from the other beings that share this planet.

I mailed Dori the six-page application to review. A week passed, and another, without hearing from her. Doubt cascaded through me. Who was I to suggest that my life experience was equivalent to a master's degree? How could animals and ministry come together?

Then Dori called. She had several questions. She pointed out that I hadn't said why I sought admission to the doctorate of ministry program, and that I'd mentioned ordination in my petition. "Do you realize that the DMin is not ordination and UCS doesn't offer it?"

Ordination? I didn't remember mentioning ordination, but there it was, in type on paper.

Dori asked another question: "Have you heard of the Chaplaincy Institute for Arts and Interfaith Ministries?" She was a student there as well, concurrent with her UCS studies. "What do you really want?" Dori asked questions that had come up at every crossroad in my path.

I felt like a little ball in the universal pinball machine, bouncing from one imperturbable obstacle to the next. What did I want? Did I want the degree so I could do something with it? Or was it just validation that I'm smart and could do it? How would I bring animals into it? Could I combine ordination with animal communication, with healing animals and their people?

Dori's words helped me reach the other side of my spiritual desert after wandering in it for so long. What I was feeling was a call to ministry. As with the prophetic "You should find a good nonprofit and run it" from Pastor Dave many years before, I'd discounted and long forgotten the career counselor's words in Boulder: "With your combination of management and compassion, you could do well in the ministry."

I needed to let it flow. Stay on the path. Life is a labyrinth.

Over the following months I visited Dori many times. We talked about her studies at UCS and the Chaplaincy Institute. She told me that people can visit the first day of an intensive Chaplaincy module to see how it feels. Each visit with Dori, and many times without seeing her, I walked the garden labyrinth. Walking it at different times of the day and year was an exercise in paying attention. Each time, I noticed something different: glass dragonflies, memorial stones for departed pets, weeds to pull, flowers that attracted butterflies.

One day Dori asked if I'd like to learn the seed pattern for a Cretan labyrinth. "Once you have the seed pattern," she said, "you can draw your own labyrinth anytime, anywhere."

 She drew the simple pattern for me: two lines intersecting at right angles. A right angle in each quadrant, equidistant from the legs. A dot in the middle of each angle. Beginning with the topmost center leg, you draw a curve to connect the end of that line with the line immediately to the right. That forms the center of the labyrinth. For the next circuit, you draw another curved line to connect the next line or dot on the left with the next open line or dot on the right. You repeat that left-to-right connection until all the lines and dots are connected. A seven-circuit Cretan labyrinth emerges.

The pattern was simple, the promise it held great. The labyrinth's curving path would lead me around the corner to the next stretch of my journey. I would find help along the way.

A few nights later, I woke suddenly from a dream, sweating, my heart pounding, the bed sheet wadded in my fists:

I'm driving along a curvy road on the cliff edge, high above the ocean. The full moon is bright. I feel no wind. I drive around a corner and see Jupiter, huge and up close, hanging above the road. Next to it is Saturn, just as large, and another planet I don't recognize. They're so big they look like digital blowups in grayscale. Suddenly the car has no lights. It's dark, foggy. I can't see the road or anything around me, not even the planets. I hold tight to the steering wheel and slam on the brakes, but can't slow or stop. The car doesn't make it around a curve and launches out into nothingness. Suspended, I grip the wheel and shout No!

I knew this dream held a significant message, but what was it? What would have happened if I hadn't resisted and woken? Would I have been killed, or learned to fly? Was it time to step off into the abyss? Was it demonstrating that I'm not the driver?

I fell back into a restless sleep and woke again to rain, blustery wind, and gray clouds. The big bell on the back deck rang with emphasis. The dream haunted me. I told Gregg about it. He didn't have any answers, but I felt better to have shared it with him.

We went to church. A quote in the guest speaker's short biography held a message:

When you have come to the edge of all the light you know, and are about to step off into the darkness of the unknown, faith is knowing one of two things will happen: There will be something solid to stand on, or you will be taught how to fly.

The quotation spoke directly to my dream about the planets and car. Did I have so little faith? In the dream I had relied only on myself, been afraid, and shouted *No*. What would have happened if I'd had faith? I hoped to have another chance. As we drove home, I told Gregg how the quotation had fit with my dream. I felt the dream had been a test, and I'd flunked.

He said, "Sounds like you're being kind of hard on your-self."

At home that afternoon, I read Tyson the snippets of thoughts I'd scribed for him. He seemed pleased, and curled up in my lap purring loudly. Our heart-and-mind connection was stronger now that I'd been studying and practicing animal communication.

Tyson's words came into my mind: *I'm pleased that she was able to hear my words, feel my feelings. There's so much more. It doesn't happen often. But she tries.* Later, Tyson curled in a spot of sun on the carpet. I heard more: *The warm sun feels good on my back. Purring sets her mind at ease. I've been doing a lot of healing; it uses a lot of energy. Just let me rest.*

Tyson was quiet. I picked up the newspaper. He left, moving to a shady spot on the floor that nearly matched his fur. Did I break the connection?

Yes. He tried to teach me to just be, to see beauty in each moment.

After reading Dawn Brunke's chapter on power animals in *Awakening to Animal Voices*, I sat in the rocking chair by the sliding-glass door upstairs and followed her meditation. I mentally stated my intention to communicate with an animal guide, slid down to my usual clearing, and anchored on a tree and rock. I heard a voice ask: *Why do you anchor yourself that way?*

"To keep me grounded, connected, and together. Who are you?"

A large bird landed on my centering rock, which now sat at the center of a labyrinth. I asked if it was an eagle or a hawk.

I am Bird. You are on the right path. Follow it.

"Does that mean working with animals?"

Yes.

"What does path mean? Does UCS or Chaplaincy have a role? How can I follow a path and not know where it's going?"

Not needed for the work, but may be helpful for humans. Just have faith and trust. You will know when you get there.

I thought of the birds near our house—scrub jays, the three-note gold-crowned sparrows, hawks, turkey vultures, mockingbirds, hummingbirds—all their voices calling out to me. I heard Hummingbird turn flips and say in a small voice: *Yes, yes!*

I asked Bird about my totem animals. Cougar showed herself. She appeared when I most needed to learn courage, and was still here to help me.

Now, though, Bird would teach me to fly, to have faith. I flew over a field, looking down without fear. I looked up to the sky and felt the wind under my wings, holding me up. I thought about my dream of the planets, and the fear I felt when the car launched out over the void. I can fly, I said to myself. I just need to have faith in my wings and in the air to hold me aloft.

It was a powerful encounter. I thanked Bird before coming back to my rocking chair to write it down, lest I forget. I said a prayer of gratitude.

Tyson, curled nearby, purred encouragement.

That night Buki visited my dreams. She showed herself, and just said *Hi*. I felt comforted. The next morning Tyson woke me early to see the full moon set. I felt hope, and knew that wherever this path was leading, the animals would be with me. I didn't have the words yet to describe this to Gregg, but trusted they would come.

The Labyrinth

Everything an Indian does is in a circle,
because the power of the world always works in
circles, and everything tries to be round. . . .
— *Black Elk*

One rock after another. Some large enough that I should have asked for help. Others easy to carry. I asked each if it was willing to become part of the labyrinth. Some were not, and I honored that. Most, though, were willing.

In late summer, I needed to *do* something physical, so I started building a Cretan labyrinth on water-district land behind our house. The maintenance workers said it was okay for me to rearrange the rocks, "so long as we can still drive a front loader over them."

That works, I thought. The bare land held native grasses, bald spots, dandelions, thistles, and many rocks. Grasses covered the stone foundation of an old barn in the eucalyptus circle farther downslope. I walked a slow criss-cross pattern across the space, using my multifaceted crystal pendulum to dowse where the earth wanted the labyrinth's center. The pendulum stopped, pointing straight down when I reached the spot. Gregg helped me stake the center and exit point. He made sure I had the tools I needed, then returned to his project of rebuilding the master bathroom. Each of us doing, creating, in our own way.

Smoke from burning sage carried my request for guidance in this project, and for resolution to the deep grief I felt. I used a thick stick to draw the seed pattern for a Cretan labyrinth in the dirt, and said a prayer of thanks for Dori's sharing the pattern with me. The opening had to face east. Entering, one would walk west, toward the place of reflection and contemplation. Exiting, one would face east, the place of new beginnings.

I knotted a length of sisal rope in two-foot lengths and secured it to the center stake. Attaching a stout stick to the first knot, I held the rope taut and drew the first circle—the center of the labyrinth—which I marked with rocks carried from the old barn foundation. Interesting things turned up in the dirt and among rocks: a children's swing, construction debris, a bronze hex wrench with standard screwdriver blade welded onto it that looked like a homemade tractor tool. I gave that to Gregg. When I finished the first day's work, I discovered I'd lost my crystal pendulum. My gift to the site.

For each circuit, I secured a stick at the next knot and held the rope taut to trace that path, then placed rocks on the drawn circle. As summer turned to fall and changed to winter, circles of the labyrinth grew until at last it was complete. I realized that I was only making visible what was already there; we just couldn't see it without the rocks. As its circles expanded, I walked it in contemplation. Each cycle brought me deeper. The questions of UCS/Chaplaincy could percolate through me for now.

Our grandchildren came to visit and enjoyed playing what Greggy dubbed "the circle game." I was pleased that

Max and Sam knew the seed pattern from a magazine they received.

One day, a group of teenagers visiting a neighbor came through the site and asked, "What are you doing with the rocks?"

I explained the labyrinth's purpose and that "walking it is simple—you just stay on the path and follow where it leads you."

In response, one shrugged and walked around it, another laughed and walked straight across it, the third walked part of it in contemplative silence, and the fourth walked it until she became disoriented. She began to panic: "Which way do I go?"

I told her, "Look at the path between the rocks, and follow it." She couldn't distinguish the path bending around a corner. My words weren't clear enough, and her vision, sense of place and direction not strong enough to guide her.

"I'm lost," she called, "I can't tell which way to go!"

One of the boys called to her: "Just walk across the rocks and come out." She did so gladly. It made me realize that one person's path is not another's, and that sometime our path is clear before us, but we can't see it.

I wanted to finish the labyrinth by winter solstice but couldn't. Then I realized that the real date was January 30—a year and a day after Buki died. I didn't have words for it at the time, but came to know later that this was my grief work, just as rebuilding the bathroom was Gregg's. We each needed to build something, to labor with our hands.

When the date arrived, a small group of friends and family gathered to hold an opening and dedication ceremony for the labyrinth. Each of the friends who came had a significant loss the previous year, most of them of companion animals, including Nikki's Irish wolfhound, Finn.

Alison's black spaniel-terrier mix, Archie, had died the previous year, too—the same day Mother died. Alison woke that morning knowing it was time to let Archie go. She said, "I looked at him and he looked at me, and I just knew." She took him to the emergency clinic, and held him while he died. I remembered Archie well, and shared her feeling of loss.

We stood in a circle and spoke about our animals. I passed around a box for people to add photos, tufts of fur, whiskers, crystals, and other mementos. Warm breeze flowed by us as Sean carried a burning sage bundle around the labyrinth's perimeter and into its paths. I gave a blessing. Nikki sang an Irish blessing song as Katy carried the memory box into the labyrinth. Gregg buried it in the center and placed a large flat stone over it. The ritual celebration of Buki's life and the opening of the labyrinth wrapped around us in my first formal ministerial ceremony.

I shared a brief history of the labyrinth, and then added: "Walking it is personal, just as one's life path is personal. Envision it as walking to the center of your self, perhaps with a question or issue you've been pondering. Wait silently for a bit in the center. Retracing your steps to exit gives you time to integrate new insights into your everyday life."

I opened the sheaf of papers in my hand to the page with our memories of Buki. I started to read it, but could squeeze only a couple of words through my tear-choked throat. I handed it to Gregg. His voice faltered as he read our remembrances of Buki. He ended with:

You are and ever will be a creature of great and boundless spirit, courage, wisdom, strength, and dignity, stubborn and headstrong! Our shaman-spirited, wolf-bear dog. You will always have velvet ears and head, a tail with attitude, and a spring to your step. You'll live forever in our hearts.

I had recovered enough to read the contribution I'd heard from Tyson:

It has been a year since Buki's crossing. There is an empty space in our home and hearts. She visits in spirit, her light shining forth unfettered by the constraints of flesh. Her fur is now the rainbow aura of pure sparkling spirit energy, as she goes on walkabouts with her beloved Finn, or plays Boo! with me, or follows the call of the red-tail hawk. We honor her and bless her and thank her for the blessing of her life and her love.

I offered closing words and then stood by the labyrinth's entrance, holding the sacred space as each person walked it in silence. When all had finished walking, we made our way back to our house for refreshments. I felt a sense of completion.

After everyone left, I completed the ritual by taking Buki's blanket out of her doghouse, washing it, and hanging it to dry. Now the doghouse stood empty, although her scent lingered. I placed her last collar on a windowsill beside those of Paddy Paws and Hendrix.

Buki in spirit became Guardian of the Labyrinth. I watched from our back deck as Tyson wandered the circle paths and curled up on the warm stone in its center. Deer picked their way across the pattern, and red-tail hawks paused in eucalyptus trees above it. I wept often during the building, yet while walking it was filled with gratitude for her love and her continued presence.

Perseverance

So much can come from a labyrinth walk. . . .
It is not always easy to be ready to perceive what
comes. That's why I pray for openness and courage.
— Jill Geoffrion.

Doubt and questions. I still wrestled with what faith is, and sometimes wished for what I regarded as simple faith. I was not able, or willing, to get to that place. I attended church with Gregg, visited many churches for Matthew House, and understood the importance of community in worship. Yet, with rare exceptions, I felt the Divine's presence most strongly in solitude or outside in nature.

I couldn't draw close to the separate, anthropomorphized God in heaven that many churches seemed to put forth. My sense of God is the I Am, the living, breathing spirit of All That Is—the birds and trees and earth, the light that is within all, the essence of life that's neither male nor female but both. Sun and moon, yin and yang. I Am what? God didn't say. Just, I Am That I Am. No need to limit the Divine and confine it to a box of church walls.

It was the same with my question of *worthiness*. When I thought of all the ills and troubles that beset many people we know, and the worldwide famine, pestilence, and war riding roughshod over humanity and the earth, I was blindingly overwhelmed with gratitude at how blessed our family was. No major illnesses, wonderful children and

123

grandchildren, a marriage that stayed together sometimes in spite of itself, and enough resources to provide for our needs. The magical place where we lived. From deep within me came welling up, "Oh Lord, let me be worthy—of these gifts, these blessings, this abundance." At last, in a heartfelt way, I understood. I'd come to an intellectual understanding before, but not like this. The cognition came from so deep within that it was a few days before I thought to write it in my journal. Life is a gift, and the goal is to live life as if we had earned it, if it were possible to strike that kind of deal. But it's not. And we all have lapses. That's the ongoing challenge.

At home after church one Sunday, I sat outside by myself and made the mental connection with Buki. I often felt her presence, but connecting with her well enough to hear messages was rare. This time, I asked for help figuring out my path after Matthew House.

Buki's response was clear: *Don't worry about it. Just let go and be. Spend this year tying up loose ends at home and at work. Keep studying. Go to the Chaplaincy Institute if you want to, but you don't need to do anything.*

I hadn't realized not doing anything was an option, and felt a tremendous sense of relief.

Tyson woke me the next morning in time to see a layer of intense rose on top of a band of turquoise over the northern hills. The colors dissipated as the sun rose. I was grateful to have witnessed that beauty. Tyson had been staying close, especially since Buki's memorial service, curled beside me or on the arm of our couch, purring. I sensed that he felt okay aside from some aches and pains, although his single eye grew tired.

Settling to hear a Tyson tale, I did my morning centering and grounding exercise. I went down into my sacred internal place, knelt in front of the big tree in the clearing, and anchored my silver cord to my grounding rock. A large, full-maned lion approached. "Tyson, is that you?" I asked.

He roared and tossed his head. His right eye was missing. Then Tyson Cat settled into my lap. "Tyson, why are you showing yourself as a lion?"

The lion is the king of beasts, he said. His tufted tail flicked. We licked our front paw and between the toes with our raspy tongue. It tasted clean dirty, salty, furry. Then he mused: *The little birds call to one another. She loves their song. To me they are prey, but only when they come close enough. Surprise is the key, before they fly. Sometimes I just acknowledge them: not now, not this time. Curled on her lap, half purring. I feel the warmth seep from me to her and back again. We are one. She wants to hear, but doesn't listen well yet. I am patient.*

The lion settled into the clearing, his head on his front paws. "Do you feel like telling a story?" I asked.

Not right now. It's naptime. I've been telling you stories in your dreams. You hear a lot better then.

"But I don't remember when I wake," I complained.

No response. Then: *We are one.*

Fog came later in the week, muffling, protecting. The sun an orb slightly brighter than the rest of the sky. I felt in between. No desire to journal, no push to ask questions in meditation, just a willingness to be. I devoured the first third of Tara Thomas's book *Opening to Animal Communication* in one sitting. I recognized much of myself in her—my inability or reluctance to open up, and not believing it when I did.

I learned that "Am I making this up?" was the most common question from beginning animal communicators.

I was getting better at hearing Tyson. He liked to be near when I journaled or studied, or read animal-communication books. He continued to teach me that such a relationship is about trust. Trust in each other, trust in this innate ability to communicate without words, and trust in the Divine of which we are all a part.

Gregg and I took a day trip up the Pacific Coast. Walking along a bluff overlooking the ocean, I knew that if I asked, an answer was given. I just needed to know what to ask, and be willing to accept the answer. Looking down at the little beach in a cove at Bodega Bay, next to a sheer cliff, I thought how the incessant action of waves against a rock wall reduces it to sand. Maybe the incessant practice of meditation would reduce the rock wall of my mind and heart to sand I could walk upon. Footprints on my soul.

The next day I connected, heart and mind, with Buki. I was concerned that my need was holding her here. I held out my hands and told her, "I love you and I know you love me. It's okay if you want to go." I envisioned her coming out of my heart and onto my hands, and then growing wings. She flew toward the sun, then in and out of my heart, circled, and hovered above me. She grew much bigger. She landed on my hands, folded her wings, and went into my heart. "You make my heart bigger, Buki."

Yes, she said, and made another copy of herself. Then there were many more copies of her flying around. I felt deep gratitude. While Buki was doing so much in the spirit world, a piece of her was always with me because she wanted to be. Buki let me know she was proud of me for *finally getting it*. She was with me when Tyson was in my lap as I read animal-communication books. She was proud of me for taking the leap of faith, and reminded me that she was the gatekeeper for our labyrinth and all the dimensions it created for us. *You're on the right path. I'm here for you.*

The brief interlude of peace kept its quiet place in my heart as the season of Lent approached. A local church sponsored a series of evening Lenten classes, beginning with a section on labyrinths. The facilitators rolled out a canvas nine-circuit modified Chartres labyrinth indoors. Before stepping onto it, I asked for clarity and understanding in my shifting world. In my mind, I heard *perseverance.* That's all. I walked to the center, where I paused to listen for the real message. Nothing. I followed the path back out, and then sat to journal my impressions.

While walking, sometimes I was side by side with another person, and then our paths would diverge. Sometimes another person appeared to be going in the opposite direction, yet we arrived at the center together. Each is on his or her own path. The journey through life and the spiritual journey are solitary endeavors even if we have companions for a time.

Perseverance came back to me often in the days that followed. The politics of funding presented increasing challenges for me and my colleagues in human services. I gave an impassioned talk to a county-level funding agency on how community-based organizations were held together with duct tape and baling wire, while providing exceptional services to increasing numbers of people. The funders acknowledged that, but no more money was available.

I came home after that meeting and went out to our labyrinth. A sliver of moon shone above the trees. Light rain misted down. I sat on the center stone, hugging my knees, rocking back and forth. Everything pointed to my giving notice of departure now, yet I had elected to stay, to complete a couple of projects and put some things in place. No organic process is ever finished, but there are points at which I could recognize I'd done my share. *Perseverance* came back to me. Spirit said to stay, yet I feared that what I saw at the end of my predecessor's time was happening to me—that irritation and frustration. It crossed my mind that when I did leave, I'd be ready. Could I make it through the year? I knew I would, somehow. I just didn't want to do any damage to Matthew House on the way out.

The Universe had its own ideas, and I had more lessons to learn. Perseverance.

A Work in Progress

Cold and somewhat damp, like leftover fog.
Seeing summer in my mind's eye,
soft early-morning sun through dew-damp grasses,
the promise of later warmth.
Cloudy is easier on my eye.
Not so much glare and piercing brightness.
I settle, invisible and motionless.
Watching. Waiting. Alert.
— Tyson Cat

Progress. I'd focused on clearing my energy centers, or chakras, envisioning their spinning colors. This is not something to play with. In my heart chakra, it felt like crusty shadow stuff was tearing, wrenching loose and floating away.

In a later meditation, I envisioned each chakra as a little colored house. The door of the indigo blue sixth, my intuitive center, stood slightly ajar. Inside, it felt like a room that had been closed up for a long time. My animal guides joined me. We sat together, humming, focused on cleaning the inside of a large round window. I knew it was time to implement the self-discipline and focus to clear my body of toxins (eat right and exercise), and meditate, so that I could cleanse my third-eye chakra and be in tune with life in all its forms.

After the meditation I went for a walk, inviting the spirit selves of Buki and Tyson to come along. We made our way down a rocky lower trail at the park, zigzagging to the creek. I felt good to be outside—a breathing need to be connected to nature in a physical way. We forded the creek and climbed up the hill to go home the back way. I heard great horned owls that seemed to move along with me. When I broke out of the bushes by a fence I looked up to get my bearings. It was past sunset and darkening fast. There at the tops of two live oaks were great horned owls, their feathered ear tufts and white necklaces visible. One looked larger than the other. I felt awe and sent them gratitude for their presence and for letting me hear and see them. Then both flew away. I continued up the hill and walked our labyrinth. I felt at peace.

That night I dreamed about Buki:

I'm in the living room in an older home, by myself, sitting in a wingback chair before a fireplace. I turn around to see Buki and another dog in the doorway. The other dog is smaller, younger, female, white, shepherd looking. They come around the side of my chair and I reach down to pet Buki. She says, loudly and clearly, "Listen to me! Listen to me! Listen to me!" I was overwhelmed. All I could do was say, "I can hear you, I can hear you, I can hear you!"

I woke suddenly. It felt like a preparatory dream.

In late February, Tyson said he wasn't feeling well: *Gray. . . . Love. Feel not quite right. Not stomach, just inside; sort of all over.*

Later, I asked him, "What is your purpose in life?"

To help you to learn, to grow, to quit doubting. Get out of your own way.

Tyson settled into storytelling mode and showed me a past life as a cat. I saw reds, a tropical setting. Wildcat, in the jungle. He surveyed his surroundings, noting details and energies. He didn't seem talkative, so I asked if we were done with the story.

I suppose so, he said, giving the impression the problem was with me.

That afternoon I made the heart-and-mind connection with Tyson again, and asked him why it was harder for me to hear Buki than to hear him.

Tyson said: *It takes a higher vibration to communicate well with one who is in spirit.*

Then I felt Buki's presence, and asked if she had something to share with me.

Just keep on, she said. *It's all from the heart. You're doing well. It will come. I'll be here.*

In this exchange with Buki, I seemed to sense vibrations more than hear words. Was that another method of communicating? I knew the answer was yes.

Tyson sat by me as I wrote in my journal, tucking his front paws just so. I understood that he was trying to share his thoughts, but I had slipped into an internal space where I could hear sounds but not distinguish words. He purred, patient. I resumed writing in my journal. Tyson purred when I seemed to get a thought right.

I'm here to help, he said.

"Would you tell me memories about being a little kitten?"

I saw images of Tyson playing with brothers and sisters, tumbling. His mother, warm fur, kneading, milk, happy. He'd been taken away too young. *But it worked out*, he said.

"And Paddy Paws?" I was curious what kind of relationship had grown between them, since their beginning together was so traumatic.

We related in our own way, just like Buki and me.

"You have a great sense of humor," I told him.

I know, Tyson said. *It's all a game.*

The next afternoon, on the hillside below our house, I leaned against an old eucalyptus tree and went into deep meditation. I journeyed down a tunnel to the interior clearing I often visit in meditations. I focused on my heart, and asked for an animal guide. Elephant came forward and trumpeted. I greeted it. "What brings you to my clearing? To my heart?

Elephant said: *Why do you always ask two questions?*

"You're right. I often feel the first one isn't really what I need to ask."

Go with your gut. You must prepare, study, practice.

I sensed animal loss, and asked about it.

Some will leave, some will stay, Elephant replied. *I will not leave. You must help bring light to the world.*

"I will, Elephant," I promised. "Is there anything else?"

No, that is enough.

He trumpeted and was gone. I sat still, feeling Elephant's message and wondering about its deeper meaning. A monarch butterfly flitted past. Blue jays called, carrying on a conversation among themselves. I listened to the breeze in the trees. I felt appreciation, gratitude, and the sense of being fully present. I was learning—really learning—what many of the things I'd been saying meant on a deeper level, such as "God in all things and all things in God."

So much of this internal adventure remained within me. I felt it and recorded words in my journal, but didn't yet know how to describe this feeling of connection to animals and nature on another level, as part of the Oneness. When I tried to describe it to Gregg, it sounded to my own ears like another of the metaphysical excursions I'd embarked on years earlier. He held the concept of animal communication in suspended disbelief, neither believing nor challenging.

A few days after my meditation with Elephant, Gregg and I met Nikki and her new Irish wolfhound puppy, Artagan, for a walk. The park was abloom with spring flowers, mosses, ferns and miner's lettuce. A fragrant bay laurel had fallen across the trail. Walking behind the others, I felt a strong sense of Buki's presence. I paused, closed my eyes, and could see her happy around-the-bench dance. My face felt her tongue as she covered it with doggy kisses. She stayed by my side, before and through me. I stopped, and she prodded: *Let's go!* When I caught up with the others at the bridge to the upper park, she left us and headed back down the canyon.

I felt happy and full of gratitude for her and for all the beauty and abundance with which we were blessed. Buki had given me a special gift, knowing I was going to need it in the days to come, when my fledgling faith and confidence in my emerging animal-communication ability would be severely tested.

Listen to the Animals

We are part of the earth, and it is a part of us.
This we know: all things are connected
like the blood which unites one family.
— *Chief Seattle*

In early March, I registered for Cathy's two-day Basic and Intermediate Interspecies Communication workshop. All of my explorations in animal communication to this point had been in the protected environment of home, and in meditation. I talked Nikki into signing up too, so I wouldn't have to go alone. She offered to drive. I felt excited about this adventure and confident of deepening my emerging ability to communicate with animals.

Nikki's turquoise-and-silver rings caught the early morning light as she steered into a drive-through espresso stand. I pushed down my irritation at this detour.

"We're gong to be late," I protested.

"We have plenty of time," she said.

When we arrived, others occupied the seats closest to Cathy. Twenty students gathered in a carpeted room upstairs in the community center. Large windows opened onto a park setting. Our metal folding chairs formed a wide, lopsided semicircle facing Cathy. From my seat at one end, she seemed a long way away. Her round, smiling face capped a short, stocky frame. The sun backlit her hair, giving her a curly red halo. Beside her, a small altar held a photo of KC, her keeshond in spirit. Kobe Bear, Cathy's current fluffy gray keeshond, presided from his place of honor beside her chair. The light gray fur that covered all but his dark gray face made him look three times his actual size. A hanging cage with a parrot stood in one corner of the room. Several dog kennels and a cat carrier lined the far wall. An older female golden retriever and her younger male companion wandered around the room, sniffing introductions. A bouncy terrier investigated the room, terrifying a white Yorkie, who thereafter wouldn't leave its person's lap. The one cat sat in regal confidence, as if challenging any dog to mess with it. We each had brought photos of our own animals, alive and in spirit. I brought photos of Buki and Tyson, and wore a Turtle T-shirt to honor my heart animal.

Saturday's basic class focused on beginner exercises designed to show us that we all have intuitive ability—a muscle that needs to be strengthened. Cathy led us through several meditations and exercises. Then we practiced being an animal and hearing what it had to tell us. Moose came to me. I enjoyed balancing the weight of his antlers, feeling the strength of his body, stepping in his hooves along a wooded pathway. We each were asked to give a word that described how we felt. I said, "Strong."

It went downhill from there.

We practiced connecting intuitively with the animals present and with one another's animals through photographs. I received surface impressions, but none of the deeper messages others received, and missed many messages entirely. A giant flunk from my perspective. One of the dogs did tell me that I was just learning: *And that is good.*

"It's all about the heart," Cathy said. "Opening your heart in love and listening from that place."

"I'm trying," I wailed. I cried whenever I tried to say something. What felt like solid barricades stood between me and the intuitive connection I sought with animals.

KC, Cathy's keeshond, and my Buki, both in spirit, said I got the message. *Relax; it will happen.* At that moment I didn't believe them.

That evening I was grateful to Nikki for driving, and for her stream of chatter about things I barely heard. I melted into the passenger seat during the forty-minute drive home, my soul threadbare. I'd let Tyson and Buki down.

I made it through dinner at home. Gregg stayed outside the invisible barrier I put up, not asking how the day went. I dragged myself on a short walk, then went to bed early, convinced of my failure as an interspecies communicator. In my journal I wrote: "I so want to hear, I'm probably my own worst barrier. Trying too hard?" I cried myself to sleep that night, with Tyson rumbling his purr nearby.

Early the next morning I communicated with Tyson: "Do I need to go back for the second day?" I hoped he would agree I didn't. I understood from him that I didn't need to go, although when I asked Buki, she said to go back.

Then Cathy called, concerned about me. She knew I'd felt terrible after the first day and wanted me to know I could do it. "It'll be better," she said. I waffled. Nikki called too. Okay, okay, I'll go. I wore my Akita T-shirt.

Nikki drove again, part of the reason I returned. We had agreed to support each other. Artagan came, too. His giant silver-gray Irish wolfhound body took up the whole back of her old brown Cadillac with a dog bed platform instead of a rear seat. Today, only a couple of animals would be there to help us practice. He would be one of them.

I felt raw and vulnerable, hopeful for a better day and fearful of a repeat of my misery the day before.

On the second day I felt immediately more comfortable in the smaller, more intimate group of seven. This time we gathered in a room downstairs; it felt as if we could walk through the windows to the outside, with its redwood trees, paths, and grassy knolls. Our semicircle of chairs was flatter, closer to the altar.

In my feedback, I said how difficult the previous day it had been; I'd even considered not returning. I shared that Tyson agreed I didn't need to, but Buki had said to come.

Cathy said I had projected my own feelings onto Tyson, although he worried about me.

And I cried—more during these two days than since Buki died. I don't like crying in public, yet when my feelings run high, or come from my heart, tears overflow the dam.

Cathy's teaching on Sunday, the Intermediate level, focused on setting clear intention to work for the highest good of all. She assured us the animals are happy to assist; they "just don't like getting the same question over and over and you not paying attention to the answer."

We reviewed the previous day's tools: Connect with the earth, open your heart, become one with the animal to experience its senses; be quiet and fully present; keep soft visual focus; be aware of energy, not the physical presence. And for me, don't project myself on to the animal. For all of us, be a clear vessel to receive impressions and messages. Cathy reminded us that there are many ways to receive information. It can come as pictures or impressions, as words or feelings that need to be translated into words, sometimes just as a knowing. Different animals communicate differently. Each student has a natural way to receive messages and needs to stretch to open to other ways.

We practiced working with others' animals from photographs. Each of us also asked a question of KC, Cathy's keeshond in spirit. He told me what it was like to be in spirit: *Life in spirit is infinite, spreading across all, with no loss of sense of self. It is ever-expanding motion, with coalescing focus of energy where and when needed for healing and growth.*

Did he have a message for me?

You're doing fine, he said.

After a meditation exercise we went outside in silence to find a part of nature to talk with. Some chose trees or a flower; I found a friendly flat rock. I lay on the ground between the rock and a redwood tree, and felt prickles of redwood twigs on my back and in my hair. I saw a rock's-eye view of the world. Rock told me: *Be steadfast. Remember me. It takes much water flowing to change me. Honor us rocks as living beings, as living energy.* Rock also said: *You must know what you want and ask for it.*

That was the question I had struggled with for years: What do I want? Am I like the rock? Will it take much water—many tears—flowing over me to change me? I wondered, from a rock's perspective, looking up through the branches of a tree, what is up, and what is down?

Then I asked the assigned questions of the tree, and received confirmation of impressions I had received. Redwood said: *You are a child of the Universe, a child of God. That is all there is. Your purpose is to learn and grow, to bring awareness to fellow beings, to teach about life, loving, and living.* I asked for guidance, and saw myself going to the Chaplaincy Institute; possibly not finishing, but it was the doorway to what would come next.

By the end of the day, I felt full of potential, reaffirmed. I'd been cracked open and turned inside out. I knew I needed to shield myself to go back to work. I knew I needed to keep practicing to get into my heart, to open that channel of unconditional love.

The world would never look the same.

Conversations

Shadows, swishing tail,
waiting for the unknown yet to come.
Paws on dry grass make no sound.
Birdsong silent, watching, as the lion hunts.
Moon rising, full, bright, doesn't help.
All can see.
I do better with just my senses.
Whiskers touch,
sense trembling movement nearby.
Dark, little eyes watch me, afraid.
I ignore. I'm after larger game.
— Tyson Cat

After the animal-communication workshop, I took to heart that I did have the ability to communicate with other species. I kept receiving the message: *Practice!*

I had been writing a journal of my conversations with Tyson and animals from the wild, as well as those that came to me in meditation. Opportunities were all around me. White-crowned sparrows flitted among the branches of creosote bushes behind our house. I asked one if it had a mate, and if there were eggs.

The sparrow said: *Three eggs this year, not yet hatched. Our purpose is to bring joy and light.* I received a picture of a heart expanding.

Tyson and I explored the hillside in late afternoon, pausing at Buki's grave. I sat on a big rock while Tyson revisited his territory. He looked back at me, the gold grasses the same color behind his grayness as the single gold eye that shone out from within. He asked: *Are you still there?*

"Yes, I'm here," I replied.

He watched a sparrow, considered it, purr rumbling, tail twitching. Which end to heed? He walked away. *Not this time.* We returned to the house together

Before Gregg and I left on a short trip to visit eldest son Jeff's family, we arranged for a trusted cat sitter to care for Tyson. He was disgruntled about our approaching absence: *Wanting to tell a story, to tell how I feel. Lonely already, and they haven't left yet. Tail swishing, wanting the closeness, the connection. Being gray outside, feeling gray inside. I do like company. I know it's important to them to see their children. But I like things to stay the way they are. My world!*

I thanked Tyson for understanding.

After our return a week later, sitting on our couch with a view of the budding liquid-amber tree in front, Tyson and I had one of our most in-depth conversations. He had spent the night outside. I asked, "How was your night out last night?"

Marvelous, he replied.

"Marvelous and sublime," I teased. "You use big words."

Big words are sensuous words, he said. He showed me a picture of his gray self blending into the shadows, senses heightened, listening to the night birds. *I think about the moon, the stars, my place in the Universe, to just be, and be part of All That Is.* He added:

Gray as evening, strong, handsome and brave,
patrolling both front and back now that Buki is not
  here.
Sitting sentry-like on the front walk,
alert in the full moonlight.
Tonight I stay outside,
listening to calls of the wild and feeling the magic of
  the full moon.
Tonight I forego warmth and comfort to feel the wild-
  ness that is my soul,
to be the adventurous cat that I am,
to be part of the tribal meeting.
I sit tall, erect, alert, watchful.
I hear the door click behind me,
and know the choice is made.

I asked, "Tyson, have you ever been another kind of animal?"

He showed me a large gray-white bird. I saw cliffs, water, and trees nearby. I had the impression of a seagull. *I love to fly, to feel the wind*, he said. *No eggs, boy. Not seeds, fish.* Then he showed me a life when he was an ocean fish: *Freedom, up, down movement.* He showed me himself swimming through sun-dappled water in shades of green. *Chain of life,* he said. *Fish hunted by birds, birds hunted by cats.*

"But cats are so grounded."

Yes, but as flexible as a fish, and you know I like high places. He showed me a picture of the irrigation creek beside our house in Boulder. *I've always been a water cat,* he said. *Being a cat allows me to interact with more species, including humans. Humans need us to teach them, or there will be no more birds and fish. Humans are breaking the balance, and it harms us all. As a cat I can purr, stretch, be myself. Being, giving, getting love. This is a good life. Thank you.*

"And thank you, Tyson!" I recorded these messages in my collection of Tyson's wisdom.

My connection with animals grew as I practiced. Yet, as time passed after the animal-communication workshop, and I re-engaged more deeply with my home and work worlds, it became harder to stay in my heart rather than in my head. As a child I had been right brained, intuitive, and heart centered. I learned over the years to be left brained, linear/analytical, and head centered. Difficult training to undo!

One sunny morning strong winds blew from the northeast. A storm coming. Our bronze bell sounded, adding extra notes of a new rhythm. I sat in the old rocking chair in our room, looking out over the trees and bird activity behind our house and listening to the wind and bells.

Tyson's message for the day: *Be at peace. Everything will come to be.*

I considered that my mother was sixty when Sean was born, and fifty when Gwen, her first grandchild, was born. I was fifty when Katy Gwen, my first grandchild, was born, and I had now passed sixty. Mother seemed much older to me than I seemed to me at those ages. Did I seem similarly old to my children, and did Mother feel younger inside herself, as I did now? I held this insight gently, and my feelings toward Mother softened.

In his advancing age, Tyson was diagnosed with thyroid imbalance and received medicine as a salve rubbed on the insides of his ear tips. He was patient, but didn't like having his ears *gunked*, as he put it. He reminded me to check in with him more. I sat with him one evening to scribe some thoughts he wanted to share.

Being a cat is sublime, he purred.

"You like that word, don't you—sublime?"

Yes, it's sensuous and sinuous, like a cat. Hmm, that's enough for now. Will you stay with me? He tucked his head and paws around, to sleep, to dream of cat things.

I scheduled a consultation with Cathy as a followup to the animal-communication workshop. I had learned a lot, and knew I had a long way to go. I'd had erratic success in connecting with Buki, and I asked Cathy about my feeling that Buki was changing.

Cathy said, "Buki says you're the one who's changing. She's excited and proud of you. She encourages you to keep going. Even Gregg is coming along for the ride, whether he admits it or not." Cathy also said that Buki was one of the strongest spirits she'd ever encountered, in all her years of animal-communication work. She added, "You're now seeing differently from a month ago, and from how you'll be seeing in a few months."

Then a message came through to me from Buki that we needed to get a dog when we returned from our upcoming trip to visit Gregg's father in Louisiana: *To continue your education. May is the month. You can't go forward without a dog. It must be a powerful spirit. Don't focus so much on the body but connect with the spirit. This is a time of expansion, very busy, strong medicine.*

Tyson chimed in: *For an old guy, I do darn well.* He wasn't sure about a new dog in our house but was willing to consider it. He just asked that wherever he slept, the dog wouldn't.

I told Cathy that now when I checked in with Tyson I knew I heard him. She said, "He thinks that's phenomenal; after all these years together, you're finally getting it. He doesn't want a lot of fussing. He's happy with the same routine. Part of what he's talking about is respect."

After our conversation with Cathy and Buki, Tyson wanted to dictate to his scribe: *When the new dog comes, nose to nose, I still want my space—the high places, sleeping on the bed.*

"That's okay," I said, "you're still the senior animal, next to Gregg. And you have to approve before it happens. Do you have any guidance?"

I'll have to teach it some manners, he said. *Just go with your heart. Size and shape don't matter.*

After a pause I said, "Tell me about another life you've lived."

Tyson showed me pictures: *Flying, wind in my feathers, bright colors, shades of green and yellow and red, blue sky, trees, lush. Monkeys chatter at me. Other parrots squawk. Freedom. Looking down from the branches, feeling the power of my wings, my strong claws grasping the tree branch. Falling from the branch with wings spread and gliding to another tree. Fruit, yum. Sparkling water in the distance, snow-capped mountain slumbering, the flock flashing colors amid the green.*

Tyson said he'd been an Egyptian temple cat too, and that it was nice to be worshipped. *But you're not loved when you're worshipped, and I'd rather be loved.*

Maundy Thursday night, the day the Last Supper is honored, before Jesus' trial and crucifixion at Gethsemane. One day away from a full moon, the Winter Circle of stars still visible. I loved those stars. This night had a special magical quality to it, like the night Buki took me on a shamanic journey. When I came home from the evening church service, I thought I heard Buki greet me from behind our fence.

After the service, Pastor Randy had handed me the letter of support I'd asked him to write for my Chaplaincy application. Three letters of support were required, from nonrelated people. I would soon get the other two: One from Esther, the Matthew House board member who had been at my side through all the ups and downs there; and one from my friend Alison, whose good questions always helped me look at things from a fresh perspective.

I felt compelled to be outside, to spread my gratitude for this natural world, to greet Big Tree and thank her for being there. Big Tree agreed it was a magical night. At the park, the creek rushed downhill, full of water on its way to the ocean. Everything was connected. I returned home and walked out to our moonlit labyrinth. I greeted the stones surrounding it, asked permission to enter, and sensed that I'd gone below the surface. I replaced stones that were out of place as I walked. Gregg joined me in the center, and then led the way out under an indigo sky.

At the outer circuit I felt a big eucalyptus call and stepped off the path. It said: *Thank you for making the labyrinth; it is a special place.* I thanked the tree for its message, and its presence.

At the exit I told the sentinel stone its lichens looked lovely, glowing like flowers in moonlight. I felt it was pleased.

I wrote all this in the journal I'd started of conversations with the wild, with a separate section titled "The Wisdom of Tyson." I read it out loud to Tyson one morning. He curled up purring in my lap like a proud, furry teacher.

Stumbling Progress

Nibbling little itches.
Maintain dignity.
You're not really here, not listening.
Too much of a hurry, need to settle.
— Tyson Cat

In late April we arranged care for Tyson so Gregg and I could visit his father in the permanently mounted trailer in Louisiana crowded with Gregg's sisters and cousins. Gregg and I felt the angst of his father in decline, seeing ourselves in twenty-something years: the loss of privacy, of independence, of mobility, of vision. Trying to age gracefully and still wanting to be of service.

We walked through the semirural town, noting many fields that had grown sugarcane in abundance on our last visit now grew houses. Humid air wrapped us. I asked Gregg, "How do you feel about the idea of getting another dog?"

"I miss Buki. There'll never be another like her. I think I'd be okay with it if one came to us like she did, but I don't want to go looking for one."

That sounded right for Gregg. Inside that well-armored exterior beat a large heart. I said, "It's getting close to time. The right dog will turn up." It was clear we both felt the need for dog energy in our house.

Back at Gregg's father's house, I checked in with Tyson, and sensed it was a low-energy day for him. He said he'd feel better after a nap.

The day before we'd left on this trip, Tyson had said: *I miss you already. Will you scribe for me now?*

I'd pulled out my notebook and prepared to write. "What would you like to say?"

He paused. *I don't like, but accept, the idea of you and Gregg being gone. I know I will be cared for, and Buki and friend Nikki and Paddy will visit, as will you. I don't like change.*

"It's only for a week—seven nights, eight days. If you go interdimensional, won't the time pass more quickly?"

That's eight days of my life. While you're there, you'll be more cut off. It will be harder for you to have the focus to hear me. You take in much just by being near me.

"I know. We need to go though, mainly for Gregg, and he needs me there. I'll focus and call out to you, at night when it's quiet."

I'll wait for your call. Think of kitties playing in the flowers, of butterflies flitting in sunlight, of green meadow grasses. Hear the birds singing. See, it makes you smile.

"Add a tree and a rock too. Tyson, you are a magical being!"

I'm a cat.

In Louisiana, I sat outside in a folding chair under a tree and connected with Buki. She urged: *Be present in the now, in the moment, in the place.* I thanked her.

That night, I enjoyed lying in bed, listening to the sound of rain falling on the trailer roof. It reminded me of rainfall on the corrugated tin roof of our house in Colombia when I was a little girl. The new day opened to the Louisiana we all remembered, hot and sticky.

We were glad to get back home. I felt suspended, though, not connected. Nature waited for me to get back to the place I had been before we left. It had taken devoted energy to be present where I was on the trip, and in so doing I had lost connection to home.

I watched Tyson dream, twitching and making sounds. I asked to join his dream: *I'm a big cat in the jungle, running, enjoying the chase. Sun dapples through leaves. I pounce and catch a bird. The prey is part of this dance, the chase and giving, and the joined oneness.*

Pulling out my notebook to write wakened the great hunter.

In the afternoon I made my way down the hill behind our house, onto the undeveloped creek-side property below. A steep ravine led down to the creek. There I met an old live oak with branches the size of secondary trunks. One branch reclined on the ground, inviting me to climb up and sit on it. It felt like a hidden magical place. I asked this grandmother tree if it was in communication with Big Tree, where the road curves on the way to the park.

The tree answered: *The one you call Big Tree is part of my family.* I felt that Big Tree would like to be in a place like this, but the grandmother tree said: *Big Tree is an ambassador, there by the path to represent us and make contact with people who pass by.*

I received a feeling of acknowledgment from Big Tree, and saw myself standing with my palms on the trunk of each. I asked the grandmother tree if she had a message for me.

Return to your studies.

"Animal communication or Chaplaincy?"

Yes, both, the grandmother tree replied.

A huge black bumblebee with a yellow cummerbund buzzed around the hillside. It joined our conversation. *Go forward. Do not doubt. The All That Is sends you on this path. All you need will be provided. Focus on your growth. There is much to do. And enjoy.*

I thanked the grandmother tree and the bumblebee, and climbed back uphill to our house.

Granddaughter Katy spent the next night with us. In late afternoon I took her and Gregg to meet Grandmother Tree. At nine years old, Katy had become a good sport about these excursions. Gregg climbed up on the branch that reclined on the ground. We reveled in how many life forms made their homes there. Gregg stayed at the tree to watch the fog come in, while Katy and I made our way home. When he came up, I was still picking grass burrs out of her socks.

My feeling of disconnection extended to work. I called Mary, our former program director, to confide my thoughts about leaving Matthew House, and to discuss the timing of my exit announcement. Good counselor that she is, Mary asked, "If you announce departure this July rather than next January, would it be for you or for the board? Does the board need more than six months to find a successor?"

Probably not. Worse, could I put up with being a lame duck for a whole year? Best to keep my mouth shut, I concluded. My frustrations were best expressed in my journal.

That afternoon, needing to walk, I climbed down to the creek and sat on a log the rains had brought down.

Eucalyptus and bay laurels hung over the creek, filling the air with their scent. The voice of wind sounded in trees. I used a thick stick to free places where debris had dammed the creek, so little side channels could flow.

I asked the creek if it had a message, and heard: *Acceptance. The river flows where it will.* I thought of all the drops of water coming together to make up that little creek, and felt the sense of letting its water wash over and cleanse me.

I connected with Buki in spirit, who had come on the walk with me, and with Tyson, and with a dog whose picture I'd seen on a local animal shelter's website. I wished her well. She wasn't our dog. Maybe these were warmup exercises. Neither Buki nor Tyson would say whether a particular dog was the right one. I had to discern it for myself.

At home, Tyson purred in my lap and then bit my fingers. He quit purring, jumped down, and sat with his back to me.

"Tyson, are you mad at me? What did I do?"

You're not listening.

I took out our notebook. Gregg was watching television. The sound funneled down the hall to our living room, where Tyson and I sat. It seemed so loud! Could I block it out?

Tyson said: *Life is so short, and so long. Today, tomorrow, yesterday—it's all the same.*

"Can you be in more than one place at a time?"

Yes, more than one reality at a time. They all overlap. It's like many things happening at once, and you just pick the one you want to be part of. It takes practice.

"Is that why sometimes when I'm out walking or looking at something I get the feeling you can see it too?"

Yes, I can see through your eyes. You carry part of me with you.

"I'm glad. Is there anything else?"

No. I hear noises from the kitchen.

That weekend, before going to one of Matthew House's coalition churches to make a presentation, I walked onto our back deck to welcome the morning and do my grounding exercise: Roots grew from my feet into the earth. I stretched my arms up to the sky, and they became tree branches. Birds rested in my branches to sing. Today my chorus of animal friends was there, grinning. My heart was so full I thought it would burst in overwhelming gratitude.

In the church, I sat on a wooden pew waiting for mass to start. Light shone multicolored through stained-glass windows. I quieted and went back to that clearing. The animals were all still there, although this time they were singing Handel's "Hallelujah Chorus"! I felt a huge grin start to grow right there in church.

Between masses, I talked with a woman who'd come to explain convoluted new prescription-drug plans to the congregation. When I was introduced to her and learned her purpose in being there, I said, "Cool."

No smile crossed her pinched face. "These plans aren't cool. They're confusing!"

I clarified that it was good she'd come to help explain it. A little later, I described what I did for Matthew House, and said it was fun.

The woman said, "There's nothing fun about homelessness."

I clarified that I didn't say homelessness was fun, but that I enjoyed my part in helping to alleviate it. What a depressing outlook, I thought, and wondered why she had picked two words and taken issue with them. The response

I would have liked to make didn't come to me until later: We need joy in our lives and a sense of humor to do this work. We take ourselves too seriously. Tyson agreed.

That afternoon I packaged my application to the Chaplaincy Institute. I felt confident I'd get in, although wondered how to pay for it and what the outcome of going there would be. Could I do it, or was this another exercise in busyness?

Gregg questioned my decision to enroll. "You talk about how much is on your plate already. How can you consider taking on a graduate program?"

I couldn't answer that. I just knew it was the right thing for me. I mailed the application.

Contemplation of the
Other Side

Grayness of fur, grayness all around.
Fog closing in, eyes grow dim.
Heart beats strong, purr rumbles, love grows,
as body loses its hold.
— Tyson Cat

Regal Tyson sat on a footstool in front of the two-person couch in our living room, watching me read. I sensed he had something to say, and asked, "Ty, are you feeling well?"

No. My time is drawing close. He stretched the long, languorous ritual that cats do so well. *There's so much to teach you; there won't be time for it all. It's all about love.*

"Does this have something to do with getting another dog?"

That's Buki's wish. Life is infinite. When I go, I will not be gone, only different. I will stay to help teach you. You have great potential, but you're just starting to open. And you backslide. That's why you must clear your body of the sugars and toxins that block communication.

"On the trip I became disconnected, didn't I?"

You were where you were, and that is good, to be present. Don't give up. You've stumbled and feel sidetracked. That's the nature of the path. It's part of the learning.

I had an image of me stretched across a sticky web, sometimes falling through the holes, but making slow progress across it. "Ty," I asked, "is the Chaplaincy Institute where I should be headed? I'm concerned about the cost."

It will give you focus and help you exit your present situation. The tuition money will come.

His tone of voice let me know that thread of discussion had concluded. Then, curious, I asked, "Tyson, after this life, will you stay a cat?"

Oh yes, I'm always a cat, regardless of the body I wear. I felt him smile.

"Do you feel you're going to transition out soon?"

Not right away, but yes. The process will begin soon.

"Thank you for your help and your love."

I'm not gone yet. Again I felt him smile.

I still felt disconnected. Not as sharply as when we returned from Louisiana, but not yet as solidly connected as before we left. Not either place. I felt best outside under the eucalyptus trees. "Focus!" I told myself.

The next day Tyson dictated another poem, which we called "Shadows." A consultation with Cathy revealed that Tyson was either going through a bad spell or was getting ready to transition, but he hadn't decided yet. "He's tired," Cathy summarized, "and sorry he's not keeping his fur up. He's happy to be spending extra time with you."

Cathy added, "Since your path is taking you to work with people on matters of spirit, what better way for him to teach you but to be in spirit, and Buki too?" She assured me that just loving him was doing a lot—letting him do it his way. There was much to be learned in holding that space for him.

Shadows

Life is ending, night draws near.
Clouds form behind the trees
and sift through their branches.
Birdsong quiets as darkness falls.
The chill of dew on grass
brushes against my belly,
wets my paws.
Color fades to gray,
and the world turns to shadow,
a gnawing sadness,
nibbling around the edges of consciousness.
I do so love being a cat.
When the leaving time has come,
I will go with grace and dignity,
welcoming the transition
to light-filled spirit and new adventures,
unfettered by body.
But would yet still miss the gentle hands
and touch that smooth my fur and whisper,
"I love you, Tyson."
We are one.
I purr; it comforts us both.

— Tyson Cat

Learning to just be there for Tyson was priming me for the next phase. Tyson wanted to teach me in a way Buki couldn't because I hadn't been ready.

Buki came through, wanting me to know she is there for all of us. *You need to get out and walk more with me. That will help you feel better about what's happening to Tyson.*

I questioned if Tyson was ready to bring a dog in, given his situation. Did he want to share the focus? He said that part of him wanted it, part of him didn't.

At the end of our call, Cathy told me, "I want to validate that you're really getting it."

After the call, I recorded our conversation in my journal, then scribed for Tyson: *Purring, the rhythm of breathing. Quiet together, gently loving, melting oneness.*

I told him, "Ty, I'm concerned about you and feel you're nearing the end of your life."

Yes, that is so. It's a passage, a transition to a higher vibration of being. I'll still be around. You're not off the hook. You have much to learn.

"I appreciate your guidance. You are a good teacher, Tyson, as is Buki. I'll miss you, as I do her. Ty, is there anything I can do to make it easier or smoother for you?"

Just be with me. It's not time yet. It has been a good life, loving, and lots of adventures. Even Buki and Paddy. A rumble of purr. *And the tuna.* Then: *Bury me in a high place.*

I needed to ask another question. Tyson had been defecating and urinating outside the litterbox more often. "Ty, can I ask you about what's happening with the litterbox?"

I don't like to talk about it.

"I understand, but it would help me to know why you sprayed in Gregg's closet, and why you leave your feces on the floor in front of the box."

I don't know. I don't mean to; it's like something snaps, and I think I'm outside. Sometimes I'm somewhere and find that I've peed.

"I'm concerned, Ty. If it keeps up, Gregg will want to make you an outside cat. Or I could put a little diaper on, but that's not dignified."

I won't be around that long.

A few days later we continued the conversation. Tyson said: *I feel a little unsure, things just don't seem quite right. The way I feel, and . . . my whole self.*

"Tyson, I want to you to know that whatever you do, whether get better or decide to go, I honor your choice."

I know; it's just the doing and changing that feels strange . . . different.

"Tyson, will you let us know, when the time comes, if you want us to help you transition?"

It won't come to that. Buki needed your help; she was so strong and full of life. But I'm more at peace with it, more at one with it. It would be nice to be held.

"Let's sit together, okay?" I picked up my beloved senior sage, aware of how bony and light he had become. I carefully separated mats that had formed in his downy gray undercoat, now that he wasn't flexible enough to groom himself all over. We sat together, his head resting on my arm, and watched light shift the color of liquid amber leaves. Change was coming.

Arrival of the Wild Child

Large, furry creature, so insecure,
so full of light and life,
feet hardly touching the ground.
Confusion reigns.
— Tyson Cat

A blue eye surrounded by a ball of multicolored fur slammed into the kennel door. *Get me out of here!* resounded in my head. Startled, I jumped back. The surrounding cacophony of dog barks, yelps, and heart-wrenching anxiety assaulted my senses. I focused, and the ball of fur transformed into a dog, with one blue eye and one brown. I felt a connection. "I can't," I said. "I have to leave now, but I'll be back to see you."

Promise, she said.

"Yes," I replied.

I left the kennel area, and asked the animal control officer on duty about the dog in kennel number twenty-four. A card on the door read "Lexi. Female. Australian shepherd mix. wt. 45 lb., age unk. approx. 4 yrs.," with a capture date. He said she had been running loose near the regional park. "They had to dart her to catch her," he added. She'd been wearing no tags or identification. No one claimed her during the required three-week quarantine period. She'd been moved into the public area for possible adoption just that morning. I told him I had to leave but

159

would be back to see her. "Sure," he said. His tone of voice said he'd heard that a lot.

It had been a year and a half since Buki died. Gregg and I felt the need for dog energy in our house, and Buki had said we needed a dog to continue our education. Tyson didn't comment at first, but acknowledged a door of possibility opening.

I had asked Buki, "How will I know if it's the right dog?"

You will know. Follow your heart.

Tyson said: *I just want to have a say in it. Change. It's a good thing. But it will take getting used to.* He admitted: *You need a dog.*

"Someone to get me out for walks," I joked.

Disdain colored Tyson's reply. *Dog energy. I do what I can, but you need dog energy.*

Timing was a factor. We'd been leaving our back gate open, halfway hoping another dog would come up out of the canyon to live with us, as Buki had. I stopped that when we visited Gregg's family in Louisiana in April. I didn't want to be gone when our dog appeared! Now it was May. Gregg would be leaving for a two-week business trip in mid-June. He needed to agree about a dog, but if more time passed we'd have to wait until he returned.

I wanted something more specific than "Follow your heart." But this was a test. I would need to figure it out, feel it, myself.

The Universe arranged three tests for us. The first had been in March. One early morning I was still in bed when Gregg called up to me, "Come see what's in the backyard!" The tone of his voice told me it was something special. I threw a robe over my nightgown, pulled on slippers, and stumbled downstairs. Two dogs were in our backyard—lean and reddish brown. The small female shivered inside Buki's doghouse. The larger male stayed nearby, licking dew from the grass. Gregg talked to them while I filled a water bowl. Both lapped the water eagerly. I sat on the concrete steps near the dogs, directing calm and loving energy toward them. The male let me scratch his head, and read the phone numbers on his tags.

When Gregg went inside to call, I tried to communicate with them. I didn't want to return them to an abusive owner. What I got from them was that their gate had been open. They'd gone for a walkabout, and couldn't find their way back. They wanted to go home.

Twenty minutes later, a car screeched to a stop in front of our house. A man leaped out, leaving the car door hanging open. His dogs were happy to see him. He thanked us again and again, and told us a workman had left the gate open. "Other times that happened," he said, "the dogs have gone out, but always came back soon." This time the pair of red Dobermans had been gone for two days. They'd wandered six miles down the canyon, to come up into our yard.

Neither Gregg nor I felt this was a coincidence. It had been a test, especially for Gregg, to see if we were ready to welcome another dog into our hearts. We passed.

The next test was finding the right dog. I scoured adoption websites, but found it heartbreaking. Over five hundred Akitas needed homes! I focused on two local animal shelters, looking for a female smaller than Buki's eighty-five pounds, and around four years old. We didn't want a puppy. In one, I found an Akita-chow mix that met our criteria. The woman fostering her said I could see the dog at the animal shelter's open house that weekend.

When I drove into the gravel parking lot that Saturday, I spotted the dog and felt a spark of recognition. We walked along a dirt trail between the summer-dry grasses and the road. I explored communicating with her. By the end of our walk, though, we knew we weren't right for each other. I returned her to the kennel and told her, "I hope you find your forever-home soon." Test two.

Discouraged, I toured the shelter's adoption area. I felt anxiety, confusion, and hopefulness from the dogs and cats. Some had been there too long and were giving up on finding a home. It was like being chosen last for a team on a school playground. Others were confused about their situation. Some wore masks of bravado or unconcern. I walked the concrete aisle between rows of double-stacked wire cages on one side, and larger kennels on the other side. As I neared the end, feeling worn by the barking my presence had caused, the ball of fur slammed into Lexi's kennel door and I looked into that wild blue eye.

I went back during lunch break on Monday. When an animal control officer brought Lexi out on a leash, she warned me, "She's shy, and doesn't warm up to people right away." I felt pressure on my leg and looked down to see the dog leaning against me, looking up at me. "Or maybe not," the animal control officer added. She said this dog was submissive, and "passingly interested in cats but easily distracted from them."

We went for a walk along the same trail. This dog, named Lexi by animal-control staff, pulled on the leash but otherwise seemed socialized. She knew basic commands such as "Sit." By the end of our walk she had started to show her personality. I went to the shelter at noon three more times that week to walk her. Lexi was glad to see me, or just to get out of her kennel.

That weekend I walked down the canyon below our house. The creek bubbled around fallen logs and big rocks. I climbed out onto a rock and sat, surrounded by flowing water. So many questions. Was this the right time to get a dog? Was this the right dog? I sensed that this sequence of experiences was meant to polish my discernment. I connected with Buki and Tyson, who still wouldn't say whether a particular dog was the right one, or if it was the right time.

The following week I took Lexi for another walk. We were comfortable with each other. I felt light and happy after being with her. She was sweet and liked tummy rubs and chasing tennis balls. I told her about the work I wanted to do in the future, helping people as a chaplain. She thought about it. She liked me, but she wasn't sure about working with me the way I described. I felt she would be good for us but wasn't quite the right dog.

This was so close to my heart that I lacked confidence in my animal-communication ability. I called Cathy. She'd said finding a dog would be easy, but it didn't feel that way. I felt confused. Cathy said, "Buki wants to know why you think Lexi isn't the right one."

I couldn't answer. Lexi was such a different dog. Buki had been earth connected and grounded. Lexi was all fire and air energy. I hadn't felt a clear sign, but did feel a connection. Cathy said there was some Nordic dog in her mix, and Northern dogs tend to be headstrong as well as smart. "Lexi has Coyote trickster spirit. She has different energy but was cut from the same shamanic cloth as Buki, and is very smart." This dog, though, had been neglected or abused and had anxiety and a strong prey drive. She needed training.

Gregg agreed to meet Lexi. I realized I'd made a decision and hoped he would agree. Lexi was hesitant around him at first, then chased a few tennis balls, and finally let him rub her tummy. Gregg liked her. Although still uncertain about getting her or any other dog, he was willing to give it a try. He said, "It's bringing stuff up for me. I know it would be easier to just bury my feelings about Buki, but I'm hoping Lexi will help both of us get past it."

When we walked her back to the kennel, I told Lexi what would happen next: She would go to the vet to be spayed, and we would pick her up from there. Then she saw some cows, and her herding instincts kicked in. She bolted to the end of her leash.

Gregg said, "She has a lot of energy. Are you sure about this?"

In another conversation with Cathy and Lexi, we talked about a new name. The shelter had named her Lexi. She didn't want to use that or her original name. She had Coyote energy, and with her coloration looked like a moving sand painting. We settled on Heyoke Katsina, which translates roughly as Coyote Spirit Doll.

The night before I brought our new dog home, I asked Tyson, "Ty, do you have thoughts to share?"

Of course, he answered. He jumped up beside me on the couch. *Someone else to share the work in keeping you focused!*

"You're putting a good face on it, aren't you?"

Yes, things will be different. It's always the new baby that gets attention.

We sat, enjoying what might be our last evening of quiet together for a while. *The change is coming,* he said.

On June 1, 2005, I brought newly spayed Sina, as we came to call her, home from the vet. Then the fun began.

When I told our vet that the shelter staff had said she was four, he said, "No way this dog is four years old! Year and a half, max!" That answered one question—I had thought it unusual that a four-year-old unspayed female would never have had puppies. There was still a lot of puppy energy in her—another aspect of the universal conspiracy! The vet's opinion was strengthened when she gained ten pounds in her first six months with us. "She's just filled out to her adult size," the vet said.

I could hear Buki chuckling to her spirit self, as Sina was clearly meant to be with us, and had much to teach us. My animal chorus was outright laughing in the background. We had connected with the right dog, and passed the third test.

For the first week I worked from home, going to the office for meetings and no longer than two hours at a time. Sina easily leaped over the baby gate we put up to keep her in our family room. Gregg stacked one gate on top of another; she broke through that. She ripped the arm fronts off Gregg's recliner, and tore down the Venetian blinds in our office. We tried one size crate and then a larger one, to help her feel secure and for timeouts.

After the recliner incident, Gregg had second thoughts. He sat on the couch in our living room. Tyson stretched beside me on the arm of my chair. Sina raced down the hallway, took a flying leap ten feet away from Gregg, flipped in the air, and landed on her back with her head in his lap, tongue hanging out and smiling up at him. Tyson and I looked at each other. We knew Sina had just wrapped Gregg around her paw.

She captured my heart during a walk on the canyon trail. Sina trotted back and forth, sniffing the underbrush. Our feet crunched on dry leaves and twigs. I thought about how often I'd walked these trails with Buki. We entered a shady spot. Sina paused, turned, and came back to me. She leaned against my leg and looked up at me, as she had at the animal shelter. I felt more than heard: *Thank you for bringing me to this place.*

It didn't take long before Sina acted as if she owned the park. She enjoyed playing with other dogs and meeting their people (especially if they carried treats). She soon earned the nickname Irrepressible Katsina. She liked Nikki's Irish wolfhound, Artagan. I would learn later that she thought him cute, and that Artagan considered Sina a flirt.

Sometimes I drove her to a fenced dog park for off-leash time. She wasn't as comfortable there with the changing group of dogs and their frenetic massed greeting at the gate. Driving home, we saw a woman walking a collie. I told Sina, "There's a collie with a tail like yours."

Sina replied: _Nobody has a tail like mine._

I corrected: "The collie with a tail somewhat like yours only not so full, fluffy, and pretty." I could feel her satisfaction. That was the clearest communication I'd heard from her since that day in the animal shelter.

We soon discovered she had more than a "passing interest" in cats—this dog had a strong prey drive. I caught her snapping at Tyson. Rule One was "Leave the cat alone!" I was emphatic: If Sina hurt Tyson, she was going back to the shelter. I was watchful, and kept her on a leash in the house. Sina had to earn our trust.

Tyson did his part too. He said: _You need help with this dog._ He had a new mission. Tyson moved in slow motion around Sina and even walked under her, dragging his tail across the underside of her belly. He knew she needed help with grounding.

Sina's ungrounded behavior gave us clues that she'd been abused by her previous owners. She had learned to pop her spirit self out of her body. I could see the shift in her eyes when that started to happen, and learned to call her back as soon as I noticed it.

When Sina had been with us for a week, Gregg left for his two-week business trip. I settled into a routine of up at 6:30, feed the cat, feed and walk the dog, then alternate work in office and work at home in two-hour stretches. It was wearing, but we were making progress.

One day a neighbor called me at work. She'd been walking her dog and saw Sina in front of our house! Sina came to her, and the neighbor put her in our backyard. After taking her own dog home, the neighbor found Sina prancing up the street again, waving her plumed tail and wearing a big smile. The neighbor returned her to our backyard, found where Sina had escaped through the fence, barricaded it, and called me. I came home and inspected  the escape route. Gregg had pulled back the chain link to move something, then rolled it into place and secured it with nylon rope. Sina figured out how to untie the knots. I secured the fence with wire clamps. Now I could add chain-link fence repair to my marketable skills.

On our walk that afternoon, another neighbor told me, "I'm glad you got your dog back." I related the day's escapade. He said, "No, I saw her out yesterday!" So she had been out at least three times. This headstrong dog was demonstrating the wanderlust of her Nordic heritage.

It was hard for Sina, but she was getting the "Leave the cat alone!" message. Tyson was a great trainer. One night, I had Sina sit in the kitchen while Tyson ate his supper. He ate slowly, his gray self hunched. His tags clinked on the food bowl. He moved in controlled slow motion, patient, letting the dog know who was boss. Sina did well, and even lay down on the brown-vinyl tiles. Then Tyson stretched and walked slowly out of the kitchen. Sina wanted to follow. We went around the corner. No cat in sight.

Tyson could slip through the stair railings to go upstairs, which was reserved for him. We kept a baby gate at the foot of the stairs, a psychological more than a physical barrier. Sina was only allowed downstairs. I was about to praise Sina and give her a treat when she jumped over the baby gate and headed upstairs. She came back when I called, and was submissive. The voice plus volume worked that time.

Walks to the park revealed more aspects of this dog. She played in the sprinklers, biting at the water, not caring if she got wet. What fun! Then I saw her prey drive at work. Sina spotted a blue-eyed feral kitten beside the trail and was on it like greased lightning. She pounced and gave it a quick shake. I pulled her back, yelling, "Drop it!" She didn't understand. I was insistent. Finally Sina dropped the kitten on the dirt trail. It sat on the path, hissing, as I pulled Sina away. I was shaken, nearly nauseated. We doubled back a short time later, and the kitten was gone. I suspected it had crawled into the blackberry canes to die. I felt terrible.

I made an emergency call to Cathy, who relayed that Sina didn't understand why I was upset. Cathy said, "When she was on her own, she hunted, and she's proud of her ability to catch her own food." Sina wanted to know why I wasn't proud of her too. We had a lot of work to do.

Tyson reminded me that he wanted his scribe back. I gathered pen and notebook. Tyson purred in my lap, and described vigilance:

Vigilance. Predator in the house, enemies outside.
Must exercise control over the large one.
It's kind of fun.
Her thoughts and feelings are scattered,
energy all around, flashing in spikes of sunlight,
sharp daggers piercing into my eye.
I am calm. I watch. I wait.
The training program is slow,
like a cell memory of kittens.
Must learn to undo and then redo the lessons.
I am safe.

I thanked Tyson for his help and told him I was glad he felt safe.

You make it so, he said.

In a later session, Tyson mused about Sina: *She's cute and clingy and needy. How could a beast be that way?* He wanted to make sure he received his share of time and attention. He was right about the patient one sometimes being overlooked. On the other hand, he said: *It's good not to be the whole focus.* I sensed he was enjoying the challenge of training Sina. Tyson said: *I'm not going to die. I'm just resting.*

Buki and Tyson warned me that Sina knew how to read me. She'd come a long way in our first month, but we were not used to having a wild child among us. She exploded with exuberance from time to time, as if someone had given her an electric shock. I had to be firm and consistent with her. She wanted direction and to be told what was expected.

For her part, Sina seemed to understand the need to get along with Tyson. She was young yet, and knew that Tyson and Buki had a paw in bringing us together. We were all still learning.

I sensed Buki's spirit staying close. She reminded me to call on her when I was upset with Sina: "Buki, fix this!" Buki assured me she's not laughing at me but with me. She said: *This has helped complete the cycle.*

In July, just over a month after bringing Sina home, Tyson gave a summary: *I am calm. I speak with the slow and steady voice of one who commands. I move slowly, with dignity, lest she think I am prey. The lessons each day, each meeting. She learns quickly, though still has that gleam in her eyes that tells me to maintain vigilance.*

I noticed subtle changes in our house. Sina seemed to bring out and reward a softness in Gregg that was easy for him to lose.

Tyson, who was tired of being an old cat and not feeling well most of the time, had considered leaving his body. Now he had a new mission—help ground Coyote-spirited Sina and teach her the rules. Our buccaneer pirate cat was invigorated and having a good time training this impetuous dog. He also knew he had to stay alert. I was glad of his renewed commitment to stay, and marveled at what a courageous and perceptive cat he had turned out to be.

I still did not know the extent of the transitions he would help me through.

Breaking Open

Transition – it's all about change,
and staying the same.
— Blue Dragonfly

My protective shell, whacked by a loving hammer, started to fracture and crumble.

The third week of January, a few days before Buki's memorial service, I'd kept a promise to myself and Buki. I had visited the Chaplaincy Institute for the free first day of an intensive module. Morning lecture on Early Christianity, afternoon art. Something clicked in place for me then, and I knew this was where my path was leading. It just wasn't time yet.

Six month later, in June 2005, I attended my first full module. It was the beginning of a period of deep inner work and spiritual growth. My heart cracked open, uncovering old wounds and limiting beliefs, and opening the path to a new way of walking in the world.

We met in the education wing library at Grace North Church in Berkeley, home of the Chaplaincy Institute. Bookshelves rose to the ceiling on two walls, above second-hand couches. Windows filled the wall across from me, giving me a connection to outside. I was grateful to see Dori, who had guided me here after I'd visited her garden labyrinth. I met Gary, who would come back to retake my last module and be part of my ordination group. Five of us

171

enrolled for the whole module. Four others came to visit the first day. I was excited and scared at the same time. Was this the beginning of a new chapter in my life?

First on the agenda was a check-in. All of us said a few words about ourselves and how we were doing. When it was my turn, I said, "I'm glad to be here. This is the first day of my first module. And we just adopted a high-energy new dog—she's a real handful."

"Welcome," they chorused. No one commented on my sharing about the dog. I suddenly felt a shadow of doubt pass over me, and questioned if this was the right place if something so monumental for me as adopting a new dog would pass by with no comment.

I slowly grasped the group dynamics. The closeness wrought by unfolding and growth stitches people together. Different students attended each module. Some took the twelve one after another; others spaced them out over two or more years, as I would. As time passed, I learned that my presence and focus on animals helped open this ever-changing group to animals. People told me this, and I was always surprised to hear it.

Rev. Dr. John Mabry gave the first lecture of this intensive module, on interfaith. He was humorous and immensely knowledgeable. His overview of world religions and their commonalities showed how salvation differs with each faith tradition.

In the afternoon the group interpreted a dream from a Jungian perspective. So far, so good.

The next day brought a challenge. We met in the church's labyrinth hall. Morning light streamed through the tall, narrow windows, shining on the seven-circuit modified Chartres pattern painted on the wooden floor. That labyrinth helped keep me from falling apart. We focused on music coming from within. Each of us had to sing or tone to the song within us. Each tone wrenched itself through my constricted throat. In the afternoon we practiced body movement to tell a story while a partner interpreted the movements. These forms of self-expression were new to me. I cried from the effort of dragging up and expressing deep feelings.

On Friday, in the process class and meditation, the group sat in a circle and discussed how the module was going for them. This too was new for me, coming into touch with my feelings in the moment and being encouraged to talk about them.

I missed Saturday's session to attend Matthew House's board retreat. With only three days of Chaplaincy Institute behind me, I could feel a difference in myself. Even though I would have another opportunity to draw and discuss my family history and go through a grief ritual, I was sorry to miss the deep sharing of other class members' stories. The board retreat was productive, though, with its focus on fundraising.

Chaplaincy's Sunday morning session met at Chapel of the Chimes in Oakland, one of architect Julia Morgan's masterpieces. After a tour, we went into a sedately fur-nished conference room for a description of the funeral and burial process. It was hard for Dori. That was the same room where she and her husband had talked over funeral arrangements for their daughter. Dori's intense feelings highlighted the importance of a chaplain's presence at such times.

Our homework had been to prepare a marriage ritual. In the afternoon, we met in the Chaplaincy office, a downstairs room with garden-level windows. Each person did it differently. I wrote a unification ceremony of three parts of myself I'd met in my last meditation with the Pathfinders in Boulder: the duke, the clown, and Grace. I couldn't read all the way through it and had to ask Dr. Mabry for help. He read the ceremony while I sat and wept. Everyone was kind. I couldn't even answer the simple and gentle questions that followed.

Sunday afternoon we held a bead ceremony, developed by students as a ritual to close each module. Each student brought beads they felt reflected the lessons of the module, and presented one to each student and to the teachers, with a blessing. I cherished those beads as symbols of learning, opening, and connection to others on this path.

This began breaking open the casing around my tender inner self. I could intellectualize that there were many un-shed tears from this life. When I stayed in my head I felt safe and in control. When I went to my heart, I was okay until I opened my mouth. This is what had happened in the sessions with the Pathfinders, in the animal communica-tion course, and in the voice/dance sessions earlier in the week. Movement stirs up the tears. Sound sends them forth.

At home after the module, I warned Gregg that I might be subject to spontaneous crying, and cried. He had his usual reaction of turning away. To him, tears were a sign of weakness, and they made him uncomfortable. He was a sensitive man who, like me, had built a shell around him-self. The well of tears wouldn't go away without being shed. I had to allow myself to cry. As uncomfortable as it would be for Gregg, the safety of home was the best place.

That evening I sat on the living room couch, furry Tyson in my lap. Sina twitched in her sleep beside me. I hadn't scribed often for Tyson since she came. We both missed it.

Three months later I signed up for the Judaism module. It had its moments, but I didn't feel the deep opening experience of my first module. I learned a wealth of information that set aside my previous impression of Judaism as a monolithic religion with uniform beliefs. It isn't. Like Christianity, Judaism has branches and sects, a complex interweaving of history and practice.

Renowned dream worker Rev. Jeremy Taylor led our dream-work session. Each student gave a dream title. I gave: "Driving Off the Cliff with Three Planets in the Sky."

Jeremy said, "Congratulations. Death dreams can symbolize a time of internal change, when some part of you symbolically dies so a new self can emerge."

"Even if I screamed *No* and woke up?"

"It doesn't matter," Jeremy said. "Some part of you is ready for that change, even if other parts are not."

Like a snake shedding its skin, I thought. The snake doesn't choose the time, and is vulnerable in the transition.

The week after the Judaism module, I dropped by Matthew House's shelter. LeRoy—the house manager and unofficial dad to families there—and I surveyed the pile of garage-sale leftovers that had appeared on the porch. A loaded pickup truck pulled up in front. "More donations," we said together. Out of the pickup stepped Aaron, the nephew of the Polish Jewish man who years before had told me of surviving the Holocaust with his brother.

Buoyant, Aaron said, "We're clearing out a family member's house. I've brought you all the sheets and towels, and some household supplies. Do you want them?"

Yes! That was exactly the kind of donation we needed. LeRoy carried the bagged linens from the truck. I thanked

Aaron and filled out a donation receipt for him, and then thought to tell him I had just completed an intensive module on Judaism. "I now have a much better understanding of Judaism," I told him.

A big smile spread across Aaron's open face. "Just a minute," he said, and loped back to the truck. He returned with a brown paper bag. "This was in the house," he said. "We wanted it to go to someone who would appreciate it." He pulled the bag off a framed oil painting, about nine-by-fourteen inches. Morning light on the shelter porch fell on a painting of the Wailing Wall in the Old City of Jerusalem, with the Temple Mount glowing gold behind it and the Al-Aqsa Mosque minaret in the distance. The most holy place of the three Abrahamic religions—Judaism, Christianity, and Islam. "It belongs with you," Aaron said, his brown eyes earnest.

I could only stammer, "Thank you! I'll honor it." My Matthew House and Chaplaincy paths had come together. That painting still hangs in my altar room.

The Chaplaincy program required regular spiritual direction. That turned out to be a further shell-cracking endeavor. I chose to work with Ron, the gentle man who facilitated Chaplaincy's process class, and who viewed the world as much through his intuition as through the thick spectacles he wore. We met in his office, a small upstairs room in a three-story brick building that had once been a laundry. The room held one small window, a tapestry showing Jacob's Ladder, two comfortable chairs, a potted ficus tree, and several boxes of tissues. I made a crack about my glaring insecurities. Ron proceeded to take it seriously and follow it. Needing to slow down, I asked for an explanation of how this worked. The pause helped. I had never been in anything resembling counseling before.

This was the first time I'd ever talked in depth about feeling wounded and invisible, and about the discrepancy between the vulnerable self inside and the strong, capable outer part I showed to the world. Ron asked about my birth family. I reached for a box of tissues and clutched it for the rest of our session. No one had ever listened that deeply before. I told him about my pretty, creative, extroverted older sister, and how I was the younger, pudgy one, the good kid, while my sister tangled with Mother, and our father stood by the side. I told him of the day my sister was getting ready to leave for boarding school. My parents were sad, and I said, "But you'll still have me." They had turned and looked at me but said nothing. How much that had hurt!

So I walled it off in my heart. Even when Mother and my sister were fighting, I learned to stay out of the way. Invisible. Alone in my room but not lonely, feeling the presence of a benevolent, loving, accepting Source that I felt more connected to than with my family. I lived with them but was not part of them. Looking at that beginning shed light on why it was so hard to leave my chosen family at Matthew House.

Ron led me on a guided meditation unlike anything I'd ever experienced. Eyes closed, I focused on my heart. It looked in my mind's eye like a piece of raw meat turned inside out—striated, broken, and chopped. In closing the session, Ron asked me to journal how my being made to feel inadequate and not valued became core beliefs. It took many pages.

Subsequent spiritual-direction sessions weren't as wrenching or deep as the first, but chipped away at my barriers and defenses. Ron and I talked about my relationship with Gregg and my family, how I protected myself from them and at same time hid behind them, using them as an excuse for not stretching myself. It all went back to my lessons of the invisible child and avoiding confrontation, not wanting to be the target of even perceived anger. Ron suggested ways I could practice deflecting anger, and ways to help others acknowledge and emphasize positives and accomplishments, rather than negatives and failures.

The animals welcomed this new channel of release for me. It didn't take long before the real issue to be addressed in spiritual direction bubbled up: fear. Not quaking in your boots fear, but self-limiting fear. Fear of change. Fear of the unknown. Just as I realized it was about fear, a red-tail hawk called, confirming fear as the topic to pursue.

In the fall, a blessing of birds! I woke to the sound of wild turkeys. I went outside with Sina in time to see a red-tail hawk fly overhead, then land in trees across the canyon. I greeted it and asked if it had a message. It said: *Work harder. Go deeper and listen; find the deeper truths.*

This felt more like a time limitation than a warning. A time was coming when I would need to be attuned to nature and the animals. The hawk flew off. Then I saw seven male turkeys doing an intricate circular dance. I greeted them, and asked why they had crossed my path.

The turkeys said: *We're just here. Listen to the red-tail.* They were sorting out who would mate with the females. They danced around bushes and through leafy growth. Gold-crowned sparrows sang their three-note song, their flock like so many ornaments in the bush. I felt blessed and reaffirmed, and reminded that my path is a serious commitment that takes work.

On the winter solstice, I sang the sun down and up again the next morning, as we passed the shortest day and longest night. And here came the seven wild turkeys again, stretching their wings and trotting down the fence line. Not a circular dance as before. I looked up Turkey in Jamie Sams's animal totems book: Turkey is the soul of selfless giving for the good of the whole tribe. To have Turkey cross your path is a blessing and a gift. When I finished reading it, I looked out; the turkeys were gone and so was the sun. And Tyson was with me.

Tyson said: *You're scattered. Get grounded.*

In meditation, all my animal chorus—Moose, Turtle, Wolf, Hummingbird, Dragonfly, Hawk, Mountain Lion, Buki, Sina, and Tyson—all the cats and animals, and birds too, were there. I asked, "What is the most important lesson for me to study and learn now so I'll be prepared?"

The simple answer: *Meditate and focus your mind.* With that focus would come the confidence to listen to my own inner wisdom.

The Gradient Stiffens

Love is the great work
Though every heart is first an apprentice. . . .
Happiness is the great work
Though every heart must first become a student
To one who really knows about Love.
— Hafiz

I planned to resign from Matthew House in January 2006. Of the three key positions—program director, book-keeper, and executive director (mine)—the agency could weather the executive director's departure with the other two positions in place.

In October our bookkeeper, Noel, told me she would be leaving after completing the annual audit. I was grateful to her for staying for the audit, and sad at losing her. This wouldn't alter my plans to announce my own departure the following January. Or so I thought.

Sina started doggy school. Basic and intermediate obedience classes. The training is as much for the handler as the dog. Sina learned quickly, although she had her own ideas about when to remember what she'd learned. She demonstrated her sensitive side the afternoon she met Marcus, a neighborhood boy with severe disabilities. Marcus flapped his hands excitedly when he saw her. Sina walked over, rested her chin on his knee as he sat in his wheelchair, and looked up at him. He couldn't speak, but a big smile grew on his face and his hand flapping calmed. When whatever it was had passed between them, she turned to resume our walk.

Buki's presence continued. One evening, as I was getting ready to close the back sliding door, I felt her. The feeling was so strong I didn't want to close the door, but Buki let me know that doors and walls meant nothing to her now. I marveled at how my love for her continued to grow. I explained to Sina that I loved her too, and appreciated her being with us. She was herself. She was not, and I didn't expect her to be, a replacement for Buki.

At Tyson's next vet checkup, I asked about his urinating on the carpet. Dr. Hackler took blood and urine samples, which showed that Tyson's kidneys weren't functioning well. "He's a sicker kitty than he lets on."

Later, I made the connection between Tyson urinating on the carpet—a deliberate action—just before all the grand-children arrived, and talked with him about it. He complained that it took so much energy to rebalance the house after the extended family leaves: *House full of little ones. I hide—too much chaotic energy. So much work to rebalance after they're gone.*

I had felt the demands of chaotic energy too. As a compromise, I asked Tyson to focus on helping me stay balanced instead of trying to do everything himself. I promised to use my pendulum to rebalance the house energy after our family's next visit. Tyson agreed. I asked if there was anything else he'd like to say.

No, you go to bed. I'll talk to you in your dreams. I'm glad to have my scribe back.

So I settled into sleep, touching him, and dreamed of ancient knowledge.

The next morning Tyson gave me an update on his work with Sina: *Katsina is dizzy. Not going easily. I'm working with her.*

Sina's erratic behavior and disregard of house rules challenged all of us. Tyson said I needed to be more on top of her, to make sure she treated him with respect. He didn't like it when she stuffed her nose in his behind and sniffed. *Treating me like a dog!*

Sina responded: *But he smells so good!* Back to basic training and earned privileges!

One afternoon I walked Sina to the horse corral in a rural area near our house. She liked the horses. That day, there was a mottled gray horse I hadn't seen before, and a chestnut. Also new to the corral, a white bull rested near the wire fence. Excited, Sina pulled me around to that side. There, all three touched noses with her, one by one, even the bull. Sina didn't want to leave. When she tried to dig under the fence I pulled her away. That interaction stuck with me. I knew it was significant, but I didn't know why. I asked Cathy about it. She relayed that the horses and bull said I had to meditate on it, journal it, and hear the message for myself. She said Buki was there too, and that Buki, Sina, and I are all members of the White Buffalo tribe.

Tyson suggested I write the way I do when scribing for him. *The answer is there*, he said. He stayed with me all that night, purring.

The next day I walked Sina down to see the horses again. White Bull said: *You're not doing your homework.* I was defensive. I was doing some, but I acknowledged not enough.

He said: You must do more. The time is coming when you will need those skills!

Walking farther, I heard: *Let the animals teach you. Especially the birds.* I asked who spoke, but received no answer.

Sina continued to lead us on misadventures as we searched for a common ground between her fire-and-air personality and apparent abuse in her former home, and my more earth-connected self. On New Year's Eve, Gregg, Sina, and I met Nikki and Artagan up at the park. We walked down to the creek, curious how much water flowed in it after recent rains and high winds. Sina was glad to see Artagan. She was bouncy as usual at the beginning of a walk, but good about coming back from the extent of her flexi-leash to check in. When we came to a steep slope down to the creek bridge, Gregg let her off leash.

"Are you sure you want to let her off?" I asked.

"The trail's steep, muddy, and slippery," he answered. "I'll put her back on in a bit."

Sina was ecstatic and ran back and forth, trying to get Artagan to play. As we walked toward the picnic tables halfway down the trail, she raced out and back. She and Gregg pulled ahead of us. Then I heard Gregg yelling at her to come back. Sina had spotted something and streaked up the hillside. We heard dogs barking at the top. Gregg climbed the hill. I stayed by the picnic tables in case she came back. Nikki and Artagan walked down to the trail's end. I couldn't hear or see Gregg or Sina. I tried to connect with her, but only received impressions of running, bushes whipping by. I sat alone as it grew dark, and called to Buki for help.

Buki said: *I'm with her.*

I asked Buki to help Sina get back to us. I didn't have a clear picture of how that would happen—whether Sina would go into someone's yard who would call us, or back to the trail, or home. Nikki and Artagan came back up the trail, and we made our way up to the park. Then I connected with Sina. "Where are you, Sina?"

I'm home. She sounded surprised that I would ask.

Then I heard Gregg's voice calling. He'd gone home to get our car to look for her on streets on both sides of the canyon. A neighbor had met him out front and told him, "I saw your dog trotting down the street. She's pretty muddy. I put her in your backyard."

Gregg thanked him. Sure enough, there was Sina in the backyard, looking quite pleased with herself. The good part, we agreed, was that she found her way home. Thank you, Buki! The bad part was that she had followed that wanderlust Nordic part of herself and run off again.

Back in the house, I flopped onto the couch. Tyson flicked his tail, irritated. *The one being who could confirm if Sina was home*, he grumbled, *and no one checked with me!*

This Coyote-trickster dog definitely had things to teach us. As Cathy had predicted: "Things are getting better in leaps and slides."

Blessing

Honor me, listen to me, feel my pain,
let people know that I too am living.
I give freely, and heal much,
though the balance is disrupted
and change is coming.
— The Voice of Earth

In my meditation, White Buffalo came close and snorted in my face. I felt his warm breath, saw his huge nostrils, felt droplets of moisture on my skin. *Just write*, he told me.

I'd gone to the grove of eucalyptus trees below our house and settled beneath one, notebook nearby. I centered and journeyed down to the clearing with the big rock where I go in meditation. Often the Council of Animals is there. Today Buki and White Bull were there. I asked Buki where she was now that my heart was so much bigger.

She said: *Still in your heart. I have more room now. Call Katsina.*

I could hear Sina whimpering back at our house, unhappy at being left behind. I called her spirit self into the clearing. She did a little dance. White Bull snorted. He tended to be very serious. I called Tyson's spirit self too. The Council says that although he's not of the White Buffalo Tribe, he's accepted and respected by them. Tyson sat to one side, tucked in his paws, and wrapped his tail around himself. I asked if White Bull was the messenger.

No; I just open the gate. He opened it, and White Buffalo came toward us.

I offered the Hindu greeting: "*Namaste*, White Buffalo. I honor the God in you."

I am God, he replied.

I corrected my greeting: "I honor God *as* you. White Buffalo, may I address you?"

That is why I am here. He breathed on me and continued. *In the beginning there were many tribes. They were all made one. Much time passed. Then the tribes were scattered. The people endured difficult times. I was to come again among my people and bring them hope. I have come many times. A few heard my true message, but their voices have been lost. Now the time is for a different way.*

"A different way of being, or a different way of telling people about your message?"

Yes. For those whose hearts are open to be in the old way, when we were one.

"Are we not one now?"

We are, although many do not know it. There is too much separation. Gather and reach out to others of the White Buffalo Tribe. You will know them. Your heart will tell you.

"Why is Tyson not a member of the White Buffalo Tribe?"

He is an honorary member because of your love for him.

White Buffalo continued: *Be aware of messages that are all around you, in the sunlight, in the wind, in calls of the eagle and hawk, in the voices of wisdom of your human teachers. Listen to Buki, who is my special messenger, and to Heyoke Katsina, whom you have chosen well. You have come far, yet you are just beginning your journey. You will find your voice.*

"How do I know if I'm listening to a true voice?"

You will know if you are truly listening. That is why I am here to speak to you. Practice. Two years to prepare, and then your journey will begin. Study well. That is enough for now.

White Buffalo came close and licked my forehead with his huge tongue, like a blessing. A shower of droplets from his breath mixed with shining sparkles of gold all around me.

The gate closed. Buki, Katsina, and White Bull gathered around. White Buffalo had withdrawn. They were silent, looking at me. In unison, they said: *You have been chosen. Awaken. We are here for you.*

I felt love and gratitude, and no fear. "I am worthy," I said. "I can walk this path." Then, "May I ask, White Bull, what you conveyed to Katsina when you touched noses at the corral?"

Recognition and acknowledgment. It was also to get your attention, so you may know you are one of us. You were talking to us with love, but you did not know us.

I gave thanks, journeyed back up the tunnel from my meditation clearing, and felt again the rough bark of the eucalyptus tree on my back. I looked up through the trees and saw a young red-tailed hawk circling overhead. I glanced at my watch. An hour had passed.

Gregg came home and released Sina from her imprisonment in the backyard. She raced down the hill and slid to a halt beside me, showering me with leaf debris.

A couple of weeks later I again meditated with White Buffalo, seeking clear direction.

White Buffalo never minced words. *You know your dreams. They are within. You want to communicate freely with me and other animals, and be acknowledged and respected for that. The need for recognition holds you back and takes you out of your heart. Like a captive dolphin, you must allow yourself to jump for joy even in captivity. Let yourself grow. The purpose of growth is to realize your full potential. The direction of growth is to find your work in the world, both as a laboratory for learning and as a way to fully experience and give back to the whole.*

I hesitated, still looking for certainty. "A lot of these things cost money."

There will be enough. You have a start; expand on it. That is all for today.

Squirrel interjected: *Learn from me. Watch as I fly from branch to branch, flicking my tail and scurrying. I look like I'm having fun, yet I get a lot of work done.*

I thanked White Buffalo and Squirrel for their support and guidance. I felt like a baby chick struggling to break out of its egg.

Best-Laid Plans

All your images of winter I see against your sky.
I understand the wounds that have not healed in you.
They exist because God and love have yet to become
real enough to allow you to forgive the dream.
— Hafiz

Up, down, sideways, turned upside down. In amusement parks I don't like roller coasters. I get enough of that on a daily basis.

I planned to announce my resignation at the January board meeting. Michael, our program director, beat me to it. He told me he'd interviewed for a position with another agency. I encouraged him to go ahead. It was a good career move for him.

Both the program director and bookkeeper were leaving. I couldn't resign until those two critical positions were stabilized. I called Esther, the board member who'd lent me her ear and shoulder to talk through the agency's challenges. She knew how to listen. We sat on the gray couch in her bungalow, surrounded by piles of projects she somehow kept straight. I'd nicknamed her Mighty Mouse for her amazing energy level and diminutive stature. I poured out my thoughts about whether it was time for me to step aside at Matthew House. I shared my plans to announce my resignation in January, and told her how Michael had just told me he was leaving. He and Noel, our bookkeeper, would exit around the same time. I couldn't go now. Did I have the strength to once again motivate myself to keep going?

Esther told me, "You're stronger than you know. You can do what's necessary!" Her support encouraged me, and I felt better after sharing what was in my heart.

We held a joint going-away party for Michael and Noel. Esther told me I was "businesslike" when I informed the board of their resignations and status of the search for replacements. Esther's support remained steadfast over the next months when I announced the hire of a new program director, who left after six weeks to return to her former agency. The new, well-qualified bookkeeper departed after two weeks, telling me he couldn't handle the stress level. He was succeeded by a series of temporary accountants, and then by Julia, a skilled young woman who wanted to learn nonprofit accounting. I felt the revolving door in our bookkeeper position had served to buy time until she became available, and was grateful.

I stewed over the staff changes and interim measures we needed to put in place. One Sunday at home, I felt off balance and disquieted. I went outside, sat on the ground, and succumbed to flowing, wet sadness. "I'm afraid," I admitted. Excitement over my new path hadn't blossomed enough to be stronger than the sadness of letting go and fear of starting something new.

I recognized my grief about leaving Matthew House. Transition means giving up something and moving to something else. There's grief in that. Leaving the agency meant giving up a major portion of my life—one in which, perhaps for the first time, I'd been successful and received recognition for it.

When I stopped crying, I deepened into meditation. Buki in spirit licked my face. Tyson came to sit with me. Sina did too, knowing at that moment my need was greater than hers. My chorus of animals called: *We love you!* and *Keep on.*

They always say to keep on, I thought, but I'm sad and afraid.

Tyson said: *Yes, and strong!* I felt their belief in me, and thanked them all. I felt better. Later, Tyson and I sat in our favorite chair in the living room.

You're growing, he said.

"Yes, thank you. I seek to be whole."

You already are whole. You just haven't opened up some parts yet.

Buki chimed in: *You are my daughter in whom I am well pleased.*

"Thank you, Buki."

I'm getting old, Tyson added.

"Only in body."

I'm a pretty old soul too.

One morning my eyes opened to a cloud bank filling the lower half of the sky, reflecting pink orange from the rising sun and last city lights, topped by a thin wiggly line of silver where the full moon hung behind it. Light indigo filled the sky above. Glory. Then I noticed the word *shaman* on a book pulled slightly out of the headboard bookshelf, and accepted it as a sign to proceed on my path. A Chaplaincy module started in two weeks. I also signed up for the animal-communication practice group Cathy was starting.

Early Christianity, my third Chaplaincy module, happened to me in late January. Familiar with the material, I was surprised when another student asked, "Who is Paul?" Christianity, even unstudied, was an undercurrent in my upbringing; yet many people hadn't been reared in that framework. Three little words—"Who is Paul?"—revealed one of my baseline assumptions.

Homework included identifying a strength and a weakness to work on, to strengthen the gift and heal the wound. My list of weaknesses was long. I finally settled on closing self off as the weakness, and allowing self to be self as the healing I sought. Picking a strength was harder. The concept of recognizing strengths and not defining myself by weaknesses bore much thought.

Writing about my grief helped me get a better grip on the transition I was going through. I'd been coming to terms with needing to express and release my feelings rather than bury them. My task was to own and honor my feelings. Then the memories—building blocks of who I am—remain, but without the attached emotions.

In spiritual direction, Ron asked if I could pinpoint an early cause. My mother's voice popped into my mind saying, "Stop crying or I'll give you something to cry about!" I internalized feelings, while my sister reflected them back. I also remembered an incident from Colombia, when I was about four years old. My family walked a jungle path and came to a swinging rope bridge with wooden foot planks, suspended over what seemed to me a deep chasm. Mother crossed it, then my sister. My adventurous older sister enjoyed the thrill of our father gently swinging the bridge while she crossed it, but I asked him not to. I stepped out on it, trembling. When I was about halfway across, my father started swinging the bridge. Terrified, I shrieked and clung to those side ropes so tightly they embedded in my hands. At first everyone laughed, thinking it funny. Then my sister asked Mother to make Dad stop. Someone pried my hands off the ropes and helped me across. They pooh-poohed my reaction, saying it was all in fun and I'd been in

BEST-LAID PLANS | 193

no danger. It didn't feel that way to me. I'd had a thing about bridges ever since. That incident undermined my trust, and showed me that what I felt wasn't important.

Ron asked if these unexpressed feelings had limited me in any way. Yes, of course, I could answer readily. How? I wasn't sure. Years ago, as far back as the 1960s, I felt frustration over never having the same level of passion and outrage about the women's movement, Vietnam War, civil rights, and so on as the people around me. Had all the years of training myself to be invisible, to not express my feelings, resulted in their being dampered, so that I didn't allow myself to experience true depth of feeling?

This dynamic carried over to my spiritual quest for oneness. The times when I'd been in the presence of God/White Buffalo/Spirit were filled with such overwhelming love I felt like I was being ripped apart. It was like that when Gwen and Sean were babies, and with the grandkids. In that ecstatic love I dared not hug them as tightly as I wanted to, for fear I'd crush them. I was trying. Buki, Tyson, and Sina helped me, loving and listening.

The mantra from a Chaplaincy class was "Be gentle with yourself." I didn't want to commit spiritual bypass and just go through the motions. I wanted to prowl around the roots of my Tree of Life and heal those wounds. Maybe that was what this process was about—healing the little girl who now wore this woman's body. What struck me most about the Chaplaincy experience was that I kept going back. I had to trust the process, trust there was a reason, trust that I would find internal resources to carry through at Matthew House, trust that my unfolding would reach a conclusion. I remembered granddaughter Katy's snail, and her patient wait for it to extend its eyestalks and begin its slow movement.

At the end of the month, I thought about how it was two years since Buki died. This year the day was beautiful and sunny, unlike the day she died, when the world seemed like it was crying. I thought of Buki gamboling in heaven, running through a field of flowers with tail outstretched, doing her shaman work in a ball of golden energy.

Tyson, Buki, Sina, and my chorus of animals kept cheering me on, and nature painted such beauty that it took me outside myself.

It's All a Process

Settled, purring, preparing to tell a story.
Peering at the world, grass at eye level.
Comfortable in a warm lap,
her hand on my back, stroking.
Rolling in the dirt, the fresh freedom of dust,
jumping to my feet at a sound, a whiff of scent.
Unseen fingers of wind touching my fur,
little tickly crawls on my skin.
Tuna!

— Tyson Cat

If the events of the previous year felt groundbreaking, this one was kicking me to a new level, of something. Chaplaincy and Matthew House worked on and in me. Cathy promoted me to advanced student of animal communication, which would bring challenges and rewards too. Through it all, Tyson kept me focused and grounded. We sat on the leather couch by the front window together. I asked if he had something to say.

A lot, he said. It turned out to be a lecture. *I've been waiting for you to settle. It's time to start scribing again. You're going to run out of paper.*

"I'll get more."

You're not focused enough! You need to practice more to hear the voices. You skim across the top and don't go deep. You want the deep to come to you. I've been trying to help you, but you must do most of it. It's not easy. It's just that

195

you have made progress and know there's much more. I know you and understand you, and you're holding yourself back.

I asked if he'd like to dictate or tell me something, but couldn't hold the connection, so we just sat together, curled on the sofa in a spot we'd made warm.

That night I woke in the wee hours and saw the moon, full and orange, about to set behind the trees. It looked like a sun in the dark sky. The next morning sunlight warmed trees from the top down, against an intense blue. Outside, a hawk flew from tree to tree. Birds sang. Peace wrapped me like a warm blanket.

The next session with Tyson was more successful. We sat together on the couch by our living-room front window, my notebook and pen ready to scribe for him.

Tyson began: *I'm here for a rest, and to help you people grow a little. It's drawing close to the time for transition. You're in good hands, with Buki and Katsina. But you need help with Katsina.* He paused. *I love being a cat. Sometimes I get tired of not feeling quite right. I'm hungry all the time, but nothing tastes good. My body is wearing out.*

"And yet you carry yourself with such dignity. You're working hard to keep things balanced and to bring healing."

Especially to you. It's a lot of work. You're confused, Gregg is unhappy, Sina is chaotic. If you're healed, you can heal the others. Don't allow Sina to scatter your energies. I'm doing what I can with her, but she looks to you. I know you're trying, and you're doing well. It just takes time.

"Tyson, I don't want you to be overlooked in the madness."

I am sometimes, but the night is my time. I do my best work when everyone is asleep. There's not so much energy to cut through. I wander freely through your dreams in this world and the next. And Buki and I play.

"Tyson, that makes me smile. Is there more you'd like to say?"

That's all for now. You got it. Let's just sit together. A bit later he added: *I'm not leaving right away. I'll let you know.* Then he jumped down and headed for the stairs.

Sunday afternoon, words from Sina came to me: *Sina is sad. Tomorrow you'll go back to work, and I'll be all alone.*

"That makes me sad too," I said. Sina and I were enjoying quiet time together. I folded laundry and she explored, one of her rare times upstairs. I asked if she would like to tell me a story, but felt that she'd like me to tell her one. She settled on the rug, and I began, out loud: "Once upon a time, there was a princess puppy who lived with some people who didn't treat her well. . . ." I continued, recounting how she ran away one day and had many adventures with cars and people and with dogs wanting to fight with her, and how she caught little animals to eat and wound up in the animal shelter. Then a woman and man came and took her home, and gave her a new special name. And Princess Heyoke Katsina learned many new things and had important jobs, and got along well with Tyson Cat. She and her new people had many adventures and lived happily together all the rest of their days.

Sina looked nearly asleep, her eyes slitted almost closed, her breathing steady. I mentally asked her if she would tell me a story.

Sina showed me a picture of a fat, sparrowlike bird with blue back and cream-colored underside, standing on a chain-link fence, singing. *The bird is my friend. When I am lonely and unhappy, it comes and sings to me. When I'm happy, it plays with me and sings to me.* I saw a picture of a young adult man, slender with dark hair, holding what looked like a dog brush. He threw it at her, hard. It hit her left flank and hurt. She spun in circles to get away and hid in her doghouse, curling into as small a ball as she could. She was unhappy and her back hurt. The little bird came and sat on the fence near her and sang to her for a long time.

I knew I'd been shown a picture of Sina's life in her former home. I asked if the bird was the same kind as the scrub jay that came to visit her here.

No, she said, *but all the birds talk to one another. My little bird knows where I am, and is happy for me.*

"I'm sorry you were hurt," I told her. "Thank you for showing me that story." I now understood why she didn't like to be brushed.

It was time to make a new story. The next day I told it to Sina: "Two little girls meet in a field filled with waving soft grass and yellow flowers. One is multicolored, and the other is pink. The little girls join paws and skip through the flowers. Then some great eagles pick up the corners of the field of flowers, as if it were a blanket, and fly with it. The little girls peek over the edge, and see their house and yard, neighborhood and city, and the whole world passing by below. They feel the air and enjoy the sights, knowing they are safe with the eagles. Then the eagles bring them back home, and replace the blanket of grass. The little girls thank them for the adventure, and skip back to their home together, holding paws."

Then Sina and I went into the kitchen together. I had her sit next to the garbage can. She watched as I picked up the wood-handled dog brush, showed it to her, and then ceremoniously dropped it into the garbage. "No more brushes," I told her. Happiness shone in her eyes as she bounded to her feet.

Sina and I had made a breakthrough to a new level—
hers of trust, mine of understanding. She communicated
through pictures and impressions, rarely words, quite different from the clear verbal messages I received from Tyson,
and the words accompanied by a sense of knowing I received
from Buki.

Tyson gave his version of my story that evening:

> *Sitting quietly on a hillside of yellow flowers*
> *Two girls—one innocent, one harlequin.*
> *I join. Wolf and Bear come from the other side.*
> *Hawk flies circles above and cries.*
> *Feathers rain down in grand celebration.*
> *The carpet of flowers lifts and soars, we all sing.*
> *Flowers melt into the singers.*
> *On each, wings spread wide, shining,*
> *lifting into the future the world we create.*
> *God grins and cheers*
> *with singing voice from mountain and lake,*
> *tree and rock, bird and snake, paw and feather.*
> *Phoenix leads to a new world.*
> *Life begins again.*
> *And there is more . . . .*

"More?" I asked.

Not now, that was a lot of work. It really flowed, didn't it?

"Yes! Thanks, Ty."

I'm happy you're getting it.

Sina added:

> *Fear loosens its grip slowly.*
> *It wants to cling and protect,*
> *shield, imprison.*
> *Love frees gently, patiently.*
> *Tears flow, cleanse.*
> *Sneezes work too.*

"Sina, is that your first poem?"

Yes! I like to write poems!

Then Buki, who was listening to all of these conversations, gave us a blessing: *May you be all that the Creator intended, open to all Creation's beginnings, to carry the message between the worlds of animal and human, mountain and sky. And so be it.*

I did feel blessed, and full of gratitude.

The breakthrough with Sina was followed by the same feeling at Chaplaincy's module on Theravada Buddhism. I flowed with the practice, and sank into chanting rhythms during our visit to a Buddhist monastery high in the East Bay hills. During chants, which the monk led and we repeated, the white temple cat visited each student. He coiled around me, rubbing, stroking my folded legs with his long tail, and curled up next to my feet. I thanked him for this blessing.

The sense of breakthrough was repeated the next week. Walking Sina around a nearby lake, I spotted a butterfly with black wings trimmed in bright orange, perched on a branch of scrub brush. It was with another, whose cream wings were spotted and striped in brown. Then the dark one moved its wings. Their underside was the cream pattern of the second butterfly, which was upside down. I wished them well, and moved on. When I stepped on a plank to cross the creek, I noticed what looked like a necklace on the ground. It was a small king snake with red, black, and cream bands. The snake looked at us and tasted the air with its forked tongue, but didn't move away. Snakes and butterflies are both symbols of change. That one butterfly was upside-down spoke of not resisting change. A powerful message—twice.

A month later, Tyson sprayed upstairs. I sat holding him, feeling his purring energy rumble through me. *I'm sorry about the hall upstairs,* he said. *I just . . . I don't know.*

"Do you want more of my time just with you?"

Yes. Quiet. The quiet one gets overlooked. Echoes of my own childhood.

I called Cathy. She said, "Tyson's hanging in there, surprised to be doing so well. He and Sina are reaching an understanding, though he feels she's still a handful. Sina keeps Tyson occupied, focused on her. He's happy she's here for the most part. Despite herself, Sina has a big heart and wants to be good." Cathy added: "Life is settling more into a pattern that hasn't been there since Buki left. Tyson's living his stately self."

I heard Buki say: *Continue to work with as many species as possible. Walk the labyrinth with Sina to help her focus. We can walk it together. Practice being grounded, connected. That will help in itself.* Buki saw a labyrinth for people and animals as part of my ministry. She added that she's proud of Gregg too. *Between us girls, he's come a long way. Sina is about lightening him up.* Buki at last confirmed that she'd chosen Sina for us.

Sina said: *I'll try hard to do better with the grandkids. I have to protect and learn and take care of them.* She was beginning to understand that she wasn't in competition with them.

Tyson had words about the grandchildren, as well: *It can be a lot of fun teaching them how to be kind to kitties and how to be gentle.*

On June first we celebrated the milestone of Sina's one-year adoption anniversary. Sina's young, wild, and free spirit needed a bigger connection to me and to Gregg, but she had a new groundedness now. She was learning what real love is.

I had the sense that everything was coming together.

"Not so fast!" the Universe let me know. It wasn't done with me yet.

Permission

I needed great courage to go out into the dark
Tracking god into the unknown,
And not panic or get lost
In all the startling new scents, sounds, sights. . . .
— *Hafiz*

Occasionally we recognize an opportunity to do something life changing. Cathy announced she would be leading a group swim with dolphins and sea turtles on the Hawaiian Kona coast in October 2006. Everything in me said yes, and yet I hesitated.

Obstacles presented themselves. I invited Gregg, who said he had no interest in going. I was reluctant to go without him, and spend family money just on me. Matthew House's annual fundraising dinner/auction was on the opening day of the workshop in Hawaii. And I wasn't sure I had enough vacation time; I'd been using it to take Chaplaincy modules. I equivocated.

At our following month's practice session, pink azaleas bloomed in Cathy's small garden, alongside plants that attracted hummingbirds and butterflies. Afternoon sun warmed the carpeted cat tree to her Siamese cat's satisfaction. Several students had committed to the trip. "What's stopping you?" they asked. I sipped hot chamomile tea and recited my list of obstacles, but I had a strong sense this would be my only opportunity; if I didn't go on this trip, there was a good chance I never would.

As I worked through my list of obstacles, I realized that most were logistical and could be dealt with. Only one was major—permission. Permission for me to say to Gregg: "I want to do this." Permission for me to spend the money and go without him. Permission for me to take this step, and either miss the fundraiser or arrive at the workshop a day late. Permission.

Returning from the park one evening after our walk, I talked with Gregg—or rather, to his back and broad shoulders. He strode ahead, keeping the pace Sina had set. Our tennis shoes crunched on loose rock embedded in the dirt pathway as we walked past the big live oak. I spoke between breaths, keeping a pace that was too fast for me: "I want to do this."

I waited. I rarely said, "I want this." My standard operating procedure was to defer to him, as I had deferred to my parents, and just about anybody else. So often Gregg had said in frustration, "Tell me what you want!" I couldn't. I didn't know.

Gregg thought for a moment and said, "I've been spending a load of money on the Ford Model A I'm building, so if you want to go you should just go. I can take care of Tyson and Sina." Just like that, it was settled.

I related this story of personal breakthrough when six of us Chaplaincy students joined for lunch, taking advantage of a late summer day to sit on the outside patio. Tiny brown sparrows searched for crumbs under the tables. It felt good to exercise my growing sense of inclusion.

My confession was met with incredulity that I couldn't just say what I wanted. Was it a generational difference? Most of these women were my daughter's age, and currently single. The only student who understood my quandary was my age and also in a long-term relationship. It made me deeply value the give-and-take growth that people in durable relationships go through. The, confession, the permission, and the revelation were added bonuses of my trip.

In preparation for the dolphin swim, Cathy encouraged us to meditate with the dolphins. At home, I settled into the rocking chair in our bedroom that still held scrape marks from a diaper-changing tray for baby Sean. I looked out the sliding-glass doors to hazy blue sky and a stand of eucalyptus trees. Without my glasses, I couldn't see details of birds among the leaves, but felt their presence. The bed next to me thumped as gray Tyson jumped onto it and curled himself just so, purr volume turned high. I closed my eyes and deepened into meditation and a vision: I was nose to nose with a Hawaiian sea turtle—*honu*—with dolphins circling around us. I asked, "Do you have a message for me?"

Dolphin replied: *You never know what to ask of us.*

"It's difficult for me to know what to ask. I'm confused and uncertain."

Dolphin replied: *All of us in the sea—you are one of us. You feel lost because you have lost connection with the soul purpose for coming into this lifetime. You try to remember, but have been so long with not remembering that it is difficult and you are frustrated.*

"Is Chaplaincy with animals and people my path? Who or what has led me here?"

In answer, I saw the succession of animals, from the jungle birds and backyard chickens in Colombia to my first dog, Misti, a white spitz who loved rides in my bicycle basket in Peru; through a long chain of cats to Tyson; to my acknowledged mentor, Buki Akita, as well as Sina and the wild animals who had come to me—Turtle, Mountain Lion, White Buffalo, Moose, Bird. My chorus of animals, trees, rocks, water, air—all of nature. Around us, dolphins, sea turtles, and manta rays leaped in a rainbow of sunlight. "Is this what I came into this life for?"

Dolphin answered: *Not all, but part. We want to lighten your energy. You have been honu, and dolphin; you have been tree, rock, bird, snake, and the furred, four-legged. Remembering this is part of your mission. Communicating with animals is part of bringing together the pieces and parts of yourself. Swim your path with us.*

Overwhelmed, I said, "I need to sit with this information. May I talk with you again?"

I felt Dolphin answer *yes,* and gave thanks. I opened my eyes to sunlight slanting through the eucalyptus trees. I felt more than heard Tyson's *I will be with you,* before he stretched and flowed from the bed to the floor and around the corner.

I wrote a proposal for my practicum on Animal Chaplaincy. The directors approved my proposal with resounding encouragement. My research would begin with the dolphin swim.

Matthew House's dinner/auction was held Saturday night. Early the next morning, while it was still dark, Gregg hefted my suitcase into the back of our station wagon and drove me to the airport. I'd tucked a pouch of tumbled rose-quartz stones and a few amethyst points into my bag, along with a fossil whale ear I intended as a gift for the place. Exhausted, I slept nearly the whole flight. I had taken a large step into the unknown, and knew that it was one of many.

The jumbo 737 touched down smoothly in Oahu and taxied to the gate. I expected the scent of flowers to greet me, as it had when Gregg and I vacationed there in the late 1970s.

The thick floral scent had reminded me of tropical Colombia where I'd lived as a child. Flower scent, though, was missing from the 2006 airport; fumes of car exhaust had replaced it.

After a short layover in Oahu, a jet-jockey airplane ride brought me to the Big Island, Hawaii. There the flower scent enveloped me. Cathy's husband, George, picked me up in their green rental van. George cheerfully told me the group had decided to postpone starting until I arrived. Our first session would be that evening.

We drove south down the Kailua-Kona coastal highway. Largely barren of trees, the land sloped unbroken to the ocean. A large shopping center on a hill seemed out of place.

The atmosphere of our hotel in Kailua-Kona was well aligned with our quest. It perched on rocks overlooking Kahalu'u Beach. Waves splashed around sea turtles sunning on lava rocks. A grove of palm trees encircled a garden and an ancient stone-lined pool fed by a spring.

At the hotel, we discovered that the snorkel-gear stand on the beach had closed and wouldn't open before our sea-turtle swim the next morning. "I'll take care of it," George said. He returned a few minutes later with a bag of gear that another guest had left for hotel staff to return. The fins fit my size-eleven feet—a sign that this adventure was meant to be.

That evening we splashed in the hotel pool, completely unselfconscious. We named ourselves the Ohana Pod for the Hawaiian word for *family*. I made up a chant of seven repetitions of the word, borrowing the melody of a Zulu chant I'd learned at Chaplaincy. Later, when we walked through the lobby to the elevator, I heard other hotel guests refer to us as "the fun people." How often I had longed to be one of the "fun people" but had been too shy to join in! Here, with no thought and little effort, I was one of them!

The adventure had only begun.

Sea Turtles, Dolphins, and Manta Rays

We hold this space in the ocean depths.
Honor the earth and all on it as Divine Creation,
constantly in motion and re-creation.
What you call God is not separate,
but is within every molecule.
Do not worship a single element.
Hold all the elements sacred and teach people to
honor all life and its cycles.
— Spirit of Whale

At dawn our group of nine met on a semicircle of beach at Kahalu'u Bay. We dropped our towels onto fine sand above the tide line and flopped on awkward finned feet to the water's edge through narrow trails between sharp black lava rocks.

I sank to my knees in the cool, shallow water, then floated face-down to adjust my snorkel. The mask leaked a little. Relax, I told myself. Float; breathe. I was glad I'd practiced snorkel breathing in the pool the previous night.

I kept my arms close to my sides and flippered into deeper water. A sea turtle wearing shades of green swam under me. As he started to move off, I remembered legends about the turtle's shell. "Wait, please," I thought to the turtle, "so I can count the number of plates on your shell." The sea turtle obligingly halted, backed up, and held still directly below me while I counted. Thirteen—just like land turtles, one for each moon cycle in a year.

"Thank you," I said, in awe at this simple but powerful validation of human-animal communication. I watched the turtle disappear into deeper water.

A smaller turtle swam close by me. I sent a mental greeting, and heard her response in my mind: *I am female, neither young nor old but not as ancient as some of the others.* I asked about a concave section of shell missing in front of her right hind fin, with a spot of infection.

A shark took a bite of it, she said. *It will heal or not. My life may be shorter than others.*

I swam toward the coral, fascinated that what appeared as jumbled rocks were complex structures built by small ocean creatures. Many carried black lines on lime green—natural variations giving the impression of ancient symbols. I reached out mentally and heard: *We grow all over the world but wouldn't want to be anyplace else. This is home, the Heart of the Earth.*

A wave carried me over a reef into a school of small black fish. The fish showed me how to flow with the water as waves swept them over the reef and back again. When I pushed myself toward them, physically or mentally, they pulled back. When I relaxed, they came closer. Underwater, I could see our group flow apart like fish, together yet separate. Two hours passed unnoticed; when the lagoon grew crowded with people, it was time to leave.

Back in our hotel, we followed Cathy upstairs, like ducklings behind a mother duck. The carpeted room gave onto an open deck. We could hear seabirds and breeze in palm trees outside. We pulled up straight-back chairs to complete a circle around the rectangular coffee table, transformed into an altar.

In a guided meditation, we practiced being an animal—merging with it, feeling with its senses. Cathy cautioned us not to project ourselves onto the animals, but to stay open and listen. Dolphin came to me. I journaled:

> *Dolphin skin is sensuous and sensitive, feels bubbles and little bumps. I see energy, light patterns. Aware of connection, I swim, weaving a widespread net. Others join me. We make patterns, play, climb up shafts of light. There's no difference between sea and sky and stars. The fish taste good; I thank them. There is only freedom.*

After journaling our experience we kept silence, and went outside to communicate with nature. Ocean called to me. I walked out a finger of rough, black lava rock that extended into the ocean, and sang the "Ancient Mother" chant I'd learned at Chaplaincy. I heard Ocean's voice: *I like your song. Waves are the voice of the ancient mother.*

"Do you have a message for me?"

I am the source of all life, she answered. *I am the cradle. Be aware of the interconnectedness of all things. Treat my children gently. I must make sacrifices. Some of my children elect to go. I can not sustain all.*

"How can I help?"

Bring awareness that we are all here together. The tide flows in and flows out; this is the natural cycle of things. The tide of awareness is shifting. When this age passes, another will come and there will be life—different. This has happened before and will again. Go and walk your walk. What happens is not as important as how it is done. All is for the growth and learning of the whole.

The next morning at dawn we gathered in a circle on a grassy knoll near the dock. Cathy led an opening blessing. We cleansed ourselves with sage smoke and set our intention for the day's encounters to be for the highest good of all. We wore purple orchid leis and swimsuits, some with T-shirt coverups, some in sarongs. Seagulls screeched overhead.

Spirits high, we climbed into the pontoon boat. The tanned captain regaled us with crusty humor. A videographer joined us. A neat blonde braid hung down her back, and a tiny gold manta-ray charm nestled in the hollow between her tanned collarbones. As we motored to our first stop, I sang our Ohana chant and every other chant I could remember.

The boat slowed to a stop in a small cove. We slipped into the water. It was early, and only a few dolphins had returned after a night of searching for food. I could see vast numbers of floating life forms in the water, and gained a deeper understanding of Ocean's message. I floated, mesmerized by sunlight shining through the water. Long beams of light seemed to come from deep within the ocean and spread out as they reached the surface. Our captain had warned us: "Do *not* go towards the light!" His echo of the words of people at death's door reminded us of the ocean's dangers. Snorkelers sometimes got in trouble swimming too deep and running out of breath trying to reach the receding point where beams of light come together.

Unaware that everyone else had returned to the boat, or that I had floated away with the tide, I was surprised to hear voices calling me. The boat idled in front of me. Familiar faces peered over the rail. Cathy said they'd started up the boat to come get me. Thereafter, the group called me Drifter. The dolphins, though, called me *Singer*, and asked if I knew more songs.

Our boat skimmed over the water, spinner dolphins cavorting in our bow wave. They lagged behind and burst ahead effortlessly. The boat glided to a stop in another cove. In the clear water, we spread out for our own interactions with the dolphins. Ripples in the sand below looked like waves. Was I up looking down, or down looking up? A large pod swam under us in twos and threes, mothers and babies, mating pairs, dark-bodied dolphins rubbing against one another for the pleasure of touch. I floated on the swell above the dolphins, just being.

On our way back to the dock I gave myself over to joy and played whale rider, straddling a pontoon and holding onto a guard rope as we bucked through waves. The ocean changed colors at different depths, from deep blue to cloudy to light blue to aqua clear enough to see sand, rocks, and plant life on the bottom below us.

We regrouped that afternoon in Cathy's room. In my meditation I asked for clarity in my work, and heard/felt, *Practice, learn, talk to the animals. Let the process work. Many things are coming together.* I felt gold light sprinkling around and through me. I told Cathy about the fossil whale ear I'd brought and my intention to drop it into the water as a gift to the ocean. Her distant look told me she was communicating with animals: "The dolphins say for you to keep it, work with it."

I became grateful for the container of the group. They watched out for me, someone at my elbow when I headed off in the wrong direction or "spaced out," as Cathy called it. I was so accustomed to being in charge and in control that when I let go, I scattered to the four winds. In the hotel's gift shop I bought a hematite sea turtle pendant strung on a thong. I hoped its weight and magnetic properties would help me stay centered and grounded.

The next day was unscheduled. I meditated in the morning, connecting with my animals at home. Sina said: *The turtles are too slow. I liked swimming with the dolphins; they go fast. I like their speed and energy. You need to listen more. Tyson stayed on the boat.*

Tyson loved the turtles. They were like him and held ancient wisdom. *Spend more time with them,* he said. *You understand a lot but need to practice more.*

Buki said: *You've come a long way, and have yet a way to go. I'm proud of you!*

All the animals said I must practice more. My half hour a day was a good start, but not nearly enough. I felt torn between staying at the hotel, letting myself sleep and integrate this information, and going to visit the volcanoes, which also had lessons to teach.

The group's discussion of possible activities included horseback riding and kayaking. As the conversation continued, I felt that my desire to go to the volcanoes had been lost, and saw myself sinking back into my familiar swamp of invisibility. No! I slammed on internal brakes. I repeated: "I still want to go to the volcanoes. I'll rent a car and go by myself if need be."

Kay reserved a rental car. A red one. I marveled at her confidence and matter-of-fact approach when she'd made a decision. She and I and our youngest member, Monica with the armband tattoo, tossed our snorkel gear into the car's trunk. Kay's windblown auburn hair and buoyant humor reflected the joy we all felt: "Volcanoes, here we come!"

The road followed the island's shoreline. Tropical growth hung on our left, and deep-blue Pacific Ocean spread to the horizon below cliffs on our right. The air felt fresh and clean. After we passed the island's most southerly point, Kay remembered visiting a Buddhist temple nearby—Wood

Valley Temple. We made our way down a two-lane unpaved road, parked under an overgrowth of trees, and were escorted by peacocks up a path to the temple.

A stocky sarong-clad bald monk greeted us at the temple. The well-worn wooden floors glowed with a soft shine. Windows on both sides let in filtered light. A large sitting Buddha dominated the altar, surrounded by multicolor cloths, a singing bowl, flowers, offerings, and candles. Kay asked permission and rang the carved bronze bowl. As the resonant note faded, the monk invited us to sit. We pulled bright-patterned cushions onto the floor from neat stacks along the walls and sat for over half an hour. On our way out, I left a rose-quartz stone on the altar. The monk invited us back for the evening meditation and chanting service. That set the timeline for the rest of our excursion.

Halema'uma'u crater in Hawaii Volcano Park is a crater within a crater, where the goddess Pele is said to live. Steaming vents smelled of sulfur but made our skin feel soft. I shared crystals with Kay and Monica, and selected an amethyst point as my gift to Pele, goddess of fire and mother of the islands. We offered silent prayers and tossed our stones into her crater. I felt timelessness envelop me as history and the land folded together.

A pair of *nene*—Hawaiian geese—walked toward us. The black and cream-gold feathers on their necks looked more like fur than feathers. The banded one made soft sounds. I told him how handsome he was, and asked what the sounds were.

He said: *It helps us stay in touch with each other.*

Kay commented: "When you talk with animals, they look at you."

We arrived back at the temple just in time. The monk said we could chant too, but "It may be too complicated, so you can just listen, quiet mind, go to place of compassion, and meditate." No one chanted with him. I was sorry we couldn't join in; I felt like an observer rather than a participant.

After we helped put away the pillows, we saw the petite temple cat. I had thought there must be one. I asked the monk if it bothered the peacocks. He said, "No, they're good friends." Then the cat added: *We all live in harmony. My job is to bring peace and healing to all who come here—including the monks!*

I thanked her, remembering how blessed I felt during my Chaplaincy visit to the Buddhist temple when the white temple cat stroked me with his tail and curled up by my crossed legs.

We drove back to our hotel in the darkening tropical night. None of us wanted to go into the lighted lobby and confining walls. We walked to the garden's ancient spring, picking sweet-scented plumeria blossoms on the way. As we dropped our blossoms into the water, I prayed to the goddess of the spring that we each ripen in fulfillment of our dreams, as the moon ripens.

The next morning we readied for our second dolphin encounter. We told the captain we wanted to go only to the cove where the dolphins came to rest. The previous trip had felt like we were chasing them. He was accustomed to finding dolphins for tourists, not inviting dolphins to come to us, but grinned his acceptance of our mutiny.

Glistening gray dolphin fins trailed foam alongside the boat. We pulled orchids off our leis and tossed them into the water as a gift. When the boat stopped in the cove, we dropped blessed crystals into the water, donned fins and masks, and lowered ourselves in.

The dolphin pod numbered fifty to seventy that day. The captain said he'd never seen so many before. They played, rubbed against one another, and swam in spirals that looked like DNA helixes. They rewarded our respect with a curtain of bubbles that felt like a blessing. I could feel waves of energy as the dolphins sonared us. I had no sense of time but was told we'd been there for ninety minutes—an unusually long dolphin encounter.

Then the boat took us to water fourteen thousand feet deep off the island shelf to look for pilot whales. No whales appeared. Cathy reminded us that when we send an invitation, the animals have their own reasons for accepting or declining. I felt woozy and swam slowly, trailing bubbles from my snorkel. Later, when we struggled to stay afloat and do the Hokey-Pokey at the same time, I received a picture of Tyson. My dignified elder statesman cat stood on his hind legs, wearing a ridiculously large Mexican sombrero with red puff balls around its rim. He too was doing the Hokey-Pokey! Was I hallucinating?

When we returned to the hotel, the inside of my head vibrated and my body tingled, as if the atoms in my body had been spread out in a thin three-dimensional film that reached from one end of the Universe to another. I had the sense of being taken apart and put back together.

Early the next morning we went to the lagoon, but I saw no turtles. We focused on the fish and coral, saw more and brighter colors than before—even a coral with stripes! Big-eyed yellow fish followed us through the lagoon. They told me we *looked funny.*

The lagoon began to crowd with people. As our group swam toward shore, I realized the quartz point I'd brought for the turtles was a gift to the whole lagoon. I thanked the lagoon and all the life forms living it, and dropped the crystal into a jumble of coral. Then thrashing water caught my attention. I surfaced to see two schools of silver flying fish splash across the surf in front of us! They curled around us and then headed across the bay—a true gift.

Our manta-ray swim was scheduled for Friday night. The captain met us at the dock. A team of scuba divers had already departed to set up spotlights on the sea floor. The lights shine up through the water, drawing the plankton the manta rays feed on.

The captain gave a stern lecture when we anchored in the cove. "Don't touch the manta rays! Humans carry bacteria that can harm mantas, as well as *honu* and dolphins. Their skin is covered with a protective barrier. Touching them can break it." He looked around our circle to make sure he had our full attention. His tone told us he wasn't kidding. His voice softened. "Float and let them come to us. . . . And they may not come. The moon is full. They don't need the spotlights to draw their food."

We entered the water with his warning in mind. While we waited, other boats anchored around the cove. Our videographer asked if I'd like to swim the periphery with her. Perhaps the dark or the swell or the cumulative impacts of this week had left me tentative. She held my hand and guided me until I felt comfortable, then let go and I swam over to our group.

The manta rays came, fully twenty of them! They spiraled up in ballet acrobatic circles with flaplike cephalic lobes gaped, funneling in plankton. We identified Lefty with the malformed left lobe, and Big Mama, about sixteen feet across. One manta ray swam toward me with lobes gaped. I could see straight through its body, the open gills, down the inside of its hollow self. Another did a loop beneath me, so close I could feel the water compress between us.

The people from the other tour boats acted as if they hadn't received the same instructions. A woman shrieked, "I touched one!" Our group swam in pairs, close to some circling mantas. Several swimmers roughed us aside, knocking loose my swim partner's facemask. Our group linked arms to keep from drifting apart, but aggressive swimmers drove us to the periphery.

Observing from the sidelines, we saw a different perspective of the mantas' balletlike flying as they spiraled upward and circled back down again. The same dance watched from a different angle gave a different and more complete perspective.

Saturday. Departure day. Up early, I meditated and connected with the sea turtles, who said: *Remember your teachers. Notice and appreciate the gifts of the present. Slow down and be still in place. Keep your heart open, and love yourself. Call on us.*

The manta rays had a message too: *We came to you because of the heart energy of your group. Spirit is with you. We did not need to come; the moon was full.* Big Mamma said: *The lesson of the ill-balanced people was to demonstrate that you can keep that love in heart even in everyday turmoil. You are blessed, my children. You are the teachers; teach the others.*

Then the dolphins spoke their message: *Remember in your heart. There is much happening at a cellular level that you are not yet aware of. You have been accelerated to a new level. Keep practicing!* I thought of the buzzing in my head that continued for a day and a half after the second dolphin swim, which I could still feel at a deep level.

During my flight home, I watched clouds outside the window, one moment appearing solid and the next a wispy vapor. Just like my sense of self—sometimes solid, sometimes intangible. Next time, I thought, it would be good to stay over a day to rest in that setting. Integrate all that happened. If I ever ran such a session, I'd include more time for unguided meditation and group processing. Without realizing it, I was considering possible expressions of my ministry with people and animals.

First, though, I needed to let it all sink in.

Letting It All Sink In

The grace of gray, soft and silky,
moving through the mists of time.
Purring, comfort, this time is mine,
wrapped in arms of warmth and love.
Clouds move, sunlight, shadow,
leaves turn red.
Life fades into winter's rest.
— *Tyson Cat*

Two days after my return from Hawaii, I dreamed of the pontoon boat, singing the Ohana chant, tossing orchids into the water, and swimming through bubbles. I held the experience close, relating only surface details at work, but shared more with Gregg. It felt important for him to know what was happening in me.

Safely in meditative sanctuary in my rocking chair by the glass sliding doors upstairs, I saw the dolphins, face-to-face, clicking to me. "What is your message for me, honored ones?"

Listen deeply. We have altered your hearing. Listen within your heart. Hear whale song. We like your singing. Aren't you going to write this down?

I reached for a pen and slid my journal from underneath Tyson.

Be diligent about collecting your tools, the dolphins continued. *Don't dissipate your energies. Keep focused on*

219

your goals and be aware of the lessons that come sideways. Journal.

Then I asked Tyson if he'd like to say anything.

I've been listening in. I can help translate the dolphins for you. Ramp it down, as it were. Tyson relayed that the dolphins said I was getting tired, and needed to rest.

Buki added: *I've been with you the whole time. You have come far. You will go farther.*

I heard White Buffalo and my animal chorus murmuring encouragement. Thank you, Buki, Tyson, Sina, dolphins, *honu*, manta rays, and my animal chorus. I moved onto the bed and sank into a much-needed nap.

The next day I asked Tyson, "How can I help you?"

He said: *I don't have much longer. I'm tired of feeling this way. But I might change my mind. Just listen to me, be with me. I have much yet to teach you. It's all intention, being what you want to be. As you spend more time with me, you'll get better at it. I am a master. You are my scribe; you can record my musings. I like that.*

"Are you related to sea turtles?"

Tyson settled into storytelling mode. *We came from the stars many eons ago, to learn, explore, to become more. There's much to do, and many opportunities for learning here. I prefer being a cat, although I have gone back to turtlehood from time to time. We feel kinship.*

"Is this how sea turtles learn more about the world?"

Yes, and through vibrations in the water. Even simple life forms like plankton have essence.

Journaling this, I realized that in our group I had worn the unseen robe of Reverend. I sang and led chants, carrying the reverence. I connected with Ancient Mother, offered prayers, and gave concluding blessings to meditations and circles opened by Cathy. I was fully immersed in my ministerial self, without realizing it. Maybe Reverend Nancy was a possibility after all.

The following Sunday Tyson wanted to talk with me. I settled onto the two-person couch beside the living room front window, savoring my afternoon cup of tea with milk. Leaves on the liquid-amber tree outside changed, each on its own schedule. I looked through green leaves closest to our house, to gold and red ones on the more exposed side. Tyson stretched across my lap, his gray head and front paws resting on my left arm. *I'm glad you're back,* he said, *though I was with you the whole time.*

"I felt you in the Buddhist temple."

The dolphins have accelerated you—your energy vibration. It's still working on you. That means you can access higher levels of learning, intuition, hearing. Don't get a swelled head; you have a long way to go! It's a life process. The dolphins have given you a boost. You must do the work: dedicated spiritual-meditative practice. Listen to me and the other animals, every day, as often as you can, not just when you feel like it.

I wondered if I kept hearing the message to *listen* because the animals felt I wasn't getting it. "Did you really show yourself to me doing the hokey pokey? And wearing a hat?"

Yes. I felt ridiculous but it got your attention. Think outside the box. You don't need to wait. Your calling is clear, but you're not listening. You can leave your job, concentrate on your studies, gain confidence, and work on your ministry. Gather your tools. Finish your chaplaincy program. You set too many obstacles. Whenever an opportunity presents itself, your first response is "I can't." I will help, but I can't do the work for you.

As I tried to absorb this, I asked Tyson if there was anything else he wanted to tell me. *I love you. I'm glad you're back. That's all for now—your tea's getting cold!*

A week after my return, I scheduled a followup call with Cathy. She said that Tyson and Sina sensed the difference in me. She suggested I ask the dolphins about my individual gifts, and how they were helping me grow. She reminded me to work with the fossil whale ear. I had told her earlier about my conversations with White Buffalo; she now told me that White Buffalo and Dolphin have similar energies.

Later that week White Buffalo came to me in meditation and said: *The dolphins have accelerated you. That brings the responsibility to communicate and to listen.*

When I checked in with Sina she said: *Your vibrational level is higher. It's kind of sparkly. It makes me feel good. Tyson, too.*

"Sina, have you ever been a temple animal?"

Oh yes, a temple cat. A big one, in the jungle. I prowled the pyramids, a jaguar. Yes, and in a Buddhist temple, like Tyson. I've been a mouse in a church, too.

"Have you ever been a coyote in the desert?" Sina radiated an unusual combination of feline and Coyote energy.

That's who I am now. Only I don't live in the desert.

I felt that since we had a good communication going, I would address her strong prey drive. "Why do you want to chase and kill prey?"

Because I am Coyote. It's part of who I am. She stated it so matter-of-factly the topic felt closed.

"Sina, you came to me. Was there a reason?"

You were chosen. We're meant to be together. I can heal. I have magic. My different eye. I can see energy patterns. That's how I know yours is different now. Besides, I can feel it.

In a quiet time, settled in my rocking chair, I breathed deep cycles of letting fresh air and energy flow in and the stale flow out. I set the intention to envision my higher purpose. I saw myself standing on steps at the entrance to a simple classical temple with columns on each side of the entry. I was facing outward with arms open, wearing my Chaplaincy stole and robe. On the grounds were a labyrinth and a meditation garden, a pool surrounded by stones, and a waterfall at one end. Turtles and fish lived in the pool. Carvings of *honu*, dolphins, and whales covered the stones. Inside was an open, breezy space where beings of all species come together to dance, sing, pray, talk, learn from one another, communicate nonverbally, honor, and respect one another as sentient beings.

Then I asked to talk with the dolphins. "What special gifts did you give me?"

Dolphin said: *We are partners. The curtain of bubbles was a group gift. Each of you received healing in whatever way each needed it. It was mostly internal for you. And we have healed your heart. You have a great responsibility. We have rewritten or, more accurately, unblocked some of your DNA. That is the buzzing you sensed. You are to be a spokesperson for us, and for others who cannot speak for themselves in the animal kingdom. We have set things in motion so that it will all come to be.*

"Thank you for your patience, Dolphin," I said. "I honor you."

Dolphin graciously invited: *Come and swim with us again; this is a blessing.*

Still swimming in the currents of my experiences in Hawaii, I enrolled in the October Chaplaincy module, on Islam. In contrast to the oneness I'd felt during and after my trip, I felt fragmented. This module was the largest I had yet experienced—eighteen students. It's easier to get lost in a large group. We met in the unfamiliar, more academic setting of Pacific School of Religion. The contrasts brought back feelings of otherness that had begun to recede as I'd deepened into Chaplaincy.

I was struck by the faith and devotion of teachers from the Islamic Cultural Center. As we sat on the floor of the mosque women's section for a prayer service, our heads covered by scarves, I was stunned to realize I didn't recognize some others in our group. Much of our identity is expressed in hair, softening features and enhancing others. When only the face is visible, a different perspective is shown. An anonymity of sorts. When I left the mosque I'd slipped back into my protective separate shell.

It didn't help that I'd returned from Hawaii to news that Matthew House's office manager, who so competently kept the office running while the bookkeeper and program director positions were in flux, was leaving. Only one person remained of our original team besides me!

I woke early one morning and sat on the couch by our front window, enjoying the sun's growing warmth. Immobile, insulated, not wanting to move out of my cocoon. Peaceful, yet unquiet. Tyson purred in my lap. Sina, trapped inside, watched out the window. My coffee cooled. I noticed that Tyson's fur had many shades and colors—black, cream, shades of gray, silver—that together made him appear gray. Like observing the bark and leaves of trees, it's a lesson in the complexity of multiple parts that make up what appears to be a whole.

Tyson mused, *The days go by, and the nights grow cold. Curled up on carpet is not the natural life, though certainly more comfortable for these old bones. Snuggling down into leaves under cover of a bush has its own warmth, and you can hear the night sounds. That's the worst part about winter in the house—I can't hear the night sounds through closed doors and windows. As I get older, I appreciate more and more the things that show caring, like your lap, the little kindnesses. I'm not long on words these days, just enjoying being.*

Early November's full moon reminded me that it had been four weeks, Friday to Friday, since we swam with manta rays. I thought about the trip every day and night, yet felt it slipping away. I wasn't sleeping well again. Tyson helped. When I slept on my side, he nestled between my shoulder blades, his purr vibrating throughout my being. He claimed lots of lap time. Sina stayed nearby. I felt disconnected, and didn't know what was wrong.

I meditated on the dolphins. I wanted to know more about my *raised vibration.*

Dolphin came to explain: *Just as the hummingbird's vibration is higher than a sparrow's, and the sparrow's vibration is higher than a slug's, we have raised you from slug to sparrow.*

I had read and been told that to step to the next spiritual level an apprentice needs to be blessed by an elder. Who would give me the blessing?

Dolphin said: *You have chosen White Buffalo.*

"Shouldn't it be a human?"

Dolphin repeated: *You have chosen White Buffalo.*

"How would White Buffalo give me his blessing?"

Dolphin replied: *White Buffalo has appeared to you, has spoken with you, and has already blessed you. He has blown his breath upon you and kissed your forehead. You have received the blessing.*

"Oh." I had felt awed, loved, and guided by our interaction the day White Buffalo had appeared to me in meditation, breathed on me, and licked my forehead, but I had not recognized its significance. I felt dense and stupid.

Dolphin spoke to my unasked question: *Your vision is in your heart. We can see it. We will help you manifest it. Yours is to walk in the world, bringing peace and wisdom, facilitating. To be that bridge between interfaith and interspecies.*

I stubbornly wanted to see the blueprint. I wanted structure. "Please clarify."

The depth of your growth will be reflected in the manifestation of your ministry. Your light is brighter than you think, but your temple is sluggish. That impedes the vibrations. Work with Cathy; practice with the animals. It is all part of growth. That is enough for now.

"*Namaste.* Thank you."

This roller-coaster feeling had become familiar, and in its way better than the downward slog I'd been in for the past few years. Perhaps lows were more apparent now because there were highs. I felt pressure from all sides, and the responding pressure of my applying internal brakes. I was still letting it all sink in. And the lessons would keep coming.

Do Be Do Be Do

There are no obstacles
except those we create for ourselves.
— Ganesha

Hinduism module! Reading assigned books for the upcoming Hinduism intensive, I felt a connection click. I would have loved to sit under a tree and enjoy it. Trouble was, I had a long to-do list and couldn't figure out how to integrate the be/do split I felt.

I took that question to spiritual direction. I sat in a chair beneath the woven Jacob's Ladder tapestry in Ron's office and giggled at the only joke I ever heard him tell: "The Buddha says 'be'; Western culture says 'do'" Sinatra says 'do be do be do.'"

Ron guided me in meditation. I saw myself within my energy field, with bands of light and colors like magnetic rays of the sun and earth, from the center up and down, right and left. My inner voice said: *Patience!* I was aware of the necessity to do justice to my commitment to Matthew House. To be fully present. I heard: *There's a difference between being and being present.* My timeline was good. I was still learning, gathering tools before moving to my next phase. I also received a message to stop stealing time for myself by procrastinating: *Just claim it, and then be present when doing.*

As we closed, Ron reminded me to be present while doing. "Do be do be do."

The Hinduism intensive provided a study in contrasts. I felt
a deep resonance with its teachings and recognition of
divinity in all things. At the same time, I wrestled with
parts of Chaplaincy and myself that were hard to confront.

At lunch break I went to an open Alcoholics Anonymous
meeting held nearby to check off one of the requirements
for ordination. We sat on donated couches and read aloud
from the Twelve-Step book. I introduced myself as a Chaplaincy student, also attending in honor of a close friend's
second anniversary of sobriety. Across from me sat Wendy,
a young woman with clear blue eyes and an honest face.
After the meeting she sought me out.

Tears brimmed those blue eyes. "Thank you," she said,
"for honoring your friend's anniversary. I just passed two
years too, and my family doesn't want to hear about it."

It was all I could do to keep from crying. I said I was glad
she and my friend had found AA to help them. Caught off
center, I missed the opportunity to be present and supportive, congratulate Wendy on two years of sobriety, encourage her to find her own path, and give her hope that her
family would come around. I felt so raw and shaken by her
gift to me and by my failure to be present for her that I
wanted to curl up under a rock.

I went outside to ground myself. This module demanded
more of me than any other, even though Hinduism called to
me in a way Western traditions had not. Sitting alone on a
white wrought-iron bench in front of the Chaplaincy office,
my eyes closed, I breathed in cool air and felt warm sunshine on my back and my feet on the ground. A birch tree

behind me rustled in the breeze. A small garden with a collection of dark smooth stones lay at my feet. One oval stone fit comfortably in my hand. I asked it if I could carry it with me during the module. The stone gave permission, although indicated it would like to return to its place in the garden afterward.

The afternoon class explored the underbelly of suicide. I gripped that stone as I thought of the people I knew who had committed suicide, intentionally or indirectly, and of the effects on those left behind. The teacher commented that the two professions that most often fail people in crisis are doctors and clergy. How present had I been for the survivors I knew?

The module continued to work on me. For one exercise, we worked in pairs to explore a form of internal suicide—walling off parts of ourselves as a response to trauma incidents. By the time it was over everyone was drained after exposing deep wounds. When we sang again, the chanting melody brought healing.

That night I said little. Gregg had come to recognize when I was sorting through deep feelings, and gave me the space and silence I needed. I went to bed with my heart sore. Tyson slept on my pillow, the vibration of his purr massaging me.

Check-ins the next day revealed deep unfolding by several people. I told about the AA meeting. Another student pointed out that talking about my friend had given Wendy what she needed. Wendy was thanking me for a gift I'd already given her. I hadn't thought of it that way, and felt better. A different student apologized for not noticing my distress when we'd talked the day before. I assured her that our conversation set a whole process in motion for me, and thanked her for it. After that check-in, the phrase "missed opportunity" crept into the group vocabulary.

The class took a field trip to a Hindu temple half an hour's drive eastward. In awe, I wandered barefoot around temples within the temple. I could see in people's eyes that devotion was part of their lives, not set aside for one day of the week. I gave offerings of apples from our tree at home. Fascinated, I watched the ritual bathing of a five-foot-tall statue of Ganesha. I was drawn to a smaller, unadorned Ganesha in a back temple. I prayed there, and surrounded it with rose petals. Hinduism felt like the air I breathe. The language difference didn't matter.

I knew I hadn't communicated with Gregg all that had been going on within me. He'd been getting snippets. I resolved to talk to him about this growing, deepening, and changing. I wanted him to come on this journey with me. At home, I told him about the temple visit, read him my home-work sermon, and warned him that I might sound like a wild woman sometimes. We both felt good about talking, each hearing the other.

I stayed up late, journaling. Tyson walked over the book, plainly telling me it was time for bed as the clock struck midnight. The next morning I woke to Tyson's purr and a chorus of the chant "I Am That I Am" in my head. I sang it out loud and the "Am" became "Om. . . ."

I had forgotten to put the stone back! I meant to replace it with thanks after our closing bead ceremony. I asked if it wanted to go back. The stone said: *I will stay with you.*

"Are you sure?" I had promised to take Sina to the dog park at Point Isabel, and could stop by Grace North on the way.

The stone repeated: *I will stay with you.*

I skimmed my journal of the last month, and my eyes fell on the direction to meditate with the fossil whale ear, to let whales speak to me directly. I had the impression of whale song as I held it. Tyson sat in my lap. The dense black fossil whale ear fit smoothly in my left hand, my thumb resting in a groove on its side. The smooth oval Chaplaincy stone rested in my right. The chant "I Am That I Am" chorused in my head. Holding the two stones, I realized that I was a bridge between interfaith and interspecies. I felt peaceful power in this validation and also great responsibility. No fear, though, not at that moment.

I'd begun the Chaplaincy program not knowing where it would go, whether I would finish, or what to do with it. Now I was deepening and growing into this role, and into the robe of Reverend in the way I went about many things. Witnessing my own growth was powerful.

Claiming Space

Why just ask the donkey in me to speak to the donkey in you, when I have so many other beautiful animals and brilliant colored birds inside that are all longing to say something wonderful and exciting to your heart?

— Hafiz

Thanksgiving approached. Indian summer days brought joy and appreciation for crisp, cool air and shining sun. I watched windblown pampas grass seeds fly from north to south. Outside, I raised my hands into the stream of seeds and began to sing "Ancient Mother" and the Ohana chant. Seed tufts flew over my head, potential plants flying off to seek their fortune. Across the canyon, the concentration of seeds seemed thicker. It reminded me of plankton in the ocean off Hawaii—the richness and many layers of life. How alive the ocean is! That same realization came on the air in my own backyard. As below, so above. Turkey vultures soared overhead. A pair of red-tail hawks circled the far trees, calling. I wanted to weep for joy.

I went upstairs to meditate, to sit and be, no questions, just gratitude and appreciation.

Before our extended family came over for Thanksgiving, I asked Tyson to help me stay balanced, "so all the energies flow around me and I don't get caught up in them. After everyone leaves, you and I can rebalance energy in the house together." I gave Sina a heads-up too, although she coped better with the often-chaotic energy level of many people in our house.

I could feel Tyson doing his work on me. He went outside when our family started to arrive, to get a good dose of earth energy. At one point, Tyson sat while Gwen's husband, Allen, stroked his back; Tyson purred loud enough for hard-of-hearing Allen to hear him. Tyson later said that Allen, a geologist, is deeply connected to the earth, and it resonates through his being.

Tyson was pleased that I took daughter Gwen and granddaughter Katy outside and taught them to sing "Now I Walk in Beauty." Hands joined, the three of us sang and did a slow clockwise sidestep, first the left foot and then the right, in a circle dance together as maiden, mother, and crone. We stumbled and giggled, lost our place and started again, until we were laughing too hard to continue. After that, whenever we felt tension, Gwen or I would start to sing an off-key "Now I Walk in Beauty," and burst out laughing.

This visit had an ease about it, with a new harmony in our extended family. When everyone had left, I thanked Tyson and Sina for being so great when our house was full. I asked Tyson if crystal dowsing was the right way to rebalance the house energies.

He said: *No need; it's done. Your singing kept it balanced. You've sung in every room. It feels fine.*

He was right. I'd sung a Chaplaincy chant everywhere I went. My prayer to stay grounded and balanced was answered, and in addition I did that for our house. Was it possible a contributing factor to everyone enjoying one another and laughing together so much was *me*? Spirit said *yes*. Blessing and responsibility, and gratitude.

On Sunday Gregg asked if I was going to church, rather than assumed. I appreciated that.

After church, I followed through on a need I had discussed with Gregg—carving out a private space for myself in our house. I complained to him, "Every space in our house is shared or yours; there's no Nancy space."

"So claim it," he said. "Pick a room, and do what you want with it!" He seemed baffled by my bringing it up. It was no big deal to him. That surprised me. We talked about how each of our mothers had determined the space usage inside her house. I could have claimed a space without talking it over with him, and recognized my internal obstacle-making machine at work once again.

I knew intuitively which room I'd choose—Sean's old room, on the southwest corner of our house, with a view to the trees and canyon. It had become a library and general "Let's put it in here until we decide what to do with it" place. I moved half of the books and a dozen boxes of storage into the hallway. We found new places for some of them, and donated much of the rest.

I smudged the room with white sage, and then emptied the closet on the east wall. Half of it would hold reorganized storage. The other half would hold my altar. I could slide the door closed when guests needed to sleep in that room. I constructed an altar out of boxes and covered it with fabrics from Hawaii. Representatives of plant, animal, and rock peoples joined my prayer beads from Islamic, Hindu, and Buddhist temples. Candles and a little bowl for offerings sat in the middle. I hung two mandalas, the wild-woman collage I'd made in Tree of Life sessions at Chaplaincy, and an interfaith Golden Rule poster. It gave the room a different feel, welcoming and more open. I felt solid as I claimed this space as mine. I lit candles and prayed for help in deepening fully into my ministry, becoming a bridge between interfaith and interspecies.

The first visitors to my altar room were Jan and Megan, the two Chaplaincy teachers I'd asked to review my midway self-assessment, another ordination requirement. Earthy Jan had greeted me warmly when I first visited the Chaplaincy Institute, and had been a grounding touchstone ever since. Creative Megan taught the Kabbalah Tree of Life and Spiritual Psychology sessions that helped me delve into the deepest parts of myself.

Sina wanted to come upstairs with us, but couldn't. The dual combination of her long multicolored fur and Megan's black outfit, and Tyson's holding firm on the upstairs as *his* territory, predominated. Sina got it. *Tyson doesn't want me there*, she pouted.

Jan and Megan sat side by side on the futon couch, surrounded by books, prayer flags, and my altar. These women represented Tree of Life pillars for me. Megan, with her colorful flowing scarf and long earrings, expressed the right, expressive pillar. Jan, in knee-length pants and untucked shirt, expressed the left, containing pillar. It was revealing and uncomfortable to talk about myself in such depth. We explored the vacuum of growing up as an invisible child and the compounding formlessness of lacking a cultural container while living in another land, away from extended family. That led to my observer state and an outsider's view of this culture.

Jan and Megan helped me develop a list of areas to focus the second half of my Chaplaincy program, part of the larger evolution they called "birthing my Self." My avoidance of conflict began in childhood: If there was conflict, I must have done something wrong to cause it, and feared it would be turned on me. Megan advised me to work on separating myself from the conflict. Identify what's mine and what's not mine. Easier said than done when dealing with a life-long pattern. I would soon have many opportunities to practice.

Jan suggested: "Put conscious attention on your observer self, and journal what you see and feel. How does that piece of you create blessings and challenges? What are its gifts?"

Journaling came easily for me. This I knew I could do. Perhaps in journaling—disengaging the logical mind and letting the pen flow on paper—I would see patterns emerge.

Megan's prescription for birthing my Self touched what had been emerging throughout my Chaplaincy program: "Check in regularly with the part of you that needs to be listened to. Give airtime to the young one who was unseen, unheard." She could see the part of me that struggled between invisibility and yearning for recognition. Acceptance starts with the self.

We said prayers of thanks and blessing to bring the session to a close.

Later, Tyson and Sina shared time together outside. Tyson said Sina learns fast, and thinks I don't love her as much as him because I don't spend as much time with her. Echoes of childhood! I'd apparently signed up for an advanced course in balancing relationships!

After a staff meeting at Matthew House, I received feedback from several people about undercurrents among staff. The new program director, Asuko, appeared to create as many issues as she solved. I woke one morning with the remnant of a dream and the words *Sometimes, even on the high road, you have to slog through some mud.*

My board-member friend Esther expressed her concern. "How are you holding up?"

"I'm operating at a steady level. I'm more concerned about Asuko." I asked for Esther's help in resolving the issues with our new program director and staff, some of which I felt resulted from dramatic differences in communication and operating styles.

The week before Christmas, a site manager gave me a five-page letter of complaint about the program director. I investigated the grievance and interviewed people involved. Versions of incidents ranged from slightly to radically different. These conversations helped me realize that I also viewed things from my own perspective. So many of these lessons now came rapid-fire, as if the window for learning them was narrow and the Universe wanted to make sure I got it.

There would be no rest over the holidays. It helped to reflect on the winter solstice, the shortest day and the longest night of the year, when the seeds of new light are sown. I added a dancing Shiva to my altar to remind me that destruction paves the way for creation.

Two highlights brought encouragement at Christmas: First, Gregg gave me an Irish bodhrán drum! The instructional CD that came with the drum would help train my hand and wrist to remember the drumbeats. Gregg suppressed a smile as he handed me the oversized box and watched me open it. His expression told me as much as the gift that he was listening to me, encouraging my growth and exploration, supporting me in his way.

The second was that I met Loretta, Kay's mother. A trained teacher of Huna, she offered to teach our pod group the introductory level. The long day filled me with a new appreciation of this native Hawaiian tradition in which the breath and heart are the center of all things.

Gregg surprised me with his willingness to go to a post-Hawaiian dolphin swim gathering at Cathy and George's home. He surprised himself by finding areas of common interest with members of our animal-communication practice group and Ohana Pod. He met Father Richard, senior pastor at Grace North Church. They became so engrossed in conversation that I was ready to leave long before Gregg. Father Richard served communion to animals at Grace North Church, and was on the list of people to interview for my practicum project.

I woke on New Year's Day and admitted I didn't want to go back to work. The demands of the nonprofit world grew more unwieldy, and called on strengths I wasn't sure I had. "Persevere" kept coming to me. At the same time, I was both exhilarated by the depth of learning and development I was going through at Chaplaincy, and torn apart as many layers of insulation I had built up over the years were pulled away.

Wheels Turning
in Different Directions

Gray as twilight, silken soft,
rising sun in my one eye, seeing all.
Purring, rumbling, I still do that well.
Gregg and I grow old together.
My soul and Nancy's take flight;
Sina fades between the realms, like a cat.
She's okay; I like her now.
She treats me with respect.
                    — Tyson Cat

Twelve years after I'd started at Matthew House—a complete Jupiter cycle through the heavens—I cycled back to the starting point, only to find that point had changed. Tyson cranked his purr up another notch, and Sina redoubled her efforts to distract us as Gregg and I entered a period that was as bumpy as a washboard-rutted dirt road.

Matthew House's new office manager bubbled refreshing enthusiasm. Asuko, the program director, had survived six months. I hoped she'd learned from the complaint lodged against her. As I started to breathe more easily, Dorita, the last of my original team, submitted her resignation. She felt "out of balance" and missed the old, smaller Matthew House.

Was expanding the agency a mistake? Client families needed the additional housing and services we now provided. Yet the internal penalty was geometric increase in budget and workload, and loss of a close-knit feel in the agency. Who now remembered the adventures, rewards, and disappointments of the early years? I went home, sat in my dark living room, and wailed: "I can't do this anymore!" Sina retreated, repelled by my intensity. Tyson listened, then turned his back and with a flick of his tail said: *Of course you can! Pull yourself together!*

And so I did. The course was set, and I had to follow. Later I realized Dorita had done me a favor. I hadn't known if I could leave my working family, but now they had all left me. I also saw how quickly pathways reshaped as soon as someone gave notice.

Balance and hope came from family and Chaplaincy studies. On my sixty-third birthday, I woke with thoughts of my mother, and knew her spirit had come to visit. Tyson curled in my lap, Sina sat at my feet, and sacred music played on the radio as we watched the eastern sky brighten and clouds change color in the west. Gregg sheepishly handed me a handmade card. He'd forgotten my birthday until that day, but made me a card with a photo of me and granddaughter Katy reading a story together, and a takeoff on "Roses are red" that he'd written himself. Life was pretty good after all. I had a challenging and stimulating (if wearing) job and was transitioning to another. Spiritual and personal growth leapfrogged through me. I felt valued by a small set of close friends and larger sets of people whose company I welcomed and enjoyed. My family was a collection of unique individuals, my sister was a friend, and my husband of forty-one and a half years still loved me. My animal family brought joy and wisdom; my spirit guides and animal chorus were always with me. Among trees and rocks I experienced interconnectedness with all the beings who shared my life.

Gregg looked forward to his retirement in February. He planned to spend a month in Louisiana with his father who, at ninety-three, was declining. Gregg wanted to do some repairs around his father's house and spend time there without the deadline of work obligations.

Back at the Chaplaincy Institute, February's module in Earth-Based Traditions touched me even more deeply than Hinduism. It started with Chief Phillip, and nothing was the same after that. Chief Phillip Scott, whose native name was *Tsunka Wakan Sapa* (Black Horse), is of Cherokee ancestry. He had a fine-tuned sense of ritual. Lean and wolflike, Chief Phillip wore a long, dark ponytail at the base of his neck. He fixed steady, dark eyes on the collected students. "Put away your papers and pens, and just be here." He turned out the lights, lit a candle, and chanted prayers in deep, resonant tones while he laid out the contents of his medicine bundle.

"Close your eyes." He sang, shook his rattles, and brought in animals, sounding each of them. Calls of Wolf and Cougar and fluttering wings swirled around us. Eyes closed, I could have sworn animals had entered the darkened classroom. I felt the energy shift and deepen.

That afternoon Dr. Diane Johnson led us through an exploration of pagan practice—*pagan* simply means "of the country" and dates to a time when people were intimately connected with the earth's cycles. From her deck of Goddess Oracle cards I drew Sheela na Gig, the ancient Irish goddess of birth and death—a gap-toothed old hag with a wicked grin who held open her vulva, vibrant and defiant in the beauty of her old age. She reminded me that a period of contraction is followed by a period of expansion, and invites the exploration of opening.

With that encouragement, I broached my fear of leaving both Chaplaincy and Matthew House. I likened it to being on a raft in a river with no rudder and no brakes, while downstream thunders a waterfall. This felt like my dream of the planets, and launching off the cliff in a speeding car. In the dream I had yelled *No* and tried to slam on the car's brakes. Now I was fully awake, and the dream was coming true. If I were to go over the waterfall, or off the cliff, I hoped to have grown wings—big ones! I felt deep gratitude for the support of the circle of fellow students.

After Friday's class, I went to spiritual direction. Ron placed his thick-lensed glasses on the table, and listened while I rambled on about change, ordination, Matthew House, and my growing acceptance of uncertainty about what comes after. I noticed that I felt completely present, comfortable in my own skin, with a sense of rootedness and confidence. I sensed sparkles of light around me, and could feel energy running in my hands. Ron said, "When you're completely present, that sometimes happens." He gave me an exercise: Check in with myself throughout the day to see if I'm fully present. If my pieces and parts have drifted off, call them back.

I told him about the balls I kept in the air and my feeling that if I stopped, some would fall. The need for movement made it challenging to stay completely present. Ron asked me to close my eyes. I went back to the incident of the swinging rope bridge in Colombia that we'd worked with months earlier. This time, rather a lot of loose and bowed planks between the ropes, there were only two—one under each foot. When my father started rocking the bridge, I stilled it by my own power. A plank materialized under my foot with each step. I kept the bridge still and safe, and gave myself a plank to support me as I needed it. Rather than feeling that my body wasn't a safe place, I saw that the best protection was to keep myself intact, fully present.

I marveled at Ron's remarkable ability to unwrap layers, and hoped I could follow his example and learn to go deep with people to reach the core of an issue.

That night I walked Sina to the park. The Winter Circle shone clear and bright in the crisp cold. I stopped at Big Tree on the way home, and told her about a classroom meditation in which I'd envisioned myself as my own Tree of Life. Birds, squirrels, and ants lived in my branches. People collected the acorns I dropped to the ground. Squirrels taunted the dog who chased them; when she leaped up I felt her paws on my bark. "I saw myself as a tree like you, Big Tree."

I already knew, Big Tree answered. I looked up. Her branches seemed to grow thicker and closer. I felt the warmth of a hug and complete love all around me.

The next morning, Tyson curled in my lap, purring, his head tucked into my arm to keep the light out of his eye, while I skimmed the newspaper. I read with sadness that dolphins were stranding themselves and dying off Long Island. Why? What was their message?

The dolphins said: *The Mother is sick. The oceans are dying. There is not much time left. We came here to die because it is close to your seat of government. We could just leave, but the people who make the laws must see. We hope if you humans see, you will understand the connection between your actions and all life. You can help with that.* I thanked them, my heart sore.

Gregg came home from work late, his shoulders slumped and his forehead furrowed. "Looks like I need to push my retirement date out to mid-March."

"Why?"

"I want to complete the circuit-boards project, and get another project far enough along to hand off to someone else. Also, the company isn't making any moves toward finding my replacement. I'll have to do it myself."

I admired his loyalty and sense of integrity, yet felt foreboding about this decision. His exit from the work world wasn't going any smoother than mine.

The next morning, Tyson woke me by gently stroking my face with his tail, and purring loudly. I felt Buki's presence. She said: *I came to see how you're doing. Your opening has slowed, though you're still moving forward. Growth isn't linear; it comes in spurts and slows as you integrate lessons. You have innate talent. Going beyond that is work. I'm here to help you. Ty is here to help you too. We speak as one voice.*

"Where are you these days?"

The dark forces have gathered. Many are dying. I have been to the desert places where there is war, and helped those souls across. I'm guiding Sina too.

"Buki, I'm afraid that I don't have a clear vision of what I want to do and be."

You do, but you're afraid. Just keep moving toward it.

Downstairs with my morning coffee, I helped Tyson with his grooming. He was patient, stretched out on my lap. For so long he hadn't wanted to be handled but now he seemed to enjoy letting me thank him in this way for all he had done for me. He said: *Tuna: It's all I can taste now. The rest is chalky, no texture, no flavor. I'm so hungry for flavor. I'll be gone soon. Plant a red rosebush over me, and give me tuna. I'll always be in your heart with Buki. Part of me is already there.*

"You are a master teacher."

Yes, it took me a while to sink into it. And for you to find out. You can do this! You just need to have faith in yourself, and practice.

"Tuna now?"

Yes, please.

On Sunday Gregg went to church. I stayed home to do Chaplaincy homework. Sina and I stepped outside. I took about fifty feet of lead to tie Sina to a tree while I meditated. I settled into a depression in leaves and shed bark, and leaned back against the sturdy trunk. Not a deep meditation, as I kept an eye on Sina and periodically untangled her, but it was nice to be outside.

Sina said: *I want to be free! So many good smells, so many sounds, so much life!*

A big eucalyptus tree joined our conversation. *Your dog is funny. Her mind is scattered, like light through leaves. You're wise to keep her tied until she settles. In earlier days she would learn lessons from us all, but this is a darker time. She knows of this, but it is not real to her.*

"Do you have guidance for us?" I felt the breeze shift to blow from the southwest.

It is all around you! We are singing the song all the time, but few listen. We don't understand why you would destroy your home! It has been so since humans banded together and made tools and weapons and lost communication with tree people and rock people and animals.

"How can I best do my part?"

Listen. Listen to the animals. Listen to the wind. Listen to All That Is.

"I try, but what I hear is to listen. I'm not getting what to listen for!"

Poor child! You try so hard. Sink into the earth, sink into my bark, and feel the pulse of All That Is. Fly with the hawk, and look down upon the land.

A red-tail circled above, calling. Buki once said: *When the red-tail calls, I go.*

Homework for the Earth-Based Traditions module was a presentation—art or music or a story. I remembered some of the magical experiences I'd shared with our grandchildren, and wrote a children's story.

When Gregg came home from church and had arranged his long frame on the living-room couch, coffee nearby, I read it to him. "That would be a good children's book," he said, sounding surprised.

I felt a flush of happiness that my ministry might bring awareness of the natural world through books! To shorten it for class, I deleted an interaction with a hummingbird. Outside later, a green Anna's hummingbird said: *I want to be back in the story!* I explained the presentation's time limits and asked if I could put him back for the one that's published. He hovered in front of me to give his approval, and then disappeared.

The feeling of completeness and happiness remained underneath, as my journey over the washboard-rutted road intensified.

More Best-Laid Plans

Like hoodwinked fools, perplexed we grope our way,
and during life's short course we blindly stray,
puzzled in mazes and perplexed with fears.
— Anonymous, "Reflections on Walking
the Maze at Hampton Court"

Sunday, March 4, 2007. The phone call came while Gregg was at church. His sister wailed at the other end. I knew before she could get the words out. Gregg's father had died. As soon as Gregg came home, I clasped his hands and told him. He turned gray. "I should have been there," he said, guilt and sorrow grating his voice.

Then anger. At the company for moving slowly to find a replacement for him, at the customer for making changes to the product Gregg was shepherding through manufacturing. Mostly at himself for delaying retirement by a month. He'd put responsibility to the company above responsibility to himself and his father. His father hadn't waited the extra month.

"If I'd retired when I wanted to, I could have spent a few weeks with Dad before he died." He felt a little better when I reminded him that he'd called his father only the day before. They'd talked for an hour, agreeing to disagree about politics and the economy.

By midweek he was on a flight to Louisiana. He spoke for the family at his father's memorial service, telling stories of life with his dad—including his pleasure in high school when his father presented him with a birthday gift of a Chrysler engine for the 1930 souped-up Ford Model A Gregg was building. After the memorial service, he spent a few days at his father's house, stepping into the role of family leader as the eldest of his siblings—a brother and three sisters—and doing repairs he'd planned. He needed to keep busy, do something physical.

I stayed home and prayed for his whole family. I was up to my proverbial eyeballs in work, Chaplaincy studies, single-parenting energetic Sina, and tending to Tyson's medications. Tyson was his quiet, supportive self. He didn't like the gunk of thyroid medicine smeared on his ear tips, but tolerated that better than pills. Sina and Tyson even sat in the front window seat together! They chose opposite ends, with Tyson's back toward Sina, but it was progress.

When Gregg came back, I asked if he'd like to talk about it.

"Not now. I'm not ready. I don't know if I ever will be." His eyes dropped to his feet. He wore his father's dark-brown corduroy house slippers. They were a perfect fit.

He agreed to go to the March 2007 Chaplaincy ordination service. I didn't want mine to be the first he attended. He went reluctantly and out of duty, but was glad he did. "That was the most truly interfaith ceremony I've ever been to. It touched me," he said afterward. I saw him mention his father to a couple of people, willingly. The sanctuary was filled with compassionate hearts. It was a natural and safe place for him to open up about his father's death.

When our children and their families came for Easter, Gregg admitted feeling unbalanced over his transition from work. He was accustomed to pushing forward with plans and schedules, and felt the approaching absence of that structure as a physical sensation. A few words slipped out at a time, relieving the pressure within him. "Inherently unstable" were the words he used. I was glad that he recognized what he was feeling, and was able to talk about it to someone!

Our bedroom became Tyson's hideaway, with litterbox, food, water, and a comfy pillow in the rocking chair. I went upstairs to check on him *(Not often enough*, he said). After our family left, he went outside to get his paws on the earth. He is himself, I thought. He and Gregg were alike in so many ways—present, self-contained, my beloved grumpy guys.

At Matthew House, packing to move from the 450-square-foot office we'd occupied for over a dozen years kept me too busy to think about it. I carried home all my personal books and mementos, and didn't move them to the new, larger office in a local church. Family, volunteers, and staff all turned out on moving day. Laboring long and hard brought a welcome physical tiredness, different from my internal exhaustion. The pastor of the host church commented that I looked tired. Many people said that. Everyone attributed it to the move, but it was more.

Big Tree said: *You need to let something go.*

"What? Matthew House? It isn't time yet. Chaplaincy? Native American studies?"

Big Tree paused. *Perhaps carve off small pieces to lighten the load.*

Friday, April 13. Gregg's last day at work. There would be phone calls and maybe days there, but this was his official Retirement Day. He struggled with the concept. "I've never done this before. I've left jobs, but always to go to or search for another." Shades of vulnerability passed across his face. He shrugged and held out his empty hands, fingers spread, showing his uncertainty about identity and concern about finances. We were entering a new way of living.

With his father's death and his own retirement, he was going through a death and rebirth cycle, as was I. How could I best support him? At least he was starting to talk about it some, especially with friends who had retired earlier. "I'm scattered. Large aspects of my life are in upheaval," he admitted. But he didn't speak his questions about his identity now that he'd left the work world, or about feeling scared. The characteristic furrows on his brow deepened. His shoulders took on a more pronounced slump.

Gregg's anxiety about the uncertainty of "life after" became almost another member of our household. Sleep brought nightmares. He thrashed as dreams ran rampant through the active mind in his sleeping body. Frustrated and helpless, I didn't know what to do. I tried to hold him, and redirect some of that energy outside and into projects. He was used to focusing his A-type energy into work and having some left over. With that focus gone, his body and mind still ran at speed, like a racecar suddenly thrust into neutral gear with the engine revved. I prayed that he find peace and new purpose for this stage of his life.

Tyson stretched across my lap as I contemplated my dual exits of retirement and ordination. He said I was brave, going off in this unknown new direction. When I answered that it was possible because he, Sina, and Gregg were with me, he added: *I won't be for long.* He flicked his tail in irritation. *Just accept the compliment.*

Yes, sir!

Paddy Paws had come in a dream and told me to remember the many things she taught me the first years we were together, and in Colorado. I asked Tyson for help. He recited a list:

Compassion;

The rocks talk, and the waters and trees;

You spent a night on the lawn and didn't feel awkward doing so;

You talked to the turtle and helped her dig her burrow;

Your soul felt freedom and you noticed stars;

You found a group of like-minded seekers, and first felt comfortable in a group;

You stretched and found you could do things you previously thought you could not;

Your soul and body felt new freedom and expanded beyond what you had known before;

You drove over the high plain and felt complete.

I wrote the first draft of my resignation letter. I planned to announce my departure on June first, after the dust had settled from Matthew House's annual walkathon fundraiser.

It wouldn't be that easy.

The Medicine Wheel

What is life?
It is the flash of a firefly in the night.
It is the breath of a buffalo in the wintertime.
It is the little shadow which runs across the grass
    and loses itself in the sunset.
    — Crowfoot of the Blackfoot Nation

Vernal equinox. Balance, elusive, like the ever-receding place where a highway meets the horizon and looks like the fulcrum of a seesaw. In my altar room at home, I prayed and lit a candle, seeking guidance. I had to choose a faith tradition, different from the one practiced by my family, for a six-month intensive study—another Chaplaincy ordination requirement.

Possible paths spread out like spokes on a wheel. I had dreams in which someone said, "Unitarian Universalist"—a friend had called me a "closet Unitarian." Hinduism resonated deeply within me. I'd already begun studying Hawaiian Huna and the Jewish mystical tradition of Kabbalah, and saw their similarities. I was drawn to Native American spirituality as a way of living with the earth, about which I had only surface knowledge. Some relief came with the realization that I could postpone my choice, thereby postponing ordination.

I quieted and asked Spirit for guidance, using my crystal dowsing pendulum. The answer came as an energetic counterclockwise circle, meaning Spirit wasn't going to tell me. Humbled, I asked for continuing support and discernment.

A break came in the rain. Sina pranced ahead of me on our walk. We stopped at Big Tree, who said: *Study me.* I thanked her, and said it needed to be a human teacher. She repeated: *Study me.* I continued the walk, pondering what that meant. Rain sprinkled like holy water. We were alone in the green and dripping park. The little creek flowed brown and full of runoff.

I stopped to pay respects to a dead raccoon, slowly being cleaned by insects, its fur still visible although its body bones were scattered among the leaves. Its skull remained intact. It said: *You can talk to me.* I thanked it, and said I was having trouble choosing which alternative religion to study. *What is the purpose?* Raccoon asked. I realized the purpose was ordination. Other studies could follow. Which would most contribute to my ministry with animals? The answer became clear: I wanted to deepen my knowledge of Native American ritual and practice, and learn animal medicine. I thanked Raccoon for its good question. Sina and I crossed the creek on a two-by-twelve-inch plank that served as a bridge, and climbed back up to the park. We walked home in a warm, steady rain, pausing by Big Tree to share my new feeling of peace.

I asked one of Chaplaincy's Native American teachers, Jane deCuir, to teach me the Medicine Wheel, with its power animals and spirit totems. Jane studied me, mischief in her coyote-dark-gold eyes. A hint of hazel flickered within them, a gift of her *metis* (mixed-blood) heritage. Beaded earrings tangled in her long, graying hair. Jane was an herbalist, working with medicine plants, and not schooled in animal lore. She agreed to take on this mutual challenge, to see where it would go. The night before my first meeting with her, I dreamed of leading a Medicine Wheel class. I knew I was far from ready to teach, but I was ready to learn.

The lessons started before the lessons. Jane gave me directions, but used points of reference instead of her street address. I found a house that fit the description. No one was home. I stayed for half an hour, and then concluded that Jane had forgotten our appointment. I left a note on the patio table and drove home, to find a phone message from Jane, asking where I was.

When we sorted out what had happened, Jane said, "It appears as if the first teaching has occurred. This is how medicine works sometimes. Once you step into the teaching, it starts working, to show where you need to pay attention. Your assignment is to look at how everything happened, how you made decisions, how you processed it through your emotions, mind, body, spirit. First teaching: Look at events with no guilt, no blame, no shame, and get the teaching."

In spite of Jane's instruction about "no guilt, no blame, no shame," I felt shame to recognize that I'd classified her as airy, challenged to have even one foot on the ground. My conclusion that Jane had forgotten or thought we were meeting at a different time was stronger than my nagging uncertainty about being in the right place. The lesson didn't start with being there; it started with getting there. And she wanted payment for the missed session!

Was the place an exact match, or a close substitute that diverted me? The redwood tree provided a clue. Jane had said to park facing the redwood. The tree where I stopped was *beside* the driveway. I hadn't insisted on a street address, even though that works best for me. I tried to call while waiting, but had no cellphone service on the mountain. When I found no one home, I could have continued up the road, but had convinced myself I'd found the right place. I went home, still thinking she would come home and find my note.

I told Gregg I felt irritated at Jane for giving me such poor directions. He tossed it back to me: "It's your responsibility to make sure you know how to get there."

The resentment (guilt, blame, shame) festered in me all afternoon.

Gregg and Sina left for a walk. I stomped up to the park half an hour behind them. This wasn't the first time I'd felt resentment about a teacher wanting payment when I thought it should be waived. A work emergency caused me to cancel a spiritual-direction appointment less than the required twenty-four hours in advance, and my spiritual director nicely said he had to hold that boundary and charge me. My animal-communication teacher was rigorous about charging for her time, even when the workshops or consultations didn't stay on target. I suddenly saw this repeating pattern as an example of my wanting to be given special consideration. This was a lesson about being fully responsible for my own actions. Did it go back to the issue of recognition and validation I'd been working on in spiritual direction? I thought I'd pretty well laid that one to rest. Apparently not. I still wanted to be special. I was finally getting it.

Like Chaplaincy itself, it wasn't about reading a few books and peeling some layers off the proverbial onion. It was deep work and commitment. Spirit gave an emphatic *yes* to that. I sighed and said out loud to whatever was listening: "There's no going back. Nor do I want to." As I worked through all this, I found myself coming back into balance again. I felt the tingling of energy flowing through my hands, and remembered the lessons the birds had been teaching me: *Listen to the birds. Pay attention.* One does not step onto this path lightly.

I drove to Jane's house that weekend with her original directions in hand. When I exited the freeway, I pulled over and prayed. Then I drove up to the correct fork in the road and found her house, with a redwood tree at the end of the driveway. When I told her later about that trip, she grinned and cautioned me again about "no guilt, no blame, no shame." I hadn't quite mastered that lesson, however, and continued to beat myself up for not going deep enough.

I told Gregg about this whole sequence of events. He listened, but made no comment. He knew I was figuring it out on my own. Gray Tyson notched up his purr.

With a new depth of respect, I gave Jane the traditional teacher's gift: a pouch of tobacco. We sat on her deck drinking herbal tea and munching almonds, surrounded by the cleansing smoke of sage and cedar. Stately bumblebees droned by. Dark-headed juncos, towhees, titmice, and hummingbirds flitted among her garden's spring flowers and trees covered in fresh green.

Each session opened another layer of the Medicine Wheel. I learned that it's multidimensional, encompassing space, time, energy, and everything that exists. An aspect of myself lives in each direction. To stay in the center is to balance all aspects of myself. In any situation, if I can locate myself on the wheel, I can find my way back to center. I began praying to the directions (East, South, West, North, Above, Below, and Within), if only to give thanks. These studies illustrated how everything is connected—not only all living things, but also all that ever has been, is, or ever will be.

In each session, Jane told teaching stories and then drummed while I went on short journeys. Beats of one of her drums—the deep-voiced buffalo drum or the lighter, more feminine elk or deer drums, whichever seemed appropriate at the time—accompanied me. After the drum journey, I'd report what I had seen and we would discuss it. On one such journey,

> *I entered the water and swam to the ocean's sandy bottom. A pod of dolphins joined me. I asked if the dolphins were my guide, and a large male said: I am. Then I was part dolphin. The dolphin and I swam over remnant buildings. I understood they were past civilizations that had risen and fallen in a cycle. From each set of ruins, bubbles rose to the surface. Within each bubble was a spark of light. I watched them float up from the sea floor, and wondered what happened to them. My dolphin guide and I swam to the surface. I could see bubbles surface and break, releasing sparks of light into the sky. The sparks then fell back down onto the land and sea. My dolphin guide and I held steady in a vertical position, with our eyes and rostrums above water. A low tropical island at first seemed uninhabited, but as I looked more closely I could see people dancing, wearing colored scarves.*

> *We swam into the lagoon. Set back from the sandy beach was a temple. A priestess waited on the top step with her arms raised. Her brownish-red curly hair fell to just below shoulder length. She wore a robe of flax-colored fabric trimmed in wide bands of patterned gold. I knew that she was me. The priestess came down the steps and walked across the beach and into the water. She slipped off her robe and swam to us, appearing to be both human and dolphin. She spoke to me. My dolphin guide asked if I understood. I said I didn't and asked for help. Then the priestess/dolphin/me swam to the beach and walked from the water, again wearing her robe. Her skin was the silver gray of a dolphin. She walked to a large tree to the right of the temple. Its thick trunk, spreading branches*

and leaves resembled an oak tree. She turned to face us, raised her arms, backed up, and became one with the tree. A large rock lay at the tree's base, and she was the rock too. I was still floating in vertical position with my dolphin guide. I turned to him and asked what was happening, what all this meant. He said: I am rewriting you.

The drum sounded, calling me to return.

I knew that the priestess became a dolphin, as did I, and also became the tree and rock, foregoing the temple. So I didn't need a temple to do my work. I also was one with all things.

My homework assignment was to remember the places where I got into trouble as a child. Jane said, "Those are your power places. How is that power manifesting?"

I wrote a long list of incidents, including the time in Colombia when my barefoot sister stepped on broken glass. Our father carried my screaming sister up a long flight of concrete steps to our house. I marveled at the bright red drops of blood on each step. They looked like flowers. When I called my mother's attention to their beauty, I was reprimanded for not being concerned enough about my sister. At three or four years old, I learned to keep such observations to myself.

Growing up in South America, we gringos were the minority. I had no concept of the racial segregation and prejudice in the States in the late 1950s. While we were in boarding school, my sister and I visited relatives in Mississippi over Christmas break. I asked them, "Why does the Negro high school look like a prison when the white students have a pretty new one?" I couldn't believe it was "separate but equal" if the buildings were so different. My aunt and grandmother called me "uppity and a troublemaker," and told me not to ask such questions.

I felt an innate sense of the equality of all beings. My natural curiosity and early questioning must have made adults around me pretty uncomfortable. I never understood why I was repeatedly punished, told not to speak, admonished to "behave yourself." Now I was learning to speak my truth.

Jane helped me gain confidence in my animal ministry as well. When I assisted a friend of hers with end-of-life concerns about her dog, I urged her to get him to a vet quickly. The dog communicated that he wasn't ready to depart this life but needed medical help to stay. For the first time, I was able to physically feel what the dog felt and describe it to the person. The vet's report matched what I had learned from the dog. This and other successful interactions increased my certainty in the value of my skills, and of this ministry.

Jane showed me how everything moves in cycles. She analyzed my natal astrological chart, overlaying it on the Medicine Wheel to show the clear pattern of my movement around it. She explained the eighteen-year cycles of the North Node, the direction in which each person moves during her life, from one quadrant of the Medicine Wheel to another.

I was struck by how my path at Matthew House had followed this cycle. At the end of 1994, my North Node transited the bottom of my chart—"the place of conception, where you're closest to hearing the voice of God." That's when I started at Matthew House. Four and a half years later, in April 1999, the baby was born—the transitional housing facility.

The next quarter of the cycle culminated in March 2003. When my North Node passed the top of my chart, the new cohousing facility had opened and reached full occupancy—my greatest achievement at Matthew House. Then we start the descent.

The midpoint of descent would be late 2007—my ordination and planned exit date from Matthew House. "The point of surrender," Jane said. "Autumn. Leaves fall, mulch, and prepare the soil for the seed that's planted in the dead of winter, when the North Node again transits the bottom of the chart." Others had called it the void. Sensing my trepidation about entering that period, she added, "The reason we have dark is that it's easier to see the point of light."

Between early 2008 and 2012, I would be steeped in reflection—the West of the Medicine Wheel. It would be a time to incorporate all that I had learned, gather tools, and practice, preparing me to emerge ready for the next cycle— the full expression of my ministry.

At the end of my six months of study with her, Jane gave me a ceramic-bowl rattle made by a friend of hers. Our work together would continue; I still had much to learn. One of the most important lessons I had already learned is that this isn't a path where you can go backward. Some aspect of travel on that path is always present.

Hope and a Hug

Purring vibrations rumbling through my body, healing.
My heart beating in unison with yours.
This is a good life.
— Tyson Cat

In a shift of perception, I realized that ordination wasn't the end of the line, but a marker on the path. Jesus was baptized *before* his forty days in the wilderness; only then did his ministry begin. I drove to Berkeley for spiritual direction. There, I broke down as soon as I started talking. It was all too much. I wasn't prepared for the upcoming Sufism module. My practicum felt half-baked, as if I were just skating across the surface and not delving as deep as the project warranted.

Ron placed his glasses on the table beside him, almost a ritual gesture, and regarded me with gray eyes. Quietly he asked, "Is this connected to your core issue of not being worthy?"

An interesting question, considering I'd recently had a revelation: "If God is in all things and all things are in God, then to be not worthy is to diminish God. That's a conundrum."

I continued my rant about everything that was going wrong. "I'm conflicted about ordination this September, and leaving Matthew House at same time," I sniffled. "I would like to steep in the ordination experience rather than grabbing it on the run. It's unlikely that I'll be out of Matthew House by then, and the fundraiser dinner is the week after ordination."

Ron asked, "Have you thought about all the things that are going right?"

I hadn't. He asked me to make a list. Some things were going right. I felt better then.

I felt a strong pull to ordination in September rather than waiting for the following March. I tried to talk to Gregg about it. Tears came. He said, "Every time you start talking about this you cry, so you obviously have something unresolved. I don't see why you can't wait."

I had to admit that doing both at the same time was a lot. And that I was afraid.

I called Karen Baldwin, who had been ordained in March. She'd been through this. At least she could provide a completely understanding shoulder to cry on.

Karen's snug home office held an array of statues and symbols of many faith traditions, books, and two comfy armchairs. A three-foot tall light-brown teddy bear sat in the guest chair. Karen wore a print silk scarf as a stole and sat with her back to the window, her legs crossed.

I clasped the teddy bear to my chest and sobbed. Words poured from me. For the first time, I spoke my fear and uncertainty about what comes after leaving the two communities—Matthew House and Chaplaincy Institute— that had given me support and structure as well as recognition and validation. Then what? I feared falling into the void and losing my way. In spite of my trust in the Divine, I still felt unworthy of ordination.

Karen let me run down and then said, "Seems to me that you're right on schedule."

Stunned, I sputtered, "What?"

"Your ordination is in five months. What you're feeling is completely normal and natural. In fact, that you're unsure tells me that you *are* worthy and you're ready to be ordained. If you were confident about it, I'd be worried about you."

The cloak of misery fell from my shoulders. At least for the time being.

A few nights later I had a dream. It was a story of a time when all beings were one and honored one another. It was my ordination sermon. I would string the beads from each intensive module's closing ceremony into one long necklace to illustrate the unity of all parts of Creation, and sound heartbeats on a drum while I told the creation story given to me: "The council fire burns bright. The heartbeat is strong in the land, and there is a story that wants to be told."

Two months later I sat beside a pond. Water lilies with pink blossoms floated on the water. Iridescent blue and orange-red dragonflies flitted in and out of shadows cast by willow trees. A bullfrog croaked. I was at MA Center, western U.S. headquarters of Mata Amritanandamayi, known as Amma, the hugging saint. Amma was in town for a few days and would be giving *darshan*, her hugging blessing, to all who came to her. I needed a hug.

At the center's main building, volunteers guided the hundreds of people who stood in line, and gave us slips of paper with our group number. First-timers were directed to the front. I left my bookbag on a chair and wandered around the assembly hall. A raised dais at one end, covered with colorful carpets and flowers, faced the wide doors behind us. Prayer flags draped from the ceiling and a balcony along one side of the meeting room. Chanting music filled the air.

The scent of roses filled the hall. Amma's disciples sang to announce her entrance. She was short, roundly built, and barefoot. Peace flowed from her, expanding her presence beyond the sari-clad space she occupied. The assembly sang her in, then quieted. People were called by group number to receive Amma's *darshan.* Each person or family group knelt before her to receive her hug. Some hugs seemed longer than others. Did she know what each one needed? Amma's face radiated unconditional love.

After a while our group was called. As I slowly advanced up the center aisle closer to Amma, the choir began singing. The opening was a song Jan had taught us at Chaplaincy: "The ocean refuses no river, the open heart refuses no love." As we came closer, we all sank to our knees and inched forward. When a space opened up in front of me, I bowed and touched my forehead to the ground in gratitude.

While I waited, I thought of the pain and grief I'd been feeling, and then of the void, the empty vessel, and how I wanted to fill it with love and light. I began to ask earnestly that the grief and pain be replaced by joy.

The group ahead of me moved out, and I was directed to Amma. She reached plump brown arms toward me and placed my head on her shoulder and bosom, nestled into the lei of flowers around her neck. She stroked my hair. I heard a male voice, and then Amma spoke to me in her native language. I relaxed, sinking deep into her bosom and her unconditional love, aware of nothing but her presence and the scent of flowers. It seemed she held me for a long time. When she released me I looked deeply into her eyes and she into mine. I thanked her and she smiled. She gave each of us the blessing gift—a Hershey's kiss wrapped in a flower petal.

I made my way unsteadily to my chair, knees not cooperating after inching halfway up the aisle on them. After, I went in search of the dining room. There I chose to sit at a table marked Silent Table to enjoy my lunch of lentils, fresh vegetables, and brown rice.

Reluctant to leave, I climbed a low hill to the labyrinth and walked it. The Cretan pattern's central circle was anchored by a large *shiva lingam* stone. The pile of rocks around it included fossils, coral, wood, a piece of quartz geode, coins, leaves, feathers—land, sea, and air creatures all represented. Then I sat by the pond to journal, solitary by choice and soaking in the precious feeling of peace, which persisted even with children playing noisily behind me.

At home, I told Gregg I wanted to stay in this bubble for a while, and went upstairs. I slept for two hours on the floor of my altar room, wrapped in the peace of unconditional love. The rest of the world would come knocking soon enough.

The Whales and the
Shatter Point

How did the rose ever open its heart
And give to this world all its beauty?
It felt the encouragement of light against its being.
Otherwise, we all remain too frightened.
— *Hafiz*

I'd been sliced, diced, marinated, and stewed.

On the heels of a Chaplaincy module in Mystical Judaism (Kabbalah), we studied Mystical Islam (Sufism). I'd questioned, "Why Sufism?" As chaplains we would probably encounter more Sikhs than Sufis. But Sufism is closest to a true interfaith practice. "There is only God." Both mystical approaches opened wide my one-to-one relationship with the Divine, and strengthened my knowing that the Divine is present in all Creation.

I flowed so deeply into this module's experience that, instead of standing at the pulpit to deliver my homework sermon, I slowly walked the burgundy-painted labyrinth on the wooden floor in Grace North's fellowship hall. With afternoon sunlight streaming through tall, dusty windows, I willingly stepped into the circle's center, wearing bright blues and greens, to be seen and heard as I offered a prayer poem I had written that morning:

Beloved: A Poem in the Sufi Tradition

Beloved, thou art the essence of my being.
Beloved, thou art the seed that grows, reaching its
branches to the sky and offering its leaves and
fruit.
Beloved, thou art the breath of life and the voice of
God on the wind.
Beloved, thou art the fire that has kindled my heart
of hearts.
Beloved, thou art in every creature and every drop
of rain, in every rock and tree.
Beloved, thou art before me and behind me, to the
right and to the left of me.
Beloved, thou art above and below and within me.
Beloved, thou art.
Beloved, I am thou.
Be loved.

We had met Shekina, one of our Sufism teachers, the first day of the course module. Her peaceful energy surpassed her small stature. She radiated compassion as she told us of her experience with "the shatter point"—that point at which a wall within breaks and the reservoir of unshed tears pours forth, with no way to stop it, until those long-held tears are exhausted.

During this week a story unfolded in the local news. A mother humpback whale and her calf were lost. They swam through San Francisco Bay and up the river system into narrower and shallower water. Nightly newscasts showed film of their dark bodies swimming through the bays and deltas, taken from shore and from helicopters. Rescue crews attempted to divert them back into the deeper waters of San Francisco Bay, and then out the Golden Gate to rejoin the whale migration. If those efforts failed, the whales would ground and die.

A beautiful May morning found us gathered in the Sufi center in North Berkeley. The wooden floor gleamed. Soft light shone through the windows. Flowers bloomed on bushes outside. We sat on colorful floor cushions and listened to the explanation of a ritual we were about to join. Sufi background music played. We followed Shekina's graceful arm and upper-body movements as she bent and reached in rhythm with the music and chant. Then we sat in meditation. Enveloped in peace and gratitude, I unexpectedly heard a clear message from the whales. I relayed this message to the group as best I could through a throat choked with tears:

> We are not lost. We are emissaries. We have volunteered to come to raise the awareness of humans to the condition of the oceans. The oceans are dying, and all life is being affected. We need your help. We came specifically as a mother and child, as we know humans have a special regard for mothers and children. Share our message, help us tell our story, and help save the oceans for all of us. We are one.

The whales were willing to sacrifice themselves to bring us this message. I assured them that their message had been heard. They were pleased to learn about the media attention they'd received. Other animal communicators heard from them as well. We all rejoiced later when the whales turned around. Their message delivered, they swam back down the river, into the deep water of San Francisco Bay, and then swam with the tide out the Golden Gate's narrow strait into the Pacific Ocean. They also had reminded me why I had embarked on my path.

I didn't know when I began this journey how much deep and painful work I would need to do. I felt ready to be ordained, but wished there were more modules because much internal work remained. I'd been a tough nut to crack.

Without the regular container of Chaplaincy modules, I would need to lean on meditation and regular practice for my growth to continue. Each cycle had gone deeper to bring healing to old wounds. I was emerging into my true self.

Big Tree said: *You are speaking my truth, and just need to do it louder and more often.*

On Memorial Day, Gregg and I stayed home and worked around the house, cleaning up piles of unfinished projects, he in the garage and family room, me in the kitchen and home office. We crossed paths over laundry and meals. I realized we were practicing hanging out in the same space together. We'd done little of this over the years; we'd both been busy with family, community commitments, and our consuming careers.

That evening, Gregg watched and I listened to a television program while I strung my Chaplaincy beads into a long necklace. The *click-click* of beads drew his attention. He looked at the wooden tray in my lap and the long coil of thin wire. "What's that?"

"All the beads from the closing ceremonies of the modules. It's going to be a prop for my ordination sermon—a demonstration of the many paths people find to the Divine, with animals and plants on it too." I asked him, "How do you feel about me getting ordained?"

"It's your thing," he said without making eye contact. "Here I've retired and was looking forward to traveling and doing things together. But instead of retiring, you're switching jobs!"

I hadn't thought of it that way. I didn't quite know how to respond. "It won't be full-time." We lapsed into silence, each occupied with our own thoughts.

That evening I signed and sealed copies of my letter of resignation from Matthew House, to hand out the next week. I felt confident at that moment, and willing to accept whatever came by way of ministry. I prayed, "May my wings unfold and grow strong in the light."

A week later I reached my own shatter point.

I told Asuko, Matthew House's program director, about my resignation when she returned from vacation. She drew back, with that deer-in-the-headlights look. Uncertainty crossed her wide face as she took it in. She'd been with the agency only six months; there was a lot yet to learn. I assured her we would spend my remaining time transferring as much knowledge as possible, and I would be available to answer questions after I left.

"We'll make do, boss," she said.

Then I met with the board president. He showed no reaction, and wished me well. My resignation letter listed my accomplishments at Matthew House and recommendations for a successor. The board didn't question my decision. Some saw it as resignation, some as retirement. I wasn't sure which it was myself. The board formed a team to facilitate the search for a replacement and the transition during my final six months. They may have seen it coming.

Telling my office staff was easy. Those I had worked with longest and most closely had already left. I appreciated the current staff, but we didn't have the depth of connection forged by years of figuring things out and making it through tough patches together.

But I wasn't prepared for the intensity of my feelings when I told the shelter staff. They'd gathered for the regular Tuesday afternoon staff meeting, filling all three couches in the shelter's living room. The sturdy furniture had held up well to heavy usage, although the green vinyl cushions wore clear sealing tape where they'd been cut or seams had come loose. The staff watched me, wondering what announcement had brought me to the meeting. Unsettled and off center, I blundered on: "I wanted to tell you myself that it's time for me to move on. I appreciate your support and hard work all these years! Matthew House has a strong reputation. I couldn't have gone out and said the things I have to the community, and raised money for us, if not for your hard work. I'm privileged to have served with you, and I thank you."

A few questions came up: "When are you leaving? Who will do your job?"

I couldn't read the group through my own barely checked emotions. It felt like a hit-and-run. A new staffer I hadn't met offered some comic relief when she asked, "Who are you anyway?" We all laughed as she and I identified ourselves.

Another staffer asked, "Does that mean Gregg is retiring too, or will he still be available to help with the computers?" More laughter, and I assured her that he would be.

Asuko later said she thought they were pretty shaken up and uncertain about the future. She told me, "I've never seen anyone take the air out of a room as fast as you did."

Gregg and I went through the motions of dinner preparation that night. I held in the tightness in my heart and throat. After he settled to watch television, I headed out for a walk.

Tears started as soon as I stepped out the front door with Sina. I tried to not make any sounds while we made our way out of the neighborhood. I paused at Big Tree, but felt exposed by the roadside. We continued up to the dark, deserted park. I sat under a welcoming live oak, leaned against it, and cried uncontrollably.

The tears came in waves, crashing and receding, and then coming again. My chaotic emotions and raw grief were too much for sensitive Sina. She sat at the end of her twenty-seven–foot flexi-leash, coming back to check on me, then returning to her distant guard post. I rocked back and forth, sobs rising from deep within. There were no words.

I kept seeing LeRoy's face, his dark skin and eyes framed by kinky black curls streaked with gray. His smooth face showed the peace he had grown into over a troubled life. A deacon in his church, LeRoy had been there longer than I; he'd had my back for years and I'd had his. Telling him was one of the hardest things I had ever had to do.

Every time I thought of him, I started to cry again. I couldn't stop, nor did I want to as long as tears wanted to come. Acting on my decision to leave had peeled away some protective layers within and broken down part of the old dam to release a torrent of long-held tears. I was grateful to be shown just how deeply I cared for LeRoy, the shelter staff, and Matthew House.

I don't know how long I stayed there. When I slid down the rough bark of that tree to sit beneath it, Venus, the evening star, shone a hand's breadth above a tall redwood tree across the park. When the tears finally slowed, Venus was close to setting. I stood and called Sina. We headed home. I felt drained, cleansed, and cold in my tear-soaked T-shirt.

At home, I thanked Sina and released her in our back-yard. Gregg had fallen asleep in front of the TV. I woke him, told him I was headed for bed, and asked if he would put Sina to bed—one night she appreciated the safety of her crate!

I took a cup of calming herbal tea upstairs to our bedroom and curled up with Papacito, my threadbare brown stuffed dog. I could smell dust on him. He'd been made as real as the Velveteen Rabbit by absorbing many of my tears and my daughter Gwen's. Gwen had embroidered a paisley design on his ears when they started to shred. Mother had bought him for me (and a blonder one for my sister, Linda) the summer before I went to boarding school for eighth grade. His three-foot-long body wore little of the soft dark-brown fur he'd had then. Papacito was fifty years old, still here, still willing. I cried myself to sleep with him.

I woke in the morning with a headache, feeling drained and sad. Over oatmeal at breakfast, Gregg said, "You should've known it would be harder to tell the shelter staff than the board." I felt his solid presence across the breakfast table, holding the space for me.

"Knowing and feeling are different," I answered. Later, in my journal, I drew a picture of my face with downturned mouth, tears falling into a puddle.

I went to see LeRoy at the shelter, to tell him I should have told him individually, and to apologize for my blunt approach. I couldn't say everything I wanted, but he got it. "I understand. We'll be okay. God bless you," he said, clasping my hand. He'd been there many years and had seen executive directors come and go. Day-to-day life at the shelter would continue.

I also spoke with the pastor of Matthew House's host church. I wanted to tell her in person. She said I'd been looking not just tired but "soul weary." That fit too.

Everyone I talked with offered support, commending the integrity of knowing when it's time to leave and initiating a smooth transition. The big hump had passed; there was no going back.

Other bouts of tears flowed, but nothing like the flood-waters I experienced the night of the shatter point, when I gave myself over to it. I drew a little heart in my journal, with me as a tree with smiling face, branches reaching up, a turtle and cat on the hill behind me, birds on the left and dolphins on the right.

The live oak tree at the park became my "heart tree." One day I saw that someone had carved a heart into its trunk. I felt strangely empty. Also expectant.

Tyson's Promise

Getting older, life is fleeting, spirit endures.
Sometimes the body is tired,
so I leave it behind and go on journeys.
I contemplate the mortality of this body
and know I, Tyson, by any name will live on.
I wonder if I want to be back in fur,
I can do so much when not.
But I do so love being a cat.
— Tyson Cat

Deep silence filled the Berkeley Friends (Quaker) Meeting. Sunlight filtered between mature trees outside the converted brown-shingled Craftsman bungalow, kitty-corner from the original Peet's coffee shop. This cloister of old Berkeley had drawn me to visit that Sunday morning. Peace enfolded me from the moment I sat on the wooden bench talking to God. I'd brought my journal to take notes, but the silence was so deep I didn't want to make even the noise of pen on paper. God said that I was nearly ready, just a few sticky places to clear.

The feeling of peace and gratitude lasted until I arrived at the office Monday morning, to news that Asuko, our program director of only six months, was also leaving. Julia, the bookkeeper, left two weeks later. The bubbly new office manager who had shepherded our office move quit abruptly. Once again, Matthew House began recruiting to fill key positions.

A board member asked if I felt like a lame duck.

"Not yet," I answered. "Too much to do." But I knew that feeling would come.

It dawned on me that this set of circumstances was similar to the set that delayed my departure several years earlier. In the midst of sorrow I felt a firming of strength and determination. Somehow I would find replacement staff and train them as best I could. But I could not, would not, delay again. It was past time for me to depart.

Leaving Matthew House as well as the intentional community of fellow seekers at the Chaplaincy Institute was a dual-death process. Both places had taught me so much, given me significant validation, and held me in community while I explored my inner self.

As these transitions came closer, I came to understand that they were gateways. Leaving Matthew House created the opportunity to discover who Nancy was, absent the role of executive director. In spite of the validation I had felt hugging that big brown teddy bear in Karen Baldwin's office, I was again feeling unworthy of being ordained and calling myself a minister.

Glimpses of another perspective—of ordination as the first step in the next phase of my life journey—teased around the edges of my mind. Another student in my ordination group shared this gem: "Regard the threshold as the door into a room in one's house that's yet to be explored." It was time to leap into the void, that place of unknowing in which all is possible. It was also time to acknowledge the deep grief of these leavings, and to accept that I wouldn't be leaving Matthew House with stable staff, financial reserves, and my legacy intact.

I said out loud to Tyson, "I feel like I'm on a train headed off a cliff, with approaching ordination and retirement."

Tyson regarded me with his single gold eye and promised: *I will stay with you through this!* He spent many hours purring my dreams, and curled nearby as I studied. He had contemplated his crossing many times over recent years, yet each time found new inner resolve to hang around. He had work to do.

I needed Gregg's support and understanding too. One night I asked if I could just talk with him. He pointed the remote at the television set, clicked a button, and it fell silent. I sat at his feet by the rust-colored easy chair that still bore evidence of Sina's destructive frenzy when she first came to us, and tried to express the deep grief I felt through a choked voice. Gregg wrapped his long arms around me and held me. He tried to talk me through the feelings, but I asked him to just sit with me. This wasn't something that fit into a logical train of thought, and I was grateful that he was willing to simply be there with me for as long as I needed him.

On Father's Day, we celebrated Tyson's seventeenth anniversary of coming to us with a new catnip mouse. I knew Gregg was thinking about his father, and asked him to talk about it.

"I'm not ready, and won't be for a long time. Everything in my life now is in a state of change." I had to honor that. Gregg runs deep, like one of the great rivers.

"Just let me know when you feel like talking about it!"

His forehead wore characteristic furrows. "You're part of the problem as well as part of the solution."

I knew he wasn't happy with the way we were living. He had to find his way outside the work world while I was still deep in Matthew House and completing my Chaplaincy program. House upkeep suffered; we had little time together.

I wasn't happy about it either, but had to focus on completing my practicum and exiting work.

Gregg's birthday fell on a Sunday. After church we went out to a favorite restaurant for omelets and fresh-baked bread. He looked relaxed on the warm summer day as we wandered hand in hand through a street fair. It was a nice day, just being together.

Back at home, Tyson waited for his scribe. I settled with my afternoon cup of tea. Gregg and I were concerned about Tyson's weight loss and poor appetite. He told me he couldn't taste food, only tuna. I knew he would keep his promise and see me through ordination, but he couldn't guarantee much beyond that. He was achy and tired, held here by sheer intent. What could I do to help him?

Practice and study, he answered.

I asked if he was going to call someone else, as Paddy had called Buki.

No, he said. *Just Sina for a while.* When the time was right, another animal would come to us. After Tyson crossed, we needed to focus on working with Sina.

As his shed fur drifted toward the ground in the shafts of sunlight, Tyson observed: *Fur drifts out like the days of our lives.*

Near the end of July I attended a workshop on dolphins held by Cathy. She'd asked me to come, as someone who'd been on the previous year's dolphin swim. We assembled in the back room of a metaphysical bookstore. I introduced myself to the dozen people present, and spoke about my upcoming ordination as an interfaith chaplain and plans to begin an animal ministry.

At the break I looked around the bookstore. Another attendee sought me out. She said, "When you told me where you're headed, I got goosebumps."

She walked with me up to the bookstore clerk. I had picked up a dark-purple sash lined with rich yellow and embroidered with gold interfaith symbols. When I asked the clerk to hold it until after class, the woman pulled out her wallet and bought it for me. "An early ordination gift," she told me, and placed it around my neck like a minister's stole. I was deeply touched, and thanked her with tears in my eyes.

In the second half of the class Cathy led us in a dolphin meditation. In that clear space, I could see my dolphin guide and feel it swim through me. I had no boundaries, no skin, only an energetic body. The dolphin guide blended with me again and again, and poked me hard in the heart with its snout. Then we swam together into the sky, surrounded by deep indigo and sparkling stars, and I knew that was home. I was slow to come back to present time after the meditation. The sense of lightness persisted for a long time.

Back at home, around midnight, I heard coyotes howling from the canyon below our house. Sina knew. The coyotes told me they're moving in, to keep small animals indoors. They liked the tasty chickens our neighbor raised. They said Sina is known to them; they wouldn't harm her. I felt tingly when I heard them singing. A touch of fear and encroaching wilderness, excitement, welcoming. It felt like the announcement of a new era.

The next morning I enjoyed the stillness of being the only human in our house. Gregg had left early to get some lab work done as part of his medical checkup, but made coffee first. One of the things he was working through in his deep-river way was concern about his enlarged prostate. This blood test was a precursor to a procedure to take samples for biopsy.

Our forty-second wedding anniversary was the first day of my last Chaplaincy course module, on Theravada Buddhism. As the module progressed, I realized I was coming into my own, stepping forth to speak my truth. In one class, the director recognized the value of animal ministry. My ministry had started at the Chaplaincy Institute. I remembered my first day's introductions, when my announcement of adopting a new dog had received no acknowledgment from the group. After the dolphin swim my voice grew. I continued to talk about animals and bring them in, especially as my ministry direction clarified. Then others started to talk about animal interactions and experiences; it became a regular occurrence. I helped make the Chaplaincy container a safe place to grieve animals and recognize the messages they bring us.

I was finally finding my voice. I was concerned, though, over how to maintain the momentum of internal and spiritual growth, and how to manifest what came after. After ordination I needed to focus on Matthew House, and then rest and reflect. That meant setting up boundaries, with others and with Gregg. It would be easy to let his stronger energy direct the time and activities. I needed to clearly establish a clear pattern, such as "From ten to noon I'm thinking and writing, so please consider me not here."

Near the end of the module, as I drove the freeway from Woodward to Berkeley, I felt bouncy with joy. During check-in at the beginning of class that day, I led the group in the new song that had come to me during my drive:

Part of the People
(A Song for Ordination, to the tune of "Rock-a My Soul")

You and I are part of the People,
and He and She are part of the People,
and They and Them are part of the People,
and Oh! Ain't it all so!

Animals are part of the People,
and Rocks and Trees and Rivers are People
and All of us are part of the People,
and Oh! Ain't it all so!

Mother Earth is cryin' great tears,
healing her is far in arrears.
Work together, the People can save her,
Oh! Ain't it all so! Yeah!

But at night I was having nightmares and anxiety dreams, as were other members of our ordination group. "Preordination dreams," we called them, showing our fear and uncertainty about finding our way through the unfamiliar place we were stepping into—dreams of things not working right, obstacles. I lay awake, focusing on breathing: in, out, in, out. As dawn came I heard from somewhere: *Heart of courage and wisdom.*

In late August, the responsibility of ministry hit me in the face. Gregg, nervous and unsure, prepared for a meeting with his doctor. His bloodwork results looked good, but his enlarged prostate demanded treatment. I tried to keep things light, and he stiffened and drew more into himself. It would have been better for me to mirror his concerns, lend presence, and encourage him to talk. What was the benefit of all this training if I didn't use it at home? I apologized for not seeming supportive enough. Women are used to having our plumbing poked and prodded, but men aren't.

In this final stretch, I was focused on myself, my needs, my project, my ordination, my exit from Matthew House. Sina and Tyson were by Gregg's side, but where was I? I prayed that we'd hang in there together as I went through all this work overload and he went through his medical processes, so that next year we could begin a new life together.

A bright spot came when a board member brought some framed art prints for Matthew House's fall dinner/auction. One grabbed my attention—an etching of stone steps leading to a white stucco building with Spanish-tile roof, and a closed, wooden door painted dark turquoise. Beside the door, the house number read: "64." Turquoise brings protection, open communication, and clarity of thought. In January I would turn sixty-four, and would step through a door I had never been through before. Beyond was the unknown, and called on deep faith. I prayed for help for Gregg, Matthew House, and me. I bought that print on the spot. It hangs today in our stairway.

The board's transition team hired a consultant to guide the search for a new executive director. I had twinges about my successor being paid more than I had been, although a higher salary would come with pressure to raise more money. During my time with the agency, we were overqualified, overworked, and underpaid. The new generation wasn't putting up with that.

At Chaplaincy, my last course module completed, I submitted my evaluation with suggestions about the program as a whole, and the packet of final ordination requirements, forms, and assessments. My sermon was ready, and my practicum project was in its final stages. Two weeks to ordination. How did that happen? It was all coming together!

At home, I lay on the wooden bench swing in our back-yard. Sina curled up on the ground below me, and Tyson climbed onto my chest. Sandwiched between cat energy and dog energy, I gave thanks for this blessing and their support. Lying there, I realized that one of the reasons I'd been having trouble with my brief bio in the ordination program was that it said what I'd done, but not who I am. It wasn't too late to fix it.

There followed a nonstop day at work, training staff, preparing for the financial audit, getting a proposal to a funder, and hurrying straight to a board meeting. I came home late, tired, and drained. I hadn't eaten and just wanted some milk and protein. Gregg had made chili, though, so I heated a small bowl and sat on the couch to eat it. The chili stopped at the bottom of my throat. I felt tightness across my chest, all the way up into my throat and jaw. I couldn't talk; I could barely breathe. Was I having a heart attack? Or angina? Tyson jumped onto the couch, walked across the tray in my lap, and climbed onto my chest. He'd never done that before. He stretched across my chest and under my chin, making me lean back and focus on breathing. He stayed there, purring, until the sensation faded away, using his cat medicine to diminish the symptoms and heal me. I realized how much stress I was under, and thanked him.

Ordination approached, and the void. I was speeding toward the edge of the cliff.

Animal Chaplain

I just wanted to say hello, since you're listening.
There are no human celebrations or grief when we
come and go. We do a dirty but necessary job.
We honor our own in our own way.
You should try soaring on these great wings.
It is magnificent.
Our message is to be aware of opportunities.
Sometimes the smellier, the better.
— Turkey Vulture

*A*nimal *chaplain* has a nice ring to it. Yet a quizzical expression crossed faces when I announced it as my ministry: "What's that?" I needed to define it more clearly.

In my Chaplaincy practicum proposal, I wrote: "Faith traditions have differing views of animals' roles in our lives, and whether or not they are spiritual beings. A person's feelings and level of grief at the death of an animal companion may be completely out of alignment with the importance assigned to animals by their faith tradition. The interfaith minister's role is to help bridge the chasm between what one should feel vs. does feel, and to honor what's in the heart."

My practicum began with the Hawaiian dolphin swim. Cathy had asked many questions before she agreed to be my project supervisor. What were my goals? What did I expect of her? Her insistence on structure from the start helped me build a framework for my project.

Cathy had met white-bearded Father Richard Mappel-beckpalmer when walking their dogs in open space near her home. I met him at Grace North Church, Chaplaincy's home in Berkeley, where he was senior pastor. He, Cathy, and I sat in his garden, surrounded by birds, buzzing drag-onflies, and the murmur of a pond that was home to frogs. Several hours under the garden's leafy arbor immersed us in a recitation of Father Richard's cosmology, and produced a list of resources for my project.

"I made a decision one day," he said in his quiet English accent. "One of the parishioners brought his dog to service each Sunday. The dog sat quietly in the pew, listening more attentively to my sermon than did many parishioners. One asked if I knew that the deacon slipped a piece of the Host to the dog during communion. I had to make a decision on the spot. I remembered the Bible lesson about the Pharisee woman who told Jesus, 'Dogs can eat crumbs that fall from the master's table' [Matthew 15:27]. I told him, 'All God's creatures are welcome at the Lord's table.' When this dog died, the church held a requiem mass for it."

Father Richard poured fresh hot tea into my delicate English china cup and continued. "The whole is present in every part. Therefore the whole is present in every creature. All creatures *are* souls," he said with a twinkle in his eyes, as one can with coconspirators. He paused and added, "Blessing animals and looking into their eyes was a spiritual experience."

Cathy referred me to Celia, who wanted a blessing ceremony for her new golden retriever puppy. Celia had been raised Catholic, and considered herself "Christian with New Age leanings." My first draft of the service included Christian elements, but was slanted in an interfaith direction. Celia didn't like it. She welcomed the earth-based elements, but wanted a more traditional

Christian service. I rewrote it. Celia was pleased with the new version, and together we shortened it to fit the puppy's attention span. The back-and-forth of revisions taught me that while the minister is the officiant, it's the client's service. Now every such service I do is cocreated.

I arrived the day of Celia's service, and met her in person for the first time. Intense dark eyes glistened in her olive-skinned face. I settled by the puppy's kennel, staying out of the way during the flurry of event setup. I felt like hired help at first, although relaxed some when Cathy and another guest came over to talk with me.

My first animal-blessing ceremony was held outdoors in the apartment's common area, circled by large trees. About twenty guests came, many with their own dogs. The small altar table held a bowl of water, feathers to represent air, candles for fire (although they remained unlit because of the breeze and rambunctious dogs), and whole-grain dog biscuits to represent earth.

I had communicated with the puppy beforehand, and included a message from her in the service: *I am a puppy. I need to learn all over again because I see life through different eyes. God is love, and dogs are love. We're little angels in fur. Humans should take our example and try to come from love. Life should be simple and fun, and if you come from the loving place it's easy. Always be in the joy of being present. Life is a gift. I'm grateful that I was allowed to come back and have this experience again. And be patient with me. This new young body is different and takes getting used to. It doesn't always do what I want it to. It's fun, though. I'm looking forward to play time. And don't forget cookies.*

I received strong positive feedback after the ceremony from guests as well as Cathy, who added tips for future events: "You need to be more attentive to surroundings."

Apparently an airplane had flown overhead and drowned out part of the ceremony's words. I never heard it.

There were laughs too. I had blessed the bowl of water before the ceremony. It took a couple of tries to get water on the bouncy puppy's forehead. Then she lunged forward to drink the rest of it, earning warm laughter from the assembly.

During the reception afterward, an elderly guest dog came to my chair at the edge of the group. I understood that this black Labrador retriever wanted a blessing, too. In Chaplaincy's Earth-Based Traditions module, Chief Phillip had taught us, "All water is holy." I dipped my fingers into my glass of water, placed my wet hand on her head, and recited a traditional blessing. The dog smiled, wagged her tail, and returned to her person.

The following week I attended Cathy's Animal Life Cycles class, one of a dozen people. Celia gave positive feedback on the blessing ceremony as a group announcement.

Close to the workshop's end, Cathy's keeshond dog came to each of us with a message. His four-word message stunned me: *Paddy Paws called Buki.* I instinctively knew the truth of it. My assignment was to talk with Paddy herself.

When I made the heart-to-heart and mind-to-mind connection with Paddy in spirit later, she said: *I called Buki. I knew I was coming close to the end of my time, and didn't want you to be alone. Or for Tyson to be alone. Another cat would take away from the memory of me. Buki is part of my soul family, and yours. You had shifted space and needed a different kind of teacher. Clear out the cobwebs in yourself so you can move forward. It's about relationships, gaining peace and clarity. Take inventory. Unbury what you are hiding. Own it and let it go with love and compassion and forgiveness. Knowing yourself well is the best way to help others.*

I felt her presence as a blessing, and knew that Paddy wanted to help me through this transition and identity crisis, as she had helped me through others.

I focused on my practicum project with renewed vigor. I learned about the grief journey, and how everyone who walks it does so in his or her own way.

Shoshana Phoenixx-Dawn, who taught in Chaplaincy's Judaism module, gave me insights into grief groups and ritual. I trotted down a corridor of the Jewish Community Center in Berkeley, trying to keep up as Shoshana multi-tasked the way to her office. When I asked about grief support for pet loss she said, "We're not encouraged to express grief over loss of a pet; we're supposed to get over it, so people hold it pretty close. People will take their bereavement to their priest, pastor, or rabbi and try to be satisfied with what they receive there, even if it does not bring them resolution."

Shoshana stressed that there are many components to loss, including changes in routine. "When someone dies we don't have to let go of the relationship. The relationship changes—now is spirit to spirit. Remember and honor what they taught you." She cautioned that where there is denial of death in general, there's less room to acknowledge grief over pets. Within families, one person may be devastated while another may be less affected.

Even people who are committed to this path can be guarded. On a visit to a pet cemetery, when I introduced myself, explained my project, and asked about their program, the proprietor was curt. After I told him my story of grief when Paddy and Buki died, he opened up, shifted his bulk on his stool behind the cemetery office's counter, and faced me. He said that many people aren't what they seem. He had encountered everything from genuine grief to those who wanted to do dark rituals in the cemetery.

He leaned forward with his elbows on the counter, wheezed, and said, "This work is a service in itself—dealing honestly with loss of pets becomes good education and practice for dealing with death of people, especially for children." He said that mourners visit their animals' graves by choice, as opposed to feeling obliged to visit a relative's grave. "At Christmas there are so many flowers on the animals' graves that it looks like a garden."

On the grounds, I witnessed heartfelt love for animal companions expressed on everything from engraved tombstones to hand-lettered scraps of wood. Messages I received from animals buried there included: *Our people were so sad. . . . Don't hold on to us; it's part of life. . . . Sadness is parting, joy is rebirth, as a snake sheds its skin. . . . Love endures.*

Including the voices of animals in such a project was, for me, a given. In meditation, I asked animal guides to share their thoughts about living, dying, and my ministry. These talks took place over many sessions. Throughout, I sensed that animals were lined up for their turn to speak. I had the clear sense that the animals' expectations of humans rise along with our awareness of them as spirit beings. The first to come forward first looked like a mountain lion. She identified herself as Spirit of Cat.

> **Spirit of Cat:** *We are all one. We are not toys, but spirit beings in different bodies and speaking another language, although all speak the universal language. We want to be honored for who we are. We do not want to be regarded*

as furry humans with four feet and a tail. Some of us cats live with you as domestics. Honor our dedication, sacrifice, and loyalty. We also live near you as wild cats to remind you of the pure spirit and the balance of things. When you have what you call a pet, recognize both the wild and tempered spirit. We do not need ritual. We participate because that is part of our agreement with you. Honor our lives when we pass, and our gifts to you in living with you. What is important is for hearts and minds to be linked together. People need to be reminded, so your services should be structured as teachings for people.

Tyson (cat): When it's my time, put me beside Buki. We became buddies. I was once a temple leopard. My job then was to connect people with the beauty and ferocity of living. They were much closer to the earth then and knew its cycles. My presence was enough. Now, fear is underground. People are farther from it in consciousness, yet it creeps through the corners of their minds. That's why I came smaller this time. You can see the fierceness but not be afraid of it. Bring your fear out into the open and look at it. Only then can you find the bravery to confront it. You can't hide from it. We agreed to come in miniature so we could teach you the ways of independence, pride of being, and walking through walls. When you are blessing, ask that this animal be brought into full awareness of its self so it may fulfill its life's purpose. When you are remembering, thank it for its work, for all contribute to the benefit of the world.

Elvis (Cathy's cat): Our job as cats is to embody the qualities that people need to develop: gentleness, love, ferocity in defense, speed in mercy, taking only what you need, and above all, being true to Self—regal. And playing occasionally. When blessing and doing memorials, bless and remember the spirit of the being, not just the body. The spirit is what lives on, and the blessings help it continue from life to life. Sometimes we get tired, especially if a life is particularly difficult. Blessings and love help heal that so we can continue our work. You have no idea how much we give to you. But we're not counting—it's in our nature.

Spirit of Dog: *We are each prey and predator, although Dog has a different kind of relationship with humans than do other species. We're more attentive to serving you in the day to day. We see all creatures and the earth as related parts of the whole. We have balance among ourselves. Your task is to help humans come back into that balance. It is a difficult task. Small steps. Helping hearts to open and recognize the cycle of life is a start. Honor each of us for the gifts we bring. Even the smallest grub makes its contribution and gives to the whole.*

Buki (dog in spirit): *You were a tough nut to crack. Remember that animals are beings who came into life in this form to learn and to teach from this perspective and with these skills. The challenge for humans is to accept us as distinct beings with feelings, needs, spiritual resources, and aspirations. We communicate all the time. We as dogs give so much—unconditional love and loyalty, so you know what it feels like. It's our special gift. Cats and birds have other gifts. Just be sure to include voices of the animals in any rituals that you develop or conduct. Put your paws on the ground and go for it.*

Katsina (young dog): *Oh yes, I've been here lots of times. I've been a cat, wild, big, and black—that's why you feel cat energy in me now. When it's my time, I want you to glorify me, tell them how pretty I am, how my independent spirit was never quenched, how I love to hunt and bring laughter. Plant a bush over me that cats can hide in so I can chase them. Ask each animal what they want to say. We're part of the whole, and we want each voice to be recognized and heard. We know who we are. We keep trying to bring you along, but it's hard work, and sometimes I just want to play.*

Spirit of Bird: *Learn from us as we fly and soar. The sparrows are constantly falling and correcting. It is their way. Larger birds ride air currents. Some days are better* *than others. We adapt to what is. Study us and our animal brethren. Learn our magic and medicine, so that you may translate that for human hearts. Be sensitive to strength within gentleness. We especially love bells. Their vibrations tickle the air on which we ride. Earth-based creatures like the drumbeats that come up through the earth.*

Rosie (daughter Gwen's parrot in spirit): *It's a challenge for one with this level of intelligence to be closed away in a cage. That magnifies the sacrifice we make to be with you. We give to you and depend on you at the same time. The intensity of one-to-one giving and receiving, teaching and learning, is like having children. We teach dedication of service, and for this give up a life of free flight. When the message is received, it's worth it.*

Sea Turtle: *I know that you loved swimming with us. It was I who backed up so you could count my plates. Do not forget those of us who live below the waters. We are often unseen and can be forgotten. That is one reason why we haul ourselves out on rocks—to be seen. Creatures of the sea have much to teach you, yet you poison our home and your own. When one suffers, all do. Bring us forth into the minds and consciousness of people so we can do our work at another level. We need the help of you and those like you.*

Sydney (Kay's guinea pig): *Took you long enough! I'm aware of your project. The animals are excited about it. Talk to Horse too! Being cute has its drawbacks. People see the exterior, and forget the profound soul that lives within. Because we're small and live in cages, we can be overlooked. Yet we can be the best introduction, especially for children who have been traumatized. Small furred ones such as I want to be honored in the fullness of our spirit—which extends well beyond the confines of flesh and fur. Elvis cat said it beautifully: Honor the being, not just the body.*

Kelly (horse): We are large and majestic; we came as helpers. Our loyalty is much like that of Dog, although it often isn't seen as such. We would like to be honored for our gifts to you. Let us die with grace. Do not break our spirits. Let us work with you, as spiritual beings and work and life partners. Honor our strength, internal and external. Honor our dedication to you. Some people are afraid of our size, but those who love us find joy in it. Honor what is unique and special about each of us.

These profound messages, and the strength and clarity with which they were offered, gave me greater insight into the wholeness of the fabric of Creation. We're connected, interconnected, and dependent upon one another. Each wants to be honored for who they are. These conversations left me with clear knowledge that the responsibility of being a voice for the animals isn't to be taken lightly. And they would have more to say.

The project gave me more confidence in my intuitive communication ability, and helped me develop a vision of my future ministry. It's important to honor people's feelings and their bonds with their companion animal(s). While ceremonies largely benefit humans and our need for rituals of passage, animals participate and want their voices to be heard, and their gifts and teachings to be honored. My particular contribution would be to bring the animals' voices to my ministry.

Ordination:
Gateway to Beginning

We are all one, living in the mystery.
We are the light for each other.
Being, becoming, I bring my whole self.
Refrain—this is my Truth.
— N.S., Cocreated ordination song

Bu-boom, bu-boom, bu-boom, bu-boom! My slender birch drumstick's padded deerskin head struck the hollow wooden pulpit in a heartbeat rhythm. Drumbeats re-sounded through the old sanctuary of Grace North Church in Berkeley. Red, yellow, and orange streamers draped from the ceiling, honoring the harvest season. Well-wishers filled every wooden pew.

"Hearken, my children, for the fires have been lit and a story wants to be told." Thus went the first words of my ordination sermon, given to me intact in a dream a few months earlier. My six fellow ordinands called it a creation story. I told how all of Creation is one, but the two-leggeds—humans—had forgotten. The animals, rocks, and trees, the air, fire, and waters—all called us to remember. The necklace I'd made of beads from module closing cere-monies hung in two wraps around my neck, a symbol and prop. I used it to demonstrate how each bead and person is different, yet strung together they make a single necklace.

In our entry processional we carried elements to the altar that were symbolic of our lives and ministry. One brought a pumpkin, one a loaf of challah bread, and one carried a three-hundred-year-old bronze Tibetan bell on a padded cushion—our group's gift back to the Chaplaincy Institute. I carried a large stuffed toy moose and wolf. I leaned them against the pumpkin in front of the altar. A short time later I squeezed the wolf to play its howl, recorded in the wild. "There's always time for a little howl," I began. People laughed. It broke the tension.

We had arrived for our four-day retreat at Presentation Center in the Santa Cruz Mountains in late afternoon, tired from the sheer effort of getting there. We'd been meeting as a group, largely by phone conference, to cocreate our unique ordination service. Each of us had arrived at the same place by a different path; we wanted to honor that journey in our service. At the retreat center, we sorted ourselves into two cottages—with three women in one, and the two other women, me, and our only male member—the same Gary who'd attended my first Chaplaincy course module—in the larger cottage. I settled into a small corner room, grateful to have it to myself. I'd had little time for solitude lately.

I called home to let Gregg know I'd arrived. I made the heart-and-mind connection to Tyson and Sina, and sensed them with me on many of my walks. I didn't call Matthew House.

We spread out to explore the wooded property with its creek, trails, and towering pine and redwood trees, and then met for dinner in the dining hall. Lovingly prepared organic foods nurtured us throughout our stay.

After dinner we went to the meeting hall to set up our retreat altar. We each added personally significant elements, including my set of prayer flags from Amma's retreat center, which we pinned to the wall to frame the space.

Our altar in place—although it would continue to evolve as the retreat progressed—we gathered in the smaller cabin and talked about what the Chaplaincy experience meant to us. I shared that I had expected a breadth of information and sampling of the world's faith traditions. I hadn't expected the rich tapestry woven by students' histories and perspectives, and our dialogue with instructors. I recalled how my carefully constructed barriers began to crumble in my first course module. We were all blessed to see the shy student who didn't dance enchant us with a danced sermon on the labyrinth; the student who couldn't sing who found her voice; the student who didn't do art who created beautiful expressions in different media; the student who was already a model caregiver who found new depths of compassion and skills.

Chaplaincy wasn't only a course of study leading to ordination. It was a deepening, enriching process that opened each of us to the core of who we truly are, and provided us with internal and practical skills so that we might better serve. I came to understand that religions are glimpses of the Divine through different windows of culture. Faith is the current that flows beneath practice—thus the importance of meeting people where they are on their spiritual path.

Early the next morning, walking before breakfast, I saw a bank of folded morning glories nestled against their heart-shaped green leaves. The rising sun lifted the shadow of night and they woke, each stretching and unfurling vibrant purple petals to embrace the sun. I suddenly understood the words of the Sufi chant we would sing at our ordination: "I am opening up in sweet surrender to the luminous love light from the One. I am opening, I am opening." Flushed with joy, I sang the chant all the way around the lake to complete my walk.

We spent all day working out our group ordination vows—a challenge with seven people! Some resisted including animals and nature as equals in Creation. Megan, the spiritual psychology teacher who'd been part of my midway assessment, was facilitating. She saw my frustration. "Nancy, this is important to you. How do you want to proceed?"

"I'm practicing acceptance and release of attachment. My personal vows might be different from the group's vows."

As it turned out, although the wording was different, the sacredness of all Creation and environmental statements became part of our group vows.

After the watershed moment of ordination vows, I found myself thoroughly enjoying the retreat. On an unscheduled morning, feeling like a little kid, I explored a long trail hoping to see evidence of the mountain lion that had been reported in the area, played by a creek, and sang songs the whole way. Each of us followed our inclinations, and crossed paths but didn't divert our wanderings. A soft, mossy place invited me to sit for awhile. Kneeling inside a burned-out redwood stump felt like being held in the womb of the Mother.

Later in our cottage, Gary played his guitar. I recognized the melody from visits to synagogues, and told him how deeply I appreciated his journey to interfaith ministry while retaining his Jewish roots. I asked to play one of his drums, and selected a small djembe. Gary sat on a low stool next to me, and devised melodies to go with my rhythms. Our session started sounding decidedly Latin. I confided to him that this retreat was a lot of fun, but I didn't feel I'd gone as deep as I wanted to. "This feels unreal, suspended from the real world."

Gary replied, "This is the real world. It's the other one that's not."

That night, someone produced a deck of Tarot cards and asked us to draw a card in answer to the question "What does ordination mean to me?" I drew the Hierophant, a card of spirituality, tradition, and finding one's own way. These evenings together became as important as sessions with our teachers. The others started referring to me as a storyteller. I liked that, and thought of the children's story I'd written for one of the course modules.

Often over these days I felt like crying but couldn't. Key words set me off. My throat tightened, or a single tear squeezed out. I needed a good, cleansing cry.

The last evening my Native American teacher, Jane, lead our session. In dim moonlight under redwood trees, Jane beat her drum and told us a story of how Coyote leads us astray and distracts us. Our assignment: Consider when we had followed Coyote rather than our true path.

Looking back, I thought I'd followed Coyote most of the time, doing what others wanted or directed, and not knowing what I wanted. I followed Coyote when I didn't know I could say no. I followed Coyote when I acquiesced and let Gregg make decisions for both of us, even simple things like sleeping in a tent when I wanted to sleep out under the stars. In Boulder, I'd followed Coyote into seeking work rather than exploring, although those lessons were good too. I saw how I had wandered in circles, yet at each turn I'd learned a vital lesson.

When hadn't I followed Coyote? Since turning fifty, I'd begun to find my own path and to recognize Coyote's influence. Returning to Woodward, I hadn't wanted to go back to work but needed to, and turned aside from other paths to follow my preference for nonprofit work. That led to many lessons. I'd followed my own path when I stepped into leadership roles and let my power grow. And I'd followed my path into chaplaincy.

Coyote was even now at my side. Finally I was able to cry!

Sunday morning we joined hands in front of our altar, prayed and sang, and removed the elements from it one by one. Each person selected one of the seven flags from the set I'd brought from Amma's retreat center as we pulled them from the cord.

We drove straight to Grace North Church for our ordination, staying in the sacred mental and energetic space we'd created, even changing clothes in the church loft.

Ordination: September 23, 2007. The first day of autumn. Time within time, suspended and yet moving too fast. Someone later commented that the service was long, but it didn't seem so to me. I was surprised by how fast it went. As a creation story, my sermon was first. When one of the directors rubbed the Oil of Transformation on my forehead, throat, and palms during the anointing of oil, it burned. None of the others said it felt hot. To me, it felt like initiation.

Even at this point of culmination, I felt unsure. Gregg, seated behind me, radiated solidity in his dark suit. I was glad to see our personal friends, Esther and Dorita from Matthew House, and unexpected but welcome guests from church. I noticed that some of the people I'd invited hadn't come. Maybe my childhood feeling of being slighted would always be with me; I needed to acknowledge and celebrate those who did come, and continue. It was probably Coyote.

Cathy, my practicum mentor, was to have presented one of my stoles. At the last minute she was sick, so my friend Nikki filled in for her. Father Richard later told me he would have been happy to present a stole in Cathy's place. I was grateful.

As each of us stepped forward, our ministerial stoles— light, raw silk lined with purple, with an embroidered purple symbol of a healing hand and labyrinth on each side— were handed to our stole presenters by Chaplaincy directors. Nikki draped my first stole across my shoulders—the purple-and-yellow sash with embroidered interfaith symbols. Then Gregg placed the official Chaplaincy stole around my shoulders.

After the general laying on of hands and blessing by the whole assembly, we processed from the church to a raucous rendition of the spiritual "Rock-a My Soul."

At the reception afterward, I wasn't surprised to find that Nikki and Jane had studied together before I'd met either of them. I was glad to have brought them together again.

Gregg organized a dinner party at a nearby restaurant, where I talked more than ate, riding high on the elation of one of the most joyous days of my life.

The generosity, love, encouragement, and witness of all who were present in person or in spirit, humbled me, and I swam in gratitude. The questions would set in later.

Now What?

When all's done and told, myths abound, life all around;
myths and legends, they're all real.
It's just the where and maybe the when.
In depth we share, our paths entwined;
your life's yours, and mine is mine.
Changing places, taking turns,
we walk the path in paws like mine.
— Tyson Cat

Interfaith chaplain—the Reverend Nancy. The next day I felt a subtle difference. In meditation, I asked the animals, "Okay, I'm ordained, now what?"

My animal guides chorused: *Now you continue. Study, learn, deepen, prepare, practice. This is only a beginning—a gateway to a new section of the path. Stay true to it.*

I reflected on my path to this point. I couldn't say when my pull toward interfaith started. I'd slowly become dissatisfied with traditional Christian approaches that boxed God within the walls of a church, in parallel with a growing sense that God is All That Is. I needed to seek, find, and speak my own truth.

Ordination had gone from the be-all and end-all to a significant marker along the way. Much study and learning remained. Ordination was a firm commitment to my path—a statement to and acknowledgment by the community that I was worthy to be in this ministry.

I'd understood at the beginning that we are all one, but I'd needed to go deep, clean out internal cobwebs, and reach understanding within. I was able to set aside the divinized Jesus that had been handed to me and find my own Jesus—a friend and master teacher, the rabbi who showed a way, but not the only way, and who didn't ask to be worshipped.

I knew too that I needed to continue strengthening the Tree of Life within myself—get myself out of my own way. I needed to climb up and down each tree rather than skimming over the top of the forest—to do the deep work rather than just wanting to get there. And I needed to create and sustain boundaries at home and with others.

I called myself an interfaith animal chaplain. I sensed that many people regarded this work as frivolous; I asked the animals for help in educating others about the importance of all parts of Creation. They gave specific guidance for developing my ministry:

Tyson and Spirit of Cat: You are already engaged in this ministry. You are preparing to enter the void. Listen to us. We will lead you through! Be attentive to opportunities for any kind of ritual and ministry. It all will be useful learning. Do not let fear or uncertainty hold you back. You have released much, and it wants to return. Stand in your truth. Discern what is right for you and follow it. Ministry is where you are. This is your time of preparation. Use it well, for your true ministry is coming. You will know.

Buki and Spirit of Dog: Practice will bring you confidence. Step forth. Others will come and follow you. Allow yourself time to rest. Changing times are coming. You may reach more in your ministry without an actual physical place. Use your teachers. Learn from them and honor their teaching, as they learn from you also.

KC (Cathy's dog in spirit): Your vision isn't limited; you just don't see all of it yet. Your role is to open the hearts of the wider community to the Divine's presence in all its fullness, within each aspect of Creation. Honor and respect the sentience of all Creation. And I love your song, 'rocks and trees and rivers are people . . .'.

Whale: *There is no turning back. Use this time to deepen, to internalize what you have learned. That will reduce your fear. Each brings her own gifts. Cathy may be better at marketing herself, while you may be better at holding the presence of Spirit. Honor your own role and gifts and those of others. This is balance and harmony. Go forth with our blessing, and know that you are of us, as we are of you. Hold out your hands to those who are seeking you; we will send them.*

Dolphin: *We swim with you always. We continue to modify your cellular structure; our bubbles and sonar work in your cells to change and expand them. Do your part to get to the next levels. Believe. You will know by looking back when you have ascended from one level to the next. You and the others of your kind who are receptive have a greater responsibility. Your work in bringing light to the essence that manifests as many forms helps raise the vibration and benefits all. People need to be reminded to honor those they cannot see.*

Bird: *Listen to us. The time of emergence will come, and your ability to reach out will be determined by how well you learn and prepare.*

The animals were right. I could only keep moving in the direction in which I was both pushed and pulled.

I met with Jane, my Native American teacher who would now become my spiritual director. Gentle Ron had held my hand throughout my studies at Chaplaincy. He and I both felt the completion and knew it was time for me to move to another spiritual director. Jane talked about how my teachers will change, coming and separating as I integrated their lessons. I remembered this later, after I'd taken every course Cathy offered and gone my separate way to study with other animal-communication teachers. Friends would go and come as well.

Jane talked about my ordination story, and noted that I shifted into a different energetic mode when speaking as the storyteller emerged. She helped me see that by using animals as key characters, people were willing to listen and perhaps recognize themselves. The teaching crept in around the edges, through the child in each of us, and worked its way into the grownup.

Gregg and I took Sina to the park, and laughed at her antics, dancing beneath an oak tree. Squirrels in the branches above held her marionette strings. Returning to work filled me with reluctance, yet I was committed to finishing the year at Matthew House and helping with the transition to a new director. Gregg held that space for me. "You can do it!" he said. "You've made that commitment, and there's an end in sight."

Back at home, I had another conversation with Tyson. "Ty, how are you?"

He answered: *I enjoy these days of warmth and comfort, each moment. I enjoy your new energy. As you deepen, so do I. I will leave, sooner or later. I'm feeling pretty good, although my system is slowing. I'm conserving energy. I'd like more tuna please. There's nothing you can do about my kidneys or my thyroid. It's getting harder, though, to get up and down for the food.*

I promised to place a step stool by the counter to serve as a ladder for him.

"Ty, I'm almost afraid to go back to work."

Don't be. Just hold onto this feeling of precious unity that we have. Just ask yourself with each moment, each decision: "Is this drawing me nearer to my destination? Is this a diversion from my main path?" Make choices rather than being swept up in another's stream.

He added: *I would like to have my story written.*

"Do you want to dictate it?"

No, but I'll contribute some poems, my perspective.

I'm a tough old cat. I've had my share of battles. Now I'm willing to teach those who listen and show me respect. Many of the feral cats aren't really feral, for they come to share my wisdom about living around humans.

At this time of year I'm returning to my primal self, connecting with the earth energies as they prepare to go underground for the fall and winter. When the world rests, so will I. I'm not leaving you, just reconnecting with the earth. There's wildness in the air now. That's what brought the coyotes. They have moved on, but the air is still full of changing seasons and senses. You can feel it too, as you let your threads go deep into the currents of the earth.

Threads of different aspects of my life wove together. The Matthew House board member from a local Catholic church asked me to participate in the St. Francis Feast Day service in October—my first official gig as clergy! The steamroller continued at work, with the transition consultant asking for reams of material. A friend organized a fundraiser to provide medical supplies following a 7.9 magnitude earthquake that hit Peru, devastating many villages. And Gregg faced his second prostate biopsy.

The week following ordination passed like lightning. Lessons sorted themselves out. I wondered why it felt so important to know where I was going from here. I went out to our labyrinth. While I was away at retreat the water-district maintenance people had driven a front loader over it, which had scraped up the stones marking paths on one side, although the center circle remained intact. I thought to myself: When they finish their work for the season, I'll re-build it. Perhaps with wider paths this time. Was this an-other ending and another beginning?

The Friday evening St. Francis service felt like my official entry into clergydom. The 150-year-old church could have been transplanted from South America or Mexico. I wore my new ivory-colored alb—a long robe with tapered sleeves worn by clergy and servers in Catholic and some other Christian churches. Instead of focusing my homily on St. Francis's communion with animals, my part was to talk about his acceptance of others' religious beliefs. I thanked the choir in Spanish, at which they beamed in appreciation. Afterward, I addressed Father Declan as "Father" and he said, "Call me Declan." I noted with awe this acceptance on a new level.

The following Sunday at our Methodist church, Pastor Randy offered me use of the church for animal blessings and ceremonies—a generous offer, clergy to clergy.

After church, Sina and I sat outside to watch turkey vul-tures resting in the eucalyptus trees. I asked if they had a message.

They said: *We're here to remind you to let go of that which is dead and doesn't serve you; let it fall away. We'll pick at it.*

"But it all sticks so hard. It doesn't want to let go."

It's all intention.

I got it.

Connections

The day grows dim, the dawn is nigh.
Moving in twilight, waiting,
the sun warms the sky.
— Tyson Cat

The week after my homily on St. Francis, that church held a fundraiser for Peruvian earthquake relief. Two Peruvian women friends organized the event—Rosalie, a dynamo of energy from the host church, and Juana, a Matthew House board member who cooked a multicourse Peruvian dinner with help from friends. Rosalie's build and unstoppable energy reminded me of an automotive piston. She prepared the church hall, made space for a music group that played on drums, guitars, and Andean pan-pipes, and compelled people to dance.

A slide presentation showed the earthquake damage, and stressed how many medical supplies would be provided by each dollar raised. Half the people at the event spoke Spanish. Even with my rusty Spanish, I could understand most of the conversation and slide show subtitles. I enjoyed myself and suddenly saw interactions in a different light—a richness of relationships, without having to wear the public role of executive director.

Gregg and I stayed to help clean up, and I talked more with Rosalie. After not seeing her for months, I'd seen her three times in as many weeks. She told me she was going to

Peru in April. Her brother runs an inn near Machu Picchu. I blurted, "I want to go too!" Visiting Machu Picchu had been a longtime dream that seemed remote.

Rosalie turned up at my office three weeks later with airplane tickets to Peru.

I stammered, "Rosalie, I didn't mean for you to take me seriously!"

She grinned, almost teasing. "Don't you want to go?"

I did. Very much! "What about Gregg?"

"Oh, does he want to go too?"

I made a quick phone call to Gregg. "Rosalie bought a ticket for me to go to Peru with her, and we need to know right now if you want to go too."

"Uh . . . yes, I'll go." I exhaled in relief. I hadn't considered going on such a trip without him.

Rosalie thought there was time to get Gregg onto the same flight. I promised to send her a check for our tickets. She grinned again. "I'll call you in a few days. We need to meet and go over the itinerary. Let me know if there's anything special you want to see."

She whirred out of my office, leaving me stunned. I was going to Machu Picchu in April! The opportunity to realize a long-held dream of going back to Peru, where I'd spent ten years as a child—especially to Machu Picchu and in the company of a friend with local connections—had materialized through generous, inclusive Rosalie!

I held Tyson that night and told him about the trip; I promised we'd make sure he was well cared for.

I won't be here, he said. That made me sad, although I knew he would always be in my heart and near me in spirit.

My next thought was that I needed to take a refresher course in conversational Spanish at the adult school.

People started sharing stories of interactions with chaplains. At church, a woman told me that when her son suffered significant scarring from an accident during basic training, the army chaplain was the one who prepared the family for reactions from the outside world. At the city's volunteer-recognition dinner, I told the coordinator of a local animal-rescue group about becoming an animal chaplain. She clasped my hands. "We need a lot more people like you!"

Some League of Women Voters friends held a luncheon in my honor. They passed around my bead necklace while I explained its significance. Through the warmth of these women, I again felt valued by people I value highly—a gift in itself. With this group, and with colleagues from other agencies, I received validation both for what I'd accomplished at Matthew House, and for moving forward to a new phase of my life. I grew more at ease with accepting goodwill and recognition.

The Matthew House board held a strategy workshop with Bill, the executive-transition consultant, whose command-ing presence kept the focus on larger ideas and trends. He asked how I'd managed to do all I had at Matthew House. I could only answer: "You do what has to be done." Bill admitted being nervous about finding my replacement. "You really are the hub of Matthew House," he said. "You do more than you realize."

After the workshop, three board members asked about my chaplaincy. I'd sent out an announcement, but with such a large ordination group we each could invite a limited number of people to the ceremony. I'd invited family and those who'd been directly involved in my project. Later, I realized that in my disengagement from Matthew House, I'd been focused on leaving, completing my chaplaincy, and worrying about what came after. I'd sometimes overlooked the support of people I'd worked with all these years, who cared about and respected me. These thoughts flowed through me as I reread cards and wrote thank-you notes for ordination gifts, deep in gratitude and humility for the expressions of love and support.

Nature reminded me to stay attuned to a world outside my own little sphere. In early-autumn mornings, a flock of wild turkeys foraged behind our house. Their gobbling sounded like laughter. An orange–and-white feral cat paused to check Sina's location, and slipped into the creosote bushes. A single bird chirped. Our furnace came on, announcing autumn's arrival.

Sina's undercoat filled in and made her look larger. Wildness grew in her brown and blue eyes as the weather chilled and squirrels teased. She longed to race into adventure, yet we restrained her to a leash. She needed a good run every couple of days to let all that energy out.

The first good rain of the season brought strong winds. I loved hearing the big bronze bell and wooden Tibetan yak bell ringing on our deck, the sound of rain falling, and water rushing down the gutters. Sitting in my favorite place in our living room as the morning sun rose, with Gregg, Tyson, and Sina nearby, I said a silent prayer of thanks for the day, the gift of life, and my journey. At that moment I felt blessed, at peace, and full of gratitude.

Then Tyson peed in the kitchen, spraying the cabinet door. Gregg told me he'd found cat feces upstairs in the bathroom, though he admitted, "My construction work made an obstacle course in front of the litterbox."

I put Tyson outside and cleaned up, then went out to sit and hold him for a long time. We didn't need to talk. His tail brushed my hand, feather light. I felt his purr rumble through my chest. Tyson had always had a large purr, even as a kitten. He'd grown into it.

Another weekend morning came. I felt myself drifting and didn't want to read anything challenging. I only wanted to sit outside where the rain had freshened the air and given it a rich feeling. In morning meditation, I lit candles in my altar room and prayed for clarity on my path. I ended with "In the name of Jesus, amen."

A voice asked: *Why do you pray in the name of Jesus when you don't believe in him?*

I answered, "I honor Jesus as a master teacher and guide, who came to show us a way. We are all sons and daughters of God."

The voice said: *Pray in your own name.*

I prayed, "I ask these things in my name, amen." I felt empowered.

At work, I admired the way our new program director dug right in. She'd accepted the position knowing I'd leave in three months, and she'd have little time to absorb all she could from me. She inserted a new level of professionalism into the agency. We promoted an internal staff member to the office manager position; I knew she would do well by it. The new bookkeeper, though, had started well but seemed to crumple under the annual fiscal audit.

Karen Holzmeister, a high-powered local reporter, interviewed me for a profile in the newspaper. Nervous, I chattered on, telling her stories about Matthew House. She prodded for stories about me outside of work, the way my friend Alison had many years earlier when she asked, "How is Nancy?" I told about being an oil brat raised in South America, going to boarding school, things I'd done before Matthew House, and what I hoped to do after. Her article ran on the front page of the local section with a full-color photo—in the *Senior Journal*! I got a good chuckle out of that. The article made me sound as if I'd gained some wisdom over the years.

High points alternated with periods when my mind churned and I couldn't sleep. When I did, my dreams were filled with details and action, test and movement on different levels. I'd had preordination dreams. Now was I having exiting Matthew House dreams? I was grateful when Tyson came to sleep with me, silken fur against my face. His deep purr massaged my heart. One morning I woke at 4:30 and couldn't go back to sleep. My focus on breathing gave way to mental chatter. I finally got up, made a cup of tea, and sat downstairs, wrapped in a blanket, to watch the sky lighten. Tyson joined me. I dozed and dreamed that Gregg came downstairs wanting to talk. Later, Gregg said he'd dreamed that too.

I went to say good morning to my altar and heard: *Pray before me.*

So I prayed. I prayed for clarity on my path, the wisdom to discern it, the courage to follow it, and income from my ministry to pay for it plus some. I gave thanks for the abundance and support that surrounded me. I prayed for Matthew House and a new just-right director to take the agency to its next level of service. I prayed for Gregg and our children and their children, that we might strengthen our bonds as a family; for Tyson and his comfort in his last years; and for Sina as she settled and deepened. And I prayed that I might hear the voices of animals, rocks, trees, and all Creation as I grew into my ministry. "Help me make wise decisions. I pray this in my name, and in the name of All That Is."

I heard: *That was a good prayer.*

Another Monday, slipping into morning from my favorite place in the living room. I continued to feel "between," neither here nor there, not connected to anything. Waiting? Was I sliding into the abyss? Tyson stayed close, in a concerted effort to make me just sit. A crystal pyramid on the windowsill cast a spot of rainbow that crept down the ivory leather chair as the sun rose. To see this visible evidence of the sun's apparent movement as the earth turned was a powerful reminder that we're continually in motion, whether we know it or believe it or feel it or not. The liquid-amber tree in front turned yellowish green, with some red leaves. It knew.

Tyson said: *I'm here. I remind you of the connection between you and all things. This is a difficult transition time for you, and I promised to see you through it. My purr heals your anxious heart. It all will come to be—your mission, your ministry, your sustenance.*

Nothing will happen to Gregg. Carve your own being separate from his, and together. I'm here to help you. I'm not going anywhere. I have my better days and my worse days, and I know you'll help me as much as you can. When my time comes I'll let you know. If I need help crossing over, I'll let you know that too.

Don't get another cat right away. I'll send the right one to you. You will know it. And I will still be here. I talk to you all the time, and you listen; you just don't know it. I want you to know it. Don't forget about writing your children's books.

"Thank you, Tyson!"

One month since ordination. It seemed longer. This also was the day of Gregg's second prostate biopsy. Even though he knew what to expect, he admitted to feeling anxious about it. I held him in a long hug before we left for his appointment. I sat in the clinic waiting room during his procedure, trying to ground and focus on sending him healing energy.

He emerged with a wry grin. "Doc said my prostate is really large! He took twelve samples." That seemed like a lot to me. I was glad I'd come to drive him home. The way he eased himself into the passenger seat and reclined it showed me he was happy not to be driving.

One morning Sina trapped a feral kitten in a hollow under a two-by-four board. It fought back, hissing, four sets of little claws extended. I could see in its eyes that it was sick. I brought Sina inside, and put on heavy gloves to protect my hands. I gently scooped up the kitten and laid it on a towel in our cat carrier. How could I help?

The kitten said: *Just leave me alone. I'm dying.*

So I sang the chant "We all come from the earth" three times, and prayed out loud to the Holy Source of All That Is to be with and protect the kitten, to welcome it back to the Source.

At that point the kitten said: *I was never separate.*

I rephrased the prayer, and asked that the kitten heal or release its soul from the body with ease, whichever was for its highest good. Then the kitten shuddered.

Inside, I asked Tyson if he wanted to see the kitten and do some healing. He said: *I have done it from here.*

Gregg and I carried the dead kitten's body to open space behind our house so that it might return to the earth and be a food source for other animals. The next morning it was gone.

As I sat upstairs to journal this experience, Tyson joined me. *You helped her. You were with her at the moment of death, and helped her soul return to the Source. That's what I want you to do for me. You honored the sanctity of the individual. I'd like a different song, though.* He wasn't sure which, but leaned toward "All I want from you is to remember me as loving you."

Samhain, All Hallows Eve, brought thick fog. Tyson stayed with me that night, purring. I woke on All Saints' Day feeling more at peace. Sina seemed gentler with me, as did Gregg, as if they were helping me as best they could to make it across the swamp I traveled through.

Settling his father's estate, the approach of his followup appointment with his doctor, and putting up with me in my funk had contributed to a darkness of mood for Gregg too. Later, we sat together in our dark living room, watching the breeze through the liquid-amber tree's remaining leaves shift patterns from a streetlight.

Tyson curled beside me. I dreamed about Peru and Machu Picchu, about clearing out my altar room and bringing my altar out of the closet. In the dream I saw my Hawaiian cloths and all the altar elements replaced by a simple white cloth, a single candle in the middle, and elements of earth, air, fire, and water. That's all. Just like clearing out and simplifying my life.

I dreaded going to work. The financial audit wasn't going well. The bookkeeper turned in circles, half doing simple tasks. I could only be of minimal help, supporting and also pressuring him to finish tasks. This felt like an uncontrolled fall through a tunnel of brambles.

Then came show-and-tell day—giving tours of Matthew House's facilities, relating its history and philosophy of services to applicants for my position. The process had taken on a life of its own. Much as I knew it was time to step aside, I still felt deep grief in leaving. But I certainly wouldn't miss the pressure and responsibility!

That night at home, bouts of sadness plagued me. I hugged Tyson. He purred healing energy to help me through it. The next morning in the shower I had a vision as warm water flowed from my head to my toes. Words to a new song to the tune of "Dark of the Moon" came to me:

> *Place of the East, new beginnings,*
> *Place of the South, where I learn to live,*
> *Place of the West, and deep reflection,*
> *to grow in wisdom as I turn North.*
>
> *Place of the Sky, home of the Father,*
> *Place of the Earth, where the Mother dwells,*
> *Place of Within, where my true self is safe,*
> *and stands in Light as I speak Truth.*

The vision that went with the song brought light and joy to my heart and helped sustain me in days to come.

Diagnosis

Breathing in, I calm my body.
Breathing out, I smile.
Dwelling in the present moment,
I know this is a wonderful moment.
— *Thich Nhat Hanh*

In mid-November, Gregg called me at work after his doctor's appointment. The hair on the back of my neck prickled.

"As I suspected, I have prostate cancer." His words hung in the air. I stared at the multicolored display of agency walkathon T-shirts secured by pushpins to a bulletin board across the room from me. They blurred together. Gregg and I had each suspected but pushed away the possibility. He said, "One of the twelve biopsy samples they took showed positive."

Suddenly nothing else mattered. It was close to noon. "What are you going to do now?"

"I guess I'll go home and have lunch."

"Let's meet at Los Compadres and eat together. We can talk about it."

I shut down my computer, cleared off my desk, and told the office manager I was leaving for the day. She nodded, understanding.

Over a taco salad for Gregg and a chicken tostada for me at our favorite little Mexican restaurant, we sorted through

317

the options and how he felt. Red-vinyl booth seats held us in familiar comfort as we talked about this journey into unexplored territory.

Gregg gave me a quick summary. "It's early yet. Some of the usual treatment options aren't available because of the size of my prostate. Also because of my age, although the doctor says I'm in better shape than a lot of younger men. I have time to investigate options. This is slow growing, though it looks like I'll probably need surgery."

With a shrug, Gregg admitted relief at the diagnosis. After months of not knowing, but suspecting, now he could act. With his characteristic engineering-mind thoroughness, he would undertake an exhaustive inquiry into treatment options, interview doctors and proponents of each method of treatment, and make an informed decision.

"How can I best support you in this?"

"Just be there," he said. His large hand covered mine on the lacquered table.

Back in our living room, we watched a red leaf fall part way down the liquid-amber tree and rest on crossed branches. Thick fog wrapped the house and mirrored what we felt. The rest of the world seemed to disappear into gray-ness at our fence; all that mattered right now was us, here. We talked on and off all afternoon and evening. That night we fell asleep in each others' arms, curled up together the way we used to before our hip and shoulder joints grew achy.

Drifting into sleep, I thought: You'll be fine, Gregg. I pray that you are healed in your body, heart, mind, and spirit, that you may find peace, joy, and new purpose for being in your retirement years. May it be so.

Research into medical options consumed Gregg and gave him a focus. He looked out our back sliding door to the sunlit trees below our house and said, "I'm more aware of changing lengths of days and nights now than ever."

Tyson continued to pee in the house, which led me to call Cathy for an animal-communication consultation. Even though Tyson's and my communication had improved, I hadn't been able to get underneath his behavior to the why of it.

Cathy said, "It's hard to get a clear reading when you're so close."

Tyson told her his peeing was mostly directed at Sina, who took liberties with rules and sneaked upstairs when we weren't looking, even though I'd cracked down on her with more obedience training. He told Cathy he was losing his power, and one way to feel better was to make his environment smell like him. He'd seen Sina's wild side and how she went after feral cats. Tyson felt vulnerable, and wasn't as sure of his safety as he had been when he was stronger.

This conversation was a good lesson for me. Tyson gave me a frame of reference for Gregg. Both felt they were losing their power. Gregg had groused about getting older and not being able to do things he could in the past. With the diagnosis of prostate cancer, Gregg said, "I feel like an old man." I hadn't realized the severity of his feelings. Tyson reframed that for me. It was difficult for these two grumpy guys—accustomed to taking on challenges, winning them, and powering their way through things—to accept limitations to their strength.

If Tyson were in the wild, he probably would have lost a battle and rejoined the cycle of life by now, but in our environment we honored him as an elder—so long as he wasn't peeing in the house! Tyson said he didn't quite belong to either the inside or the outside world—witnessing the law of the wild outside with the feral cats, and also inside with rule-testing Sina.

Gregg saw himself as over the hill without reaching the height he had envisioned. He acknowledged that his own nature had contributed—he'd made some mistakes out of stubbornness and misplaced loyalty as well as the reality that he wasn't a bloodthirsty, unethical corporate climber. His sense of integrity and fairness led to being a better person, not necessarily a wealthy one. Still, we were in better financial shape for retirement than many, due almost entirely to his efforts. That's what I asked him to focus on. We needed to appreciate our gifts and the contributions we'd each made and continued to make, even if they were different from our original dreams and visions.

Gregg's diagnosis added a new wrinkle to an already difficult time of transition. The synchronicity of timing struck me. If Gregg's diagnosis had come before the invitation to go to Peru instead of three weeks after we'd bought tickets, would we even have considered the trip?

Gregg emailed his doctor a long list of questions. Dr. Gavallos provided frank and honest answers. The size of Gregg's prostate and location of the cancer increased the risk of some treatments. Gregg intensified his investigation into surgical and nonsurgical approaches. He took Sina to the park. Sitting on the hill watching the sunset helped calm him.

Tyson peed on the floor again, giving us both something else to think about.

A few days later, I took Tyson to our veterinarian for his checkup. Tyson trusted Dr. Hackler's *direct approach and orderly mind.* The blood tests showed Tyson's T-score was extremely high. Dr. Hackler was fairly certain Tyson had thyroid cancer, although he also said his kidneys weren't working well. "That may be what does him in." We agreed the best course of action was to keep up with what we'd been doing, watching, helping Tyson be comfortable, and encouraging him to keep eating and drinking. Other treatments ranged from extreme to invasive.

Tyson told me: *I've known for a long time, and I knew that you wouldn't subject me to that other treatment. Just honor me and love me.* So I kept giving him tuna water, diluted so the high protein concentration wouldn't overload his system.

At the mention of possible cancer in Tyson, I told Dr. Hackler that Gregg had been diagnosed with prostate cancer. Dr. Hackler leaned back against the stainless-steel examining table, arms folded across his chest. "Has he looked into robotic-assisted surgery?"

"I don't know. What's that?"

"It's a high-tech procedure where the surgeon remotely operates a robot that does the actual surgery. The surgeon has a better view and can make more precise cuts than using hands. I had that surgery three years ago, and I'm fine. I'd be happy to talk with Gregg about it."

I left the veterinary office in high spirits, knowing Gregg would want to investigate a high-tech option, and grateful that Dr. Hackler was willing to discuss it with him. They talked the next day for over an hour. Gregg appreciated hearing about the procedure from a doctor who'd had the surgery himself. He sought out the surgeon who trained others in this new procedure and asked, "Do you play video games?" The answer was yes. That convinced Gregg that he had the dexterity and reflexes to operate the delicate machinery in an even-more-delicate surgery.

After hours of sifting through data on various options, Gregg liked to take Sina to the park and sit on the grassy hill to watch the sun set. He came home one afternoon with a new lightness in his face and step. "Sitting there," he said, "I realized that doing nothing is an option too. I feel a greater level of peace with that." He paused. "The cancer is slow growing. I probably have ten years before it does me in. It's a question of quality of life. That puts a new slant on it."

I could feel that a weight had been lifted from him, and could see the wheels turning in his engineering mind, sorting and sifting. A decision was needed. Until he decided on a treatment, Gregg was ambivalent about going to Peru. Sina and Tyson sensed it. If Gregg stayed home, Tyson would stay with him. Sina reflected the uncertainty in her wild eyes and ungrounded behavior. If Gregg couldn't go to Peru, would I feel right about going on that spiritual pilgrimage without him?

The Last Dregs

Twilight is coming, death stands nearby.
Warmth of body comforts me.
I purr; it comforts you.
Together we love, healing each other.
— Tyson Cat

In late November, the sun shone bright and warm. The air felt crisp and cold. Tyson purred at my side, his fur silver in morning light. Gregg made breakfast noises in the kitchen. Outside, a lone turkey vulture perched at the top of a eucalyptus tree, watching a spiked buck stroll behind the house. Sina settled as I said morning prayers to the directions. Cycles continued in my internal dance between strength and despair, life and rest, clarity and subtlety.

The day after Thanksgiving, Gregg and I donned the closest garments we owned to nineteenth-century garb and ventured to South San Francisco for the Dickens Fair. Period-costumed servers at the teashop brought delicate china cups and pots of tea, scones and crumpets with dabs of honey, lemon curd, and preserves. Awkward in the unaccustomed long black skirt and long-sleeved, ruffled white blouse, I spilled my tea and felt clumsy.

Gregg removed his Irish wool cap and set it on the table. "How're you doing with exiting Matthew House?"

323

"Sad and frustrated" was all I could say. I didn't want to give a blow-by-blow of dancing with depression, not connecting, having to make an effort to be present.

He didn't press, showing his support by giving me space to speak, or not.

At home later, I sat with Tyson. He said: *Softness, shielding my one eye from the light, I curl, feeling protected and comforted like a kitten. It's nice to trust.*

I reflected on developments at work. We'd held final interviews with the two lead candidates for my position, including time for each of them with my office staff, as I'd requested. Bill, the consultant, said, "You really know how to push for what you want."

"I'll take that as a compliment. Thank you."

I spoke with Esther, my board-member friend. "This exiting is really difficult."

Concern wrinkled Esther's forehead. "I couldn't imagine your thinking it wouldn't be."

"True," I said. "It's just that the extendedness of it is wearing."

She paused, touched my hand, and said, "You'll make it!"

I came home despondent. That night I prayed, "Just help me please." I felt like I was slipping into the void, and doing little to stop my fall—maybe even hastening it by not taking care of myself, not getting home early enough for dog walks, and not even leaving the office in daytime to walk in that neighborhood. Concern about Gregg flowed under my own feelings. I dreamed of being trapped and under assault.

After church Sunday I paused to talk with Pastor Randy. He adjusted the cincture on his alb and commented, "We've seen a lot of Gregg but not you. Are you out doing Matthew House things?"

"No, actually I'm hiding under a rock." I couldn't find the words to say that Sunday morning was the only time I could be alone.

Randy nodded, then asked, "Would you do me a favor? Each week, I want a congregation member to give a presentation on how God is moving in your life. Would you go first?"

My mind immediately started turning. I realized I'd lost sight of how God was moving in my life. Did Randy sense I was walking through the valley of the shadow?

Two weeks later, I stood at the lectern facing a round stained-glass window of a dove descending, and laid bare my vulnerabilities. I spoke slowly through a tight throat.

How God Is Moving in My Life

God is tap-dancing on my soul, laughing, and at the same time holding me in compassion and guidance. This is a time of great transitions. Gregg retired earlier this year, and I will soon. We are rediscovering how to live together after so many years of all-consuming jobs. God lives with us too, and helps us to be gentle with each other.

We have been the filling of the "sandwich generation," watching out for elderly parents and our children at the same time. This year, the last of our parents died—Gregg's father. Suddenly we moved from being the filling to being a piece of bread, and our children have become the sandwich filling. It's a new way of relating to the world, and God is helping us to do that.

I'm leaving Matthew House after many intense years, and God is holding my heart sacred as I grieve that leave-taking. God strengthens me and gives me courage as I finish projects, train others, and prepare to take that practical and deeply symbolic action of handing over my keys.

I have been ordained as an interfaith chaplain—the Reverend Nancy. God has been with me through that journey, hearing my doubts and questions, wearing many faces,

*and answering to many names. I don't know where the
path will lead, only that I must follow. As I step into the
unknown, God is the wind beneath my wings, helping me
to fly.*

*Whether the day and my outlook are dark and gloomy, or
bright and cheerful, I'm reminded that God is all things—
wind that rings our bells and rattles leaves; raindrops
and tears that fall; sunbeams that cast morning rainbows
in our living room; solid earth under my footsteps; the purr
of a cat, the soft nuzzle of a dog, the warmth of a hand.*

*This is Advent, the time of waiting. The dark time of year.
God is with me as I walk through the dark, holding a candle to lead me into daylight. And so it is.*

I stepped down in silence. Gregg clasped my hand tightly
to say, "It's okay; I'm here." I felt vulnerable, yet knew I was
strong. I appreciated the way Gregg's strength balanced my
own.

The world at work stumbled on. The new bookkeeper continued his downward spiral. On my watch. I had wanted to
hand over an agency in good order! That wasn't going to
happen.

I churned on that all night, listening to great, howling
gusts of wind ring our big bronze bell outside. Trees danced
and swayed, flexible and strong. Some branches would fall
to nature's pruning. I sensed that the trees enjoyed dancing
in the breath of God. Wind cleared the sky and let winter
stars shine forth.

At some point a purring Tyson curled by my head. I
prayed that energy would flow through me as it did around
the Medicine Wheel: "Oh Great Spirit, help me give flow to
emotion and action, and hold strength in my body. Help me
receive with my mind the information needed to discern,

and determine with Spirit what needs to be done. Help me let go of the outcome and know I can't fix it all. In the name of all that is holy, including me, amen." Finally, as dawn neared I felt a sense of letting go and was able to sleep. I dreamed that I was the tree, and the rock on which it stood, and the cougar crouched below it.

My eyes opened to a sky full of cotton-ball tufts with light gray bellies and peach-colored tops, drifting in a field of light blue. They bunched together, and then cleared to release sunshine. I marveled at how I could go to bed feeling so disheartened and wake feeling so blessed.

Winter solstice came. I placed a green pillar candle on the deck railing outside our bedroom. Given the fog and general dampness, I had no concerns about fire safety. I woke from time to time to see the glowing tip of flame change through the night, dancing against dark sky and fog. Candle in the blackest night, candle against the lighting sky. When I woke the last time, sun had not touched the treetops but the sky was bright. I stepped onto our frost-covered wooden deck in my bare feet, held the still-lit candle, and gave thanks, greeting the directions on this first day of winter. I'd kept a candle burning through the longest night, holding the promise of return of the light in a journey of time and reverence.

Our family celebrated Christmas on Christmas Eve day so the younger generation could go to their other families on Christmas Day. I remembered that my mother died on Christmas Day four years ago, and noted that this year's celebration seemed quieter than previous holidays.

Tyson surprised us by staying downstairs most of the day. He went outside a few times to get his paws on the earth. He said the energy was better this time, and he wanted to be with the family. *I won't see them all again. For me it was goodbye.*

The big news was that granddaughter Katy's first menses began that week. Daughter Gwen showed her a yoga posture to relieve cramps, which helped Katy feel better. After dinner daughter-in-law Elizabeth, Gwen, and I took Katy up to my altar room for a rite of passage. Katy sat in the East. I sat across from her in the West, and Gwen and Elizabeth in the South and North. We lit a candle and created an impromptu ritual. I told about the thirteen moon cycles in a year, and explained the symbolism of a carved black African goddess figure Katy had given me years before. She'd said she liked it and that it reminded her of me. The figure represented the four stages of womanhood—child, maiden, mother, and crone. We told stories about our first menses. Gwen dripped oil for purification on our crown chakras. It smelled like flowers. We sang "Now I Walk in Beauty," and welcomed Katy to the sisterhood. She appreciated it, and each of us felt we had filled a gap in our own evolution, for none of us had received such a ritual.

The next day I sat with Tyson, watching him twitch in sleep. *Reliving my younger days*, he said. Even a senior master teacher can frolic in dreams. In the midst of my fog, sadness, and tiredness around my own transitions, I felt the need to listen more to patient Tyson. He helped me so much. What was it doing to him? I received snatches, but hadn't heard a discourse from him in quite a while. He spent more time outside, with his paws on the ground.

Tyson purred: *Sun on my fur, a warm hand, purring, together. It's a good life. Tail twitching—there's always some dissatisfaction, some incompletion. That's the Zen of it. From one end to the other contained in one package whose energy is boundless. I have passed the point of storytelling. Now is the time to just be.*

Later, I sat in silence on our backyard swing, watching a flock of turkey vultures soar. Their red heads swiveled, scanning the ground below; their beaks gleamed in the late afternoon sun. They landed heavily in eucalyptus trees overlooking the sloped land below. I sent them thanks: "You're beautiful."

They answered: *No one ever calls us that.*

"Perhaps," I said, "but I think so. You are majesty in the air, and you do a great service in the cycle of life." I felt their thanks and knew they were pleased. I asked if they had a message.

They said: *We're here to remind you to be like us, patient, and alert to opportunities.*

The final countdown began at work. My last board meeting as director had a strange unreality. My successor was there to be introduced to the full board. She seemed restrained, but then so would I in her place. I felt that the board had already moved on.

At the staff meeting, I said what a privilege it had been to work with them, then walked through the room, calling each person by name and giving them a red rose (two to those who had been there as long as or longer than I had). They were touched by my personal tribute. It felt right, a completion.

That evening one of the churches held a holiday party for shelter staff and residents. The pastor gave me a blessing. My friend Juana, who had helped organize the Peruvian fundraiser, presented a gift from the congregation—a Peruvian tapestry in an unusual dark-turquoise color. Then she read a quotation that ended with: "To the one who always keeps her door open, her ears listening, her hands working, and her feet walking . . . may she walk slowly, because her pace is the pace of change, and change, real change, always takes time."

I had to focus on breathing to keep from crying. Humility flowed through me.

Deep in gratitude, at home I wrote thank-you notes for retirement gifts and tributes. All these folks truly cared for me and valued the work I'd done with Matthew House.

New Year's Eve, after an intense day at work, I surveyed how much was undone, and what I could hope to finish. My tenure ending with a ragged whimper. Last to leave the building, I walked down the dark stairs. Empty, alone, and sad, I sat in my car in the deserted parking lot.

At home, I went upstairs, curled up with Papacito, my old stuffed dog, and gave myself over to grief and sadness. I eventually came downstairs to sit with Gregg, Tyson, and Sina, and gradually came into present time and place. We ate our traditional New Year's Eve dinner, with thanks to the crab and shrimp for giving themselves for our nourishment. The next morning I made a long list of things I wanted to do now that I theoretically had time.

January second: my successor's first day. Now I was officially a lame duck. I welcomed Whitney, and made the practical and symbolic gesture of handing her my keys. She received them in hands much like mine—unadorned except for one simple ring, nails short and unpolished. She asked practical questions: "How does this contract work? Could you brief me on your direct reports and how they're doing?" I went into the staff office to give Whitney and the program director privacy to talk; everyone was busy. I felt like a fifth wheel. A strange, dispossessed feeling. I was glad when Bill, the consultant, came to see how we were doing.

The next morning Tyson sat with me in our couch. His tail flicked to show he wasn't at ease. The last two leaves fell from the liquid-amber tree, accepting their time or perhaps not. I searched for some feeling. No tears, no laughter, only numbness. I journaled, "This has to be one of the hardest things I've ever done. I feel dead inside." I prayed for guidance and deliverance.

That day at work was better. The host church's music director gave me a big hug and urged me to do something fun for myself. He understood the difficulty of long leaving. At home, the mail brought a note from a Chaplaincy friend, thanking me for my "solid, serene, grounded presence, a true gift." I certainly didn't feel grounded, solid, or serene! But I did feel valued. Had it taken these heavy-duty affirmations to bump me out of my gloom?

Tyson slept with me that night. He was fading, having kept his promise of staying with me through ordination and my last full-time days at work. He wandered, phasing in and out, sometimes seeming disoriented. Perhaps he needed to rest after the last few weeks of me.

On Friday I came home from work and suddenly felt much lighter. I still had a couple of things to wind up, but I felt the agency was in good hands with Whitney.

Sunday: my sixty-fourth birthday. "Will you still need me . . . when I'm sixty-four?" I stood on our stairs contemplating the print of a turquoise doorway with the number "64" beside it. I was indeed passing through a door I'd never been through before.

Gregg presented a gift he and daughter Gwen had conspired to get me: a wood sea turtle, ten inches long, carved by Nonu, a native Hawaiian artist. I named the turtle Nonu Honu. The wood glowed soft gold with light traces of grain through the thirteen plates carved on the turtle's back. Its neck was extended, reminding me that a turtle has to stick its neck out to move forward.

Time expanded and slowed. Suddenly I didn't feel pressed to do a lot; I didn't feel like doing anything, but I didn't want to just sit either. Interesting, watching myself.

Monday: the last day of my overlap week with the new director. Whitney and I felt we had accomplished as much as we could, although she said she'd undoubtedly call with questions. I left at noon, feeling complete.

"Wahoo!" I yelled from our backyard, and heard an answering yell echo back. I was officially done. I'd never thought it would feel so good to be unemployed! My euphoria would pass, but at that moment I felt light and free. Now what? In fuzzy slippers, with a cup of tea and Tyson and Sina nearby, I read the newspaper's comic strips. The rest of the world could wait.

There Is Life After

My tree keeps on growing, flowing and growing,
my tree keeps on growing, each sacred part.
Roots to sustain me, trunk to strengthen me,
branches to uplift me, tree of my heart.
— N.S.

What day is it? Within a week of walking away from Matthew House, I'd lost the sense of which day it was. Moving from the external motivator of a daily hour-by-hour calendar to an internal motivator was like removing fences and letting the sheep roam free.

Gregg and I went on mundane excursions—grocery shopping, the post office, lunch. "It's nice to have my play partner and soulmate back again!" Gregg said with a lop-sided grin. He looked sheepish and admitted to bouts of loneliness when I was still working. He worked hard to accommodate me, asking which shows I'd like to watch and if I'd like to go with him on errands.

Matthew House staff called to ask a few little questions, but nothing major. With no meetings, no obligations, I found I didn't want to do anything but felt compelled to some action. Tyson didn't claim much lap time, but when he did, his weight helped me to ground. I now understood Gregg's "not able to get traction" when he first retired. I felt no traction yet, but slept well for the first time in many months and succumbed to naptime often. I entered an extended resting period, and waited for an energy spurt that never came. I spotted corners to clean up, and cleared out closets, the pantry, and my work area in our home office.

Waking one morning, I was surprised by a fleeting sense of emptiness. Disquieted, I went onto our back deck to honor the directions, then lit a white candle on my altar and prayed: "Help me go within, to be in this dark place for as long as I need to, and prepare for what comes next."

I heard: *Be with your self.*

How do I spend time with my self if I'm spinning in circles?

Saturdays brought focus: two back-to-back Spanish classes at the adult school—conversation and intermediate grammar. I must have been asleep in school when we covered body parts! It was time well spent as my ear and tongue retuned to a language of long ago.

My friend Alison offered to keep Sina while Gregg and I went to Peru. That relieved us of a huge concern, and Sina loved their yard. It was fun to sit with Alison, a woman who is completely at peace with herself and self-contained. I told her I wanted to know who I am in the core of me. Alison looked at me and said, "You've been consistent in behavior, leadership, and integrity over the years at Matthew House. How is that different from the core you?"

"Maybe it isn't, though I want to find that out for myself."

Near the end of January, the Matthew House board held a going-away party for me. They needed a ritual sendoff as much as I did. Organizers decorated the room in shades of purple, and prepared a delectable spread of finger foods. Friends, staff and board members, and colleagues from other agencies came. Pastors wished me well in my new ministry. One surprised me, saying I'd been an inspiration to him—I'd always regarded him as an inspiration to me! In the brief program, speakers represented clients, staff, board, churches, and funders. Ornate framed city and county commendations listed Matthew House's accomplishments under my leadership.

I told my truth—that I was the front person, representing the solid team of board, staff, community, and the families themselves. I introduced Whitney: "Matthew House has come a long way, and has much yet to do. The person to take us there is our new director, Whitney." She stood and received a round of applause. The baton had been passed.

Whitney told me later, "You'll be a tough act to follow."

Sleep claimed me for many hours that first month. But at last I woke from a nap one afternoon and felt rested. It felt good to be alive. I stepped outside to pray to the directions, and felt complete. I also had a cognition: South is home to water, where one flows with emotion. I suddenly understood that crying from my heart comes from the place of water! That insight made me happy. I was collecting the pieces and parts of myself, and felt more solid than I had in a while.

Tyson made sure that I sat with him often. One day he dictated another poem, which we called "Thoughts on Leaving."

Life carried on with a to-do list, but no agenda. I moved slowly, with low energy. Was this how I would recover from the intense last years? I felt a push-pull of wanting to answer the call of animal chaplain, and equal reluctance to commit to anything. Anxiety crept in. What wanted to birth from the core of my being? I recalled no dreams and received no answer. Spirit said it was the right question; the answer would come when I was ready.

Thoughts on Leaving

I'm leaving soon, with some reluctance.
I do so love being a cat and being with you.
I don't like being an old cat.
I'll come back, bright and new,
to play, and fight, and love.
I will always be with you, my spirit self
purring your dreams.

There's so much to tell . . .
Tales of being a pirate cat,
swashbuckling on the seven seas.
Tales of being a temple cat,
my claws the mark of power.
Tales of being a star-born cat,
and the flight through space to come here.
Tales of being other things,
and their adventures too.

But I like being a cat best,
small in this life, to hold and love,
my heart much greater than this body can hold.
Purring your dreams, training your dog,
sustaining your spirit.
Transition is all about being present in the Now
as that Now changes.
Be the rock that time and all things pass over,
under, around, and through.
I am that.

— *Tyson Cat*

A container for internal work came via Chaplaincy's spiritual psychology and Kabbalah teachers, Megan and her husband, Jim. They began a series of workshops on the Tree of Life model, over seven months from February through September. Weekend journeys to their home across the bay gave me the structure to continue unfolding, and a series of initiations that brought me face-to-face with the deepest parts of myself.

Gregg began the Disciple course, a depth study of the Bible from the Christian perspective. We found many commonalities, for Christianity and Kabbalah come from the same roots. He said, "This is helping me reframe my view of God." We volunteered to carry communion to homebound church members. That felt like a chaplain thing to do.

January 29 was the fourth anniversary of Buki's death. How much had happened since! Gregg planted the little redwood that had been our living Christmas tree at the head of Buki's grave as a symbol of continuing life. I cried. Gregg put his arms around me and held me. Tears shone in his eyes too. Buki lived in our hearts, but we both still missed her warm, furry self.

Later, I talked with Tyson. He seemed to be in such good shape, I asked if he had changed his mind about leaving. He said he hadn't. What could I do for him?

Just be near. My world is closing in. I'm trying to get Sina to come into partnership. She has much to learn. You need her to help in your ministry, but she hasn't settled into that.

I continued to float, yet knew things were sorting out underneath, like sitting on the deck of a ship while that ship chugs across an ocean. In a Tree of Life ritual I drew Eagle from the deck of power animals. Eagle's medicine is far vision. The next morning, in prayer to the directions, I connected that Eagle is guardian of East, the place of inspiration and new beginnings.

In another Tree of Life ritual I had promised to return a stone taken from Mother Earth. My attention rested on a round flat stone on my altar, gray with a lighter markings that looked like a dancing goddess. I dug a hole under the large stone in our still-intact labyrinth center circle, said prayers for the little stone, the earth, and myself, and returned Mother Earth's child to her. I sang the "Uma Parvati" chant to honor feminine energy.

Standing in the center of our labyrinth, with half its stones missing, I knew it existed without stones to mark it. I thought of the circles within circles its undulating path traced, and understood how the Medicine Wheel is an organic, living entity too. I had recognized the emotion of South in water and the inspiration of East in Eagle. I was entering West for an extended period of reflection. What about North, the place of wisdom? We receive with the mind in North. Each time I opened to animals and listened to my intuition, I was in North. My Medicine Wheel lives within me. I gave thanks to Mother Earth for this lesson. The ritual complete, I followed Gregg and Sina to the park, walking slowly and singing all the way.

Matthew House called in early February. Whitney had fired the bookkeeper. Could I help the temporary accountant with the still-ongoing audit? I stepped back into the famil-iar office. It looked the same, but felt different. *I* was differ-ent. I realized I didn't need to be there anymore, and in fact didn't want to. The contract wage would help pay for our trip to Peru, though. I set to work catching up on service invoices. It was good to focus on something I knew how to do. It felt even better to not be in charge, and leave it at the door each evening.

At home that weekend, a tableau formed: Three male wild turkeys did their circular hierarchy dance. Three deer watched them. The turkeys promenaded down to the canyon and out of view. The deer moved farther down the hill. I wanted to get past the stand of trees to watch sunset. As I entered the trees I heard a great horned owl call, and answered it.

A red-shouldered hawk landed in branches above me, received my greeting, and flew off. I stepped out from under the eucalyptus trees. The sun had just set, turning the sky marigold yellow and orange. A sliver of crescent moon hung above the horizon. I welcomed it, sang "Dark of the Moon," and realized that when I'd buried the little stone, it was new moon. My seed—my request to see clearly what wants to be born of me, and manifest it—had been planted in the dark of new moon, to come to fruition in full-moon light. I felt so much gratitude it was hard to bear; wave upon wave washed through me. The whole episode felt as if I'd entered another dimension.

I met with Jane on her back deck for a spiritual-direction session, and talked about my shift from being externally to internally driven. Jane told me about the resting place between death and rebirth. People don't mention that as part of the cycle of life, but it's there, like the hesitation at the top of an arc when momentum has ceased and gravity hasn't yet taken over.

"This disconnected feeling is part of the growth I'm going through, but it doesn't rest easy. I want to *do* something!"

"You've already *done* enough," she said, with that characteristic twinkle in her eyes. "In stillness we can hear the voice of God."

I carried these thoughts back home. Praying for clarity and guidance, I heard that I'm in a resting phase now, to study and learn.

Tyson waited for me to settle. *Took you long enough! Curl up with me. I spend a lot of time in the spirit world these days, visiting, preparing to transition. I can manage my body and still be off journeying. I'm not magical; I just know how to use skills I was born with. So were you, but most humans don't remember.*

He gave me another poem, which we called "Night Journey." Tyson said: *It's hard to let go, even when it's time.* I understood that. He added that I hear him just fine. *You can't rush these things.*

> ### Night Journey
>
> *Prowling, sensing,*
> *whiskers stretching out beyond,*
> *brushing the auras of trees and grasses.*
> *Snakes walking, snails galloping,*
> *birds curled in the heather to sleep,*
> *eggs contemplating what they will become—*
> *all are possible.*
>
> *You join me, body safely asleep;*
> *hand in paw, we fly into oblivion and beyond,*
> *returning by dawn's first light.*
> *The stars and I remember;*
> *you dimly recall a strange dream.*
>
> *— Tyson Cat*

Tyson, Sina, and I all sensed Gregg's ambivalence about going to Peru. He admitted to mixed feelings, but knew it was a spiritual journey for me and was committed to going. He said, "It's not the trip itself so much as the long plane ride. Once we're there, I'll be glad."

I talked to Sina, out loud and mentally, to assure her we weren't looking for a new home for her. This was her forever home! Staying at Alison's was like a vacation for her, with different sniffs and things to investigate. We would all come back home together after our trip. Getting a firmer sense that Gregg was going—with admitted reluctance—helped Sina accept her temporary arrangement. It showed her that sometimes we do something we don't want to, because it's important to someone we love.

Tyson knew there was big energy around this trip. He confirmed he might leave his body. It would be easier for him to go with me, and stay connected with Gregg and Sina, if he were in spirit. *Leaving soon. There's not enough time to say it all. You think you're ready to see me go. Your tears will still flow. Sometimes—a surprising amount—I go within. Half here and half there, preparing to cross and leave the body I've had so long. Stray thoughts: What color will I wear next time? The luxury of easing from this life to what is between. Different when accident cuts life short—for a while you don't know if you're alive or dead, it's so sudden. This way is better, when there's no fear. The sweet sadness of leaving, the welcome release, and rest.*

March 6, two months after my retirement date, I left Matthew House again. At midafternoon I briefed Whitney on the status, and told her I'd run out of projects.

Whitney paused and said, "Well, we'll just have to send you home then."

Released! I had helped correct some of the damage done on my watch, sending out thousands of dollars in back invoices to get funds flowing into the agency again, with a cost of one month's modest pay. Fair enough. I felt that a stuck place had been released.

The next day, sitting on our back swing with a cup of tea, Tyson and Sina nearby, I admired how a red-tailed hawk fell out of a tree into a graceful glide, and climbed to cruising altitude. Later I walked Sina to the park. Plum trees blossomed along the creek, volunteers from years of bird droppings and an old orchard. White petals fell like snowflakes. I dug trenches to let puddles of trapped water escape into the creek. I felt myself flowing freely too. I slept well that night; I didn't remember enough of my dreams to record, yet I knew there was ease to them, as if issues I'd been dream-struggling with were resolved.

I reviewed my Chaplaincy practicum project notebook and saw a note that Tyson wanted a stone from Colorado for his grave. He was pulling back, pulling in. He often stayed in my altar room. He liked its energy, and the light wasn't too bright. He spent time in our family room, where classical music played on the radio. I sensed his energy as more magical, yet more grounded. Sometimes I wanted to hold him, but honored his preference to be alone. He barely ate, and was skin and bones. He still drank water, though. He said: *I'm starving, but I don't want you to do anything about it—no vet, no pills or shots, no subcutaneous fluids.* I knew he was tired, yet his heart was strong. He said he might wait until our return to transition, or he might go while we were gone. *It depends on when the angels come.* He would spend time in deep meditation, connected with Buki. His soul would travel with me. I added Tyson the Brave to his list of names.

I arranged for a recommended cat-sitting service to visit daily while we were in Peru. The service was expensive, but worth it for peace of mind. The cat sitter came for a tour and orientation. We sat at our cluttered kitchen table to go over her checklist. One question was what to do with Tyson's body if he died while we were away? No hesitation: "Curl him up and put him in the freezer." I wanted to see him, hold him, and bury him if that happened. I learned later that my response caused quite a discussion among the cat-watch team.

Alison and her husband took Sina for a three-hour walk, and brought back a tired, happy dog. I knew Sina would be fine with them while we were gone.

The week before departure, we reviewed trip details with Rosalie. I could barely contain my excitement! She told us about the school in her brother's town, struggling to get by on donations. We emailed friends, requesting children's clothing and school supplies. Donated clothing filled an old suitcase, and we tucked school supplies into our bags. I hoped our home scale was accurate. Our bags were only ounces below the weight limit.

I contemplated what to take to Peru as my spirit gift. I lit candles and spread the collected elements in front of my altar. I sewed a pouch from fabric with a Native American pattern from Colorado, with a dominant color of sandstone red. Into the pouch went a nest of my gray hair, and a picture of me in Colombia, four years old and wearing a rumba costume. A rose-quartz stone to represent my heart, an amethyst for connection to the Divine, and a raw-quartz crystal to show how all come from the earth, perfect in our imperfection with fractures and inclusions. Then a small turkey-vulture feather in homage to the condors, a tuft of Buki fur, and a claw sheath from Tyson as thanks for these two great teachers.

The same fabric wrapped a fossil whale ear. When Nikki gave me the whale ear I took to Hawaii, she'd told me about giving them to sacred bodies of water in her travels locally and in Europe. I asked for one to give to Lake Titicaca. The fossil she gave me was large and heavy, with scallop-shell remnants. I secured the red fabric with a strip of leather, and gave thanks to it for bringing the ancient wisdom of whales to high Lake Titicaca.

I filled a small baggie with dirt from the rock garden I'd built when Mother and Buki were in their final days. Other bags held fur from Buki and Sina, and a tiny bit that Tyson allowed me to snip from him. These, a bag of dried lavender blossoms, and a few extra snack-sized baggies, went into the pouch from Peru that had been holding my Chaplaincy necklace. I would carry them in reverence, as gifts to the land.

At night, I dreamed of rituals and flute music, of animals and dances under the moon, and of recovering shamanic training I'd learned in previous lifetimes.

Gregg and I took Sina to Alison's house the afternoon before we left. It felt like sending our child off to summer camp for the first time. She needed reassurance, but I knew she would be fine. Alison called later to tell us Sina had settled in and was on patrol for squirrels.

Tyson looked stronger than I'd seem him in a while, although he kept to himself a lot. He seemed to miss Sina. I hoped he'd be okay while we were gone.

The moon would be in its dark, new-moon phase when we arrived in Peru, waxing to full on our return. New beginnings growing to fruition. This trip was already doing its work on me.

Return to Peru

The landscape changes.
Places that held me, gently let go.
Memories, whispers on the breeze,
jiggling the cobwebs of my soul.
— N.S.

The vision at Sacsayhuaman made my knees buckle. I left my companions behind in the ancient ceremonial center at the head of Cusco, passed through the remains of a trapezoid-shaped entryway, and climbed curved stone steps to the second level. Around a corner, grasses and yellow wildflowers grew atop a stone wall. Suddenly, remembrance of this place entered me like a lightning bolt from another time. *I looked down and saw my legs, brown and bare under a cloth skirt woven in a bright pattern. I leaned against the wall to keep from spilling fluid from the heavy bowl I held, as warriors in feather headdresses ran in tight formation down the steps. I mustn't spill. It was a great honor to carry the bowl to the upper level.* Tears came to my eyes. I pulled on sunglasses to avoid questioning looks from Japanese tourists making their way down the steps. I stumbled up to a knoll in the ruins of the next level, plopped cross-legged onto the earth, and wept. The place had recognized me, and welcomed me back.

After too short a time, Gregg came looking for me. He towered over me, his long shadow foreshortened by the noon sun. "What's going on?"

"I've been here before!"

Gregg paused. "Well, I'm sure when you were here before you were acclimated. You're getting sunburned! Better put on a hat." He turned and walked back to the stone steps.

I was reluctant to leave but didn't want to delay Gregg and Rosalie. I asked permission of the place to take some soil, and scraped a little hard-packed dirt into a plastic baggie. I gave thanks, and poured water from my bottle onto the parched earth as my giveback.

Unsteady, I made my way back to ground level and the eight-sided stone that radiated energy. I leaned against it, feeling an internal vibration as strong as when the dolphins sonared me two years earlier. Visiting Machu Picchu first had probably prepared me for this awakening.

Our first full day in Lima, I'd wanted to see the cathedral in the main plaza. My family had made only one trip to Lima when we lived in Peru, when I was in elementary school. I remembered seeing the *conquistador* Francisco Pizarro's bones in a glass casket. I was taller than he, even if his head had been attached. Was that tenacious recollection real or did I make it up? I needed to know. I ran up the steps and into the colonial-architecture cathedral. Yes, Pizarro's bones are still there. The alcove was now gated, but I could see the glass-sided coffin. That was enough. I felt a connection snap in place—click, reconnection.

That afternoon our driver took us to the beach. I felt the ocean's pull and wanted to gather some beach sand. This was the closest I would get on our trip to Talara, where I'd lived during my primary-school years, and had been caught in the undertow of the southern Pacific Ocean one terrifying day. I'd clawed my way sideways as the current sucked at me, and had been spit out of the riptide. I'd learned a healthy respect for the ocean.

Gregg and I threaded down the crowded beach to a clear spot. The sun hung low, nearly touching the horizon where ocean and sky met. At a space that felt right, Gregg watched while I offered soil from home to the cardinal directions. I knelt and smoothed the sand, feeling grains slide under my palm, and drew a Medicine Wheel with an inner circle where the East-West and North-South roads connect. I scooped a handful of sand from the circle into a baggie, sprinkled dried lavender blossoms over the wheel, and gave thanks to the Earth Mother, *Pachamama.* I felt another click—reconnection.

That night Tyson visited my dreams, assuring me he was with me, sitting on my right shoulder. He said he would send a dream jaguar to help me see. *You've been a great student—and it only took eighteen years!* I checked in with him and Sina every day and felt their presence. Buki's too. Sina seemed happy, and said Alison and her husband took her to a place with grass and cows. I told Sina she could connect and see through my eyes.

The next morning we rose at 5:30 for our flight to Cusco (I'm using the Spanish spellings here). The plane landed hot, engines roaring in 11,000-foot-high thin air. From above, every building seemed to have a red tile roof. Cusco was the navel of the Inca world, the center of their Medicine Wheel, surrounded by four *apus* (sacred peaks). Rosalie's brother, Jim, met us at the airport, and gave us coca leaves to chew to help with the altitude adjustment.

We drove down the mountain into the Urubamba Valley, stopping at the famous Weavers of Chincheros. The women wore traditional clothing and demonstrated how alpaca and sheep wool is cleaned and spun, how plants are used for dyes, and weaving on different kinds of looms. I felt light-headed. After lunch we continued to Quinta Patawasi inn (at roughly nine thousand feet). I could see why this richly beautiful valley is considered sacred. We slept well to sounds of the river below.

The next morning, we visited the little school. The town and church each paid for half of the six teachers—$200 U.S. per year for a college graduate. The children sang for us. Many wore colorful, hand-woven native dress, which I understood marked them as a lower class than those wearing store-bought clothes. The teacher was happy to receive our school supplies, and asked me to distribute the pencils. Her students had none. I walked around the classroom, giving each student a sharpened pencil. It was heartwarming and heart wrenching. That evening we left part of the retirement and travel money we'd received to help pay for one of the teachers.

After the school tour, we piled into the van with our guide to drive up the Urubamba Valley. Our destination, a camelid reserve, held small herds of llamas, alpacas, guanacos, and soft-haired vicuñas. The llama is taller with a face more like a camel; the alpaca is shorter, with a sweeter, rounder face. Our guide assured us that the wild guanacos and vicuñas are captured and shorn every two years, then released. They don't breed in captivity.

I offered grain to a llama with multihued dreadlocks hanging from its back down to its hooves. I asked, "Do you feel like talking?"

The llama asked: *Why?*

"I bring greetings from me and my friend Cathy."

I accept your greetings and return them.

"Do you have a message for me?"

Open your eyes, open your ears, open your spirit. Pieces of the puzzle are all around.

"Thank you," I said as the llama turned away.

Early the next morning, our driver took Gregg and me to the rail station. The narrow-gauge train tracks followed the Urubamba River, with jaw-dropping scenes all along its narrowing canyon to Aguas Calientes, or Machu Picchu pueblo, at roughly seventy-eight hundred feet.

We checked into our hotel and met Gilberto, who like all of our guides was small of stature, of Indian heritage, and bristled with wiry energy. He helped us secure tickets to Machu Picchu. By 11:30 our bus had climbed the narrow switchback road to the entry gates at 8,072 feet. Clouds hung low, emphasizing the site's mystery. Rain was falling by the time our tour started.

Gilberto spoke English well enough to explain what we were seeing. He took us first to the Temple of Water, crowded because it was the only place with a roof. Rain-water pouring by in a system of water-transport canals demonstrated the Incas' masterful engineering.

The site crawled with tour groups, led by multilingual guides giving spiels in English, French, German, Chinese, and other languages. We noted many markers aligned to solstices and equinoxes. The diamond-shaped compass stone mirrors the Southern Cross constellation. Its south end is slightly elevated; the north points toward Cusco. Gregg checked the alignment with his GPS; it was exact.

The Intiwatana stone ("hitching place of the sun") is on the highest level. When the crowd thinned, Gilberto invited me to cup my hands around the north-pointing corner, "if you believe." I first asked permission of the stone. I could feel strong energy radiating from the granite altar. The stone is aligned with the cardinal directions and four sacred *apus*; at noon on equinox it casts no shadow. Spirit told me this was where to give my offering.

The Temple of Condor was so crowded we could barely make our way through. Gregg and I had already decided that this first day in Machu Picchu we would get the general layout and select places we wanted to visit the next morning. At the Temple of Condor, we could see rock carved to look like an extended wing on the right, facing a stone carved to represent a condor head. Our guide pointed and said, "Some say there is a cave underneath."

We climbed the path to a guard tower above the Inca Gate. The path wound through jungle, reminding us that Machu Picchu sits at the edge of Amazon rainforest. We shared the path with llamas trotting down to graze now that the rain had stopped. Their hooves sounded like castanets on the stone path.

I saw repeated instances of the Inca cross built into walls. Gilberto said the three steps represent the three levels of spirit. The first level is the underworld, ruled by Serpent. The second level is the earthly world, ruled by Puma. The third is the heavens or overworld, ruled by Condor.

Three llamas grazed by the high guard shack, one nursing a young llama. The young one was lovely and curious, with a spotted neck. *A girl*, the mother llama said. Tourists wanted their pictures taken with her and kept trying to touch her. I warned them not to get too close, but they ignored me. The mother llama's ears were laid back, and she didn't look happy. I attempted to communicate with her, but she was on guard duty with her young one. After the people took their pictures and faded away, I thanked the mother llama for being with us, and asked her forgiveness for the rudeness of my kind.

She said: *I don't like it, but I'm used to it. Come back early tomorrow.*

The next morning at 4:30 we joined a long line of people already waiting by a fleet of buses. We squeezed onto the third bus and arrived at Machu Picchu a little after six. Dawn hinted in the eastern sky. Gregg went to climb Huayna Picchu, the 8,860-foot peak at the end of Machu Picchu. I headed for the Intiwatana hill for my ritual.

A few other people were there, each of us on our own mission, wrapped in our own thoughts. I said prayers to the directions, and felt as if some long-held part of me was being unlocked. I gave soil from home and some Buki, Tyson, and Sina fur to each direction. Three steps carved into the Intiwatana stone's east side face the distant Gate of the Sun, where the sun rises through two barely visible stone columns at solstice.

I climbed over a low stone wall to a terrace one level down. I asked for guidance and connection, gave thanks, and tossed my spirit gift in its red-patterned fabric package as far as I could. Tears slid down my cheeks as my prayers and gifts nestled into the jungle canopy below. I sat there, listening to birds and watching clouds, hidden from view of people who came and went on the other side of the rock wall above me. I began to understand that it was not the temples, but the land itself that was sacred to the Incas. The mountains are the ancestors.

Feeling a need to move again, I took a trail up to the high guard tower, jumping out of the way as three llamas clattered across the trail on their way to sweet grasses below. I sat on an inviting rock to rest, and asked if I could take some soil. Understanding permission, I scooped a little into a plastic baggie, and left the rest of my soil from home there.

Continuing up that trail, I discovered the meaning of trudge. Squadrons of big black bumblebees droned over yellow flowers, a vibrating buzz in the background. Llamas grazed by a large stone sculpted to represent a llama, with three steps leading up one side.

I thought of Tyson's love of high places. "This is for you, Ty," I said, as I put aside my fear of heights and sat on a terrace overlooking the river gorge far below. I sank into a peaceful light meditation and connected with Tyson, Sina, and Buki. Did they want me to leave some of their fur here too? They all said *yes*, so I gave their fur to the wind at the terrace edge. I felt the energy of the stones I leaned against seep into me.

From that place I could see the Inca Gate, the main entrance to Machu Picchu, and descended to pass through it, feeling respectful and thinking of the sandaled feet that had come this way after running the Inca trail.

RETURN TO PERU | 353

Gregg and I had agreed to meet by the main gate at noon, so I continued my circuit. The western section across a wide grassy plaza felt older but isn't—rather, it's not constructed in the high style, so looks more weathered. The Pachamama stone stands there, mirroring the sacred mountain behind it and with an altar across its front. I placed my hands on a corner I could reach (all places of worship are roped off), and felt energy radiating from it. These stones still hold energy stored from many years of worship.

The Temple of Condor was deserted. I noticed an arrangement of stones that appeared to cover an opening into the ground, and appreciated the chance to be alone, silent and reverent in that place.

Gregg waited at the main gate, already crowded with tourists emerging from busses. We both felt complete and returned to town, grateful that rain the first day and sun during our second visit gave us two different perspectives of this sacred site.

Gregg told me about climbing Huayna Picchu, and his admiration for ancient workers who had carved a trail out of that vertical hillside. He was grateful for ropes to hang onto in some places. I shared my adventures of the day.

The next morning our driver took us back to Cusco, then to Sacsayhuaman. Cusco is laid out in the shape of a crouching puma, with Sacsayhuaman at its head—the Inca three-step world in massive physical form. Spanish conquistadors thought it was a fortress because of the many soldiers there and tried to demolish it, but could destroy only the top two levels.

Our new guide, Jorge, showed us a many-sided rock surrounded by eight other rocks, which held a special energy. He told us so many people wanted to put their hands on it that the caretakers had roped it off. "But," he said with a grin, "there's an even better one around the corner." And so there was. A stone half again taller than Gregg, surrounded by eight smaller stones, built into the wall. We could feel energy radiating from it even without touching it.

We climbed from the open, grassy plaza up stone steps to the first level. I asked, "If this is the first level, where's the serpent?"

Jorge grinned again, pleased that I had listened. "Around the corner, over here," he said, gesturing with his arm. The two-foot-tall serpent shape, carved about two inches deep into the stone, had a seven-segmented undulating body with its head at a right angle to its body. Jorge said that when people rest a compass on the head, the needle spins. Gregg tried it with our GPS. Its direction changed by fifteen degrees and the satellite signal strength went down.

Jorge hadn't planned to take us to the upper levels. "Not much left after the Spanish tore it down." I had to go, though. Then I had my lightning-bolt experience of having been there before. As we gathered to leave Sacsayhuaman, I still felt the vibrating buzz of energy flowing throughout my body.

Back in Cusco, we visited the Temple of the Sun complex. As in other places throughout Latin America, the Spanish tore down temples and built cathedrals on the foundations. Temple of the Sun's curved, smooth stone foundation is still in place. Temples could be destroyed, but not the earth's power or the reverence in which people held it. In the temple's main room, now a gallery where portraits of church fathers hang, I felt strong energy flowing through me. Every cell in my body vibrated.

We looked forward to a daylong train ride the next day, from Cusco to Puno on the shores of Lake Titicaca. The train cars had an old elegance from the late 1930s, with wood paneling and little lamps on cloth-covered tables. The train lurched out of the station, and rolled southeast beside the Vilcanota River. The river flows north and merges with the Amazon River, then empties into the Atlantic Ocean. My balance on the rocking train was poor, but it was fun to stumble up and down the cars. I felt better after a cup of hot tea. I wondered what the time in Machu Picchu had opened up for me. Something happened there. How had my feeling that I'd been at Sacsayhuaman before been triggered at that particular curved stone stairway? What was I dreaming last night that made my sleep so fitful? What words would I say for the whale ear when I gave it to the lake?

The train climbed onto the *altiplano*'s high mesa, surrounded by still higher mountains. Llama herds scattered before the train's whistle. At La Raya, the continental divide at 14,172 feet, Gregg and I took pictures of each other with two little girls in colorful native dress, and their baby llama. After La Raya, the river flowed south, finding its way to the Pacific Ocean.

Winded by the slight exertion, I drank more coca tea and noted the effects of high altitude—slight headache, restless sleep, loose bowels, the need to focus on breathing. Gregg had adapted easily, and wasn't showing any of these symptoms.

At teatime we shared impressions of what we were seeing and experiencing. Gregg and I mostly noticed different things. One of his insights: "Incas worshipped the sun, and the royal staff had an ear of corn on top of it. Corn absorbs the sun when growing. The natives ingest it by eating and drinking, then plant corn seeds again. So the sun provides them with food and sustenance." I hadn't put it together that way, and appreciated that he had.

Lake Titicaca came into view at dusk—flat, with *totora* reed lining its edges. We would learn that the bottom part of *totora* reed is used for food, the top to build islands and boats.

The next morning we visited the lake at the top of the world, 12,500 feet. Blue ibis and black cormorants flew by. Squadrons of dragonflies buzzed over the water. Our launch motored by the remains of a large steel trawler. Gregg asked, "How did people get that up here?"

Our guide, Dulio, grinned. The guides liked it when we asked good questions. "Piece by piece," he answered, "by train. Then assembled here."

Our boat tied up at a small island and we climbed on. The sensation of walking on the slightly spongy island surface, which is wet only a couple of inches down, felt a little like walking on a trampoline. We sat on bales of *totora* reed for a presentation about the Islands of Uros. A kitten with black, white, and gray stripes emerged from a hut, rubbed against Gregg, and settled on my lap. I breathed deep of its purr, and realized how much I'd needed a cat fix. I sensed that Tyson had sent it, and thanked him and the kitten.

A sense of peace rests on the lake among the islands. I told Dulio I had a special stone as a gift to the lake, and asked him to show me the right place to give it. He directed the pilot of our launch to a lesser-used channel. I unwrapped the fossil whale ear and told Dulio that it had been prayed over to bring the ancient wisdom of whales as a gift to Mamacocha (Mother Lake) and Pachamama (Mother Earth). I said a prayer of thanks to the whale ear, and tossed it as far as I could. A circle of bubbles came up from the bottom where it landed. Ripples radiated out.

Exploring the city of Puno later, I found a wall carved with the symbols for Snake, Puma, Condor, and a woman's breast. These symbols are everywhere when one knows how to see.

The next morning, Dulio drove us to the Chullpas de Sillustani, circular stone burial towers built by pre-Inca peoples. At the top (12,800 feet), he showed us a circle of stones with its opening facing east—a ritual center, where shamans buried the hearts of black llamas as offerings. At the summit's base we came to a granite stone about five feet high, chiseled into the rough profile of Puma, with a circle of Snake carved into it. I asked Dulio about Condor.

He said, "This is a burial place, so it is concerned with burial, earth and the underworld. It's the province of Puma and Snake, so Condor is not represented here."

I commented to Gregg, "I'm starting to see faces and animals in every rock."

Our short flight to Arequipa passed El Misti, a smoking volcano that dominates the skyline. I remembered our flight on the visit to Lima when I was a child. We'd flocked to the airplane windows to see El Misti, excited because our little white spitz dog was named Misti too. The volcano had snow on it then; now it was brown, with a crown of cloud vapor.

We could see smog on our landing approach. At seventy-seven hundred feet, the air felt thicker. My body felt more comfortable at this altitude than it had at twelve thousand feet.

At the hotel we repacked our suitcases. We were both grateful to Rosalie. This trip had been an important pilgrimage for me, and Gregg had gotten a glimpse into a world that was significant to me. He'd gained deep admiration for Inca builders, for a part of the world that was new to him, and for how the people seemed to be slowly taking back their country. I was grateful for his way of looking at things, his photographer's eye for detail, and his broad baseline knowledge. He helped weave a fabric out of scattered pieces of information.

"One of the reasons I climbed Huayna Picchu was to show myself that I could," he said. I knew he was motivated by what he saw as declining strength, and his upcoming surgery.

"I'm glad. I feel like some kind of void I hadn't fully been aware of has been filled."

Back home, Alison had already delivered Sina to our house, where we had a joyous reunion. Tyson rubbed and purred, greeting us in his quiet way. I thanked him for his presence on our trip. His caregivers told us he was social during our absence, ate regularly if not much, and spent a lot of time in the family room listening to music. Our return marked the real beginning of my retirement phase. Tyson led the way, settling back into a comfortable pattern.

That night the dreams began, full of trapezoid-shaped stones, black pumas, barking plume-tailed dogs, rituals with shadowy shapes:

> *I journey with a group to an Inca site on a mountain. A circle of trapezoid-shaped stones stands on the grass, connected by a rope. One stone is rectangular and thicker than the others, with a hint of llama in relief on it. That one is for me. It stands in the center of the circle; it's part of this setting but doesn't have a fixed location.*

I knew I had been initiated into another level, another phase of my circle of life. Whatever that was, I said yes.

Surgery, Purrs, and Preparation

I am gray, halfway between here and there,
aware of diminishing power,
aware of expanding spirit;
the time is coming.
Stars of home shine brightly,
through the veil of this life.
I will be back, and ever with you.
I do so love being a cat.
— Tyson Cat

Gregg's surgery came less than a month after our return from Peru. It began with the long day of surgery prep, then the gauntlet of early-morning hospital admission. I sat beside his bed at Kaiser Hospital in Walnut Creek and clasped his hand while the medical staff ran final checks. "You'll be fine," I told him. "I'll be waiting."

He squeezed my hand. "I know."

Attendants pushed his gurney through the double swinging gray doors. They slapped shut like an exclamation point. The surgery would take about five hours, followed by another couple of hours in recovery.

I stood in the silent, empty hallway, suddenly feeling desolate.

The hospital's quiet meditation room, tucked into a corner on the ground floor, was deserted. I sat there for a long time, praying for Gregg; for the hands, hearts, and training of his surgical team; for the equipment and support staff; for our family and for Tyson, Buki, Paddy, and Sina; for our relationship and how it had changed over the years; for all the things we'd done together and would do in years to come. I asked that all Gregg's guardian angels and spirit guides be present to watch over him, that a cocoon of pearl-gold light and protection be around the operating room and hospital for his entire stay. I asked especially that his soul be guarded while his body was asleep, and that all be accomplished for Gregg's highest and best good. Suddenly I felt lighter and at peace.

I could have asked someone to wait with me. Several people offered, but I needed to be alone. I went for a walk and found handsome deciduous trees outside. I didn't know what kind they were, but appreciated their stately presence. Waiting, my mind returned to Peru and all that had happened. It had truly been the trip of a lifetime. Some days Peru seemed far away. Other days it folded into us and reminded us of the power of that experience.

I asked myself: How do our lives take shape now? How would we continue to grow? How do we give back? Neither of us wanted to rest on our accomplishments. Gregg volunteered many hours, largely at church, continuing as treasurer and the go-to fix-it guy for anything electronic. He helped with the Boy Scout troop and coordinated a weekly breakfast program for homeless people. I had committed to one morning a week as an animal caretaker at Sulphur Creek Nature Center, and to another nonprofit agency as cofacilitator of grief support groups for children who'd lost a parent. It was the start of a new way of life. I prayed that we engaged in it consciously, with forethought and intention.

Snake, Puma, and Condor crossed my mind. Puma, or Mountain Lion, with its message of courage, had been a totem for me since we lived in Colorado. In recent years I'd gained new appreciation for turkey vultures, our local close relative to Condor. As guardian of the mysteries, their message was of purification and new vision. My internal work seemed to be in Snake's domain, underground, working with my shadow and roots, with cycles of death, rebirth, and transformation.

After we returned from Peru I meditated with the dirt from Sacsayhuaman. In the meditation, I knew that place was holy ground. I had been there, on our trip and in an earlier lifetime. Knowing that I belong there, it was okay for me not to be there now. It remains a home where I'm deeply rooted. Whatever I was doing in that lifetime at Sacsayhuaman, it was an honor, and I was concerned about doing my job well. What vessel did I carry now?

My immediate purpose became clear: Learn to sit comfortably in the void. Listen, practice animal communication, and focus. My longer-term purpose: Come into my own power. Stand in my truth and spread it through writing and services with and for animals. I asked for sufficient abundance so that my ministry would be self-supporting, and not draw down resources carefully laid by for our retirement. I asked for help to grow into my full potential. I received assurance that I am supported in these things.

Intuition let me know when to go back into the hospital. Gregg was in the surgery recovery room, but I couldn't see him until he started to wake. I held his hand. Disoriented, he asked: "I'm awake?" He looked around, gathering impressions. "How long was I out?"

"It's been seven hours."

"Wow! Last thing I remember was lying on the table and someone said, 'We're starting the drip now.'"

I followed the attendants as they wheeled his gurney to the ward where he'd spend the night, and marveled at the care staff and their efficiency. The other patients—all men—lay in their beds, vulnerable and dependent on staff sworn to care for them.

In a few short months I would be in a similar state, weakened, dependent, and vulnerable from a food-borne intestinal bacterial infection acquired in Peru. Recovery would be slow. The infection would sap my energy and require that I ask for and accept help, as Gregg did now.

Serving as sentinel for the rest of the day, I kept Gregg supplied with ice cubes to suck on. He couldn't have anything solid to eat, but he told me later that he'd begged for coffee. The orderly asked if his stomach could handle it. Gregg's response: "My stomach will be fine. It's the rest of me you need to worry about if I don't get some coffee!"

Early the next morning I brought sweatpants and a loose shirt for Gregg to wear home. Under protest, he acquiesced to hospital rules and rode to the entrance in a wheelchair; the staff extended the footrests to fit his lanky frame.

At home, we settled the wounded warrior into his recliner— the same one Sina had ripped the arm fronts from when she first came to us. Sina and Tyson suffered in the ninety-nine degree heat, but for Gregg it was perfect. The surgeon said Gregg's outcome from the surgery was the best possible, and now he needed healing and recovery. He warned Gregg not to try to do too much too soon. At that moment it wasn't an issue.

The downstairs futon became Gregg's bed. Sina stayed near, sleeping in her crate at the foot of the futon. Tyson slept beside or under the bed, purring Gregg well. I added

Master Healer to Tyson's list of names. It took a couple of nights to work out logistics. Gregg needed light at night to check his tubing and drainage bag, so we left the bathroom light on and pulled the door nearly shut. When Tyson went in to use the litterbox, he pushed the door open and light flooded the room. A long string attached to the doorknob solved that problem, allowing Gregg to pull the door closed again after Tyson finished.

Tending to both Gregg and Tyson, I was acutely aware of their discomfort. We'd been feeding Tyson on top of our kitchen counter, with a stool to climb up, to keep Sina out of his food. Now he had difficulty getting up the stool, so I put his food on the floor and reinforced Sina's "Leave it" command.

Tyson came into the living room to sit near me. Holding him made him uncomfortable. I wiped him with a soft cold towel, hoping to give him some relief from the heat. He staggered a little, and sometimes walked into a room and seemed to forget why. Elderly humans do that too. He started listing to one side. He spent time out front after it cooled down in the evening. At bedtime, I held him gently for a while—two heartbeats, just being together.

Gregg complained of a knot and stiffness in his shoulder, probably from lying inverted at a slight angle for five hours during surgery. Daughter Gwen, now a certified corrective-exercise practitioner, came down for the day. She bustled in, fully professional, and massaged his shoulders, releasing the bunched muscles.

Gregg complained: "It feels like you're ripping them apart strand by strand!"

Gwen's strong hands kept working. She assured him he'd feel better when she finished. And he did. Gwen cleaned the downstairs and kitchen while she was at it, and left us both with instructions—exercises for Gregg and oils for me to massage into his shoulders.

Sean and his family came over and cooked a big meal for us, with enough leftovers to last a couple of days. I was grateful for all the support.

Two weeks after his surgery, Gregg was relieved when the doctor removed the catheter, but disappointed that his abdominal drainage tube had to remain. "I guess I'm just a juicy guy," he said, trying to make light of it. "I feel like a great weight that I've been carrying for six months has lifted." We bought Vietnamese sandwiches for lunch on the way home, a treat to celebrate more freedom.

He made his longest walk that afternoon, half a mile to the corner of a busy street by our neighborhood, to meet Sina and me coming back from our walk. His swift recovery was aided by the robotic-assisted surgery requiring a smaller incision than traditional surgery, his overall physical condition, and the combination of his determination and religious adherence to the exercise routine the doctor and Gwen prescribed.

June first brought the third anniversary of Sina's coming to us. At this point we could laugh about the devastation our "wild child" had created with office blinds, baby gates, fences, books, and Gregg's recliner. She'd calmed noticeably since our return from Peru. She stayed closer when walking and came back when called.

Released from his abdominal drainage tube, Gregg wanted to go to a classic car show at the county fairground that weekend. Sina and I dropped him off early at the front gates, and then she and I investigated dog parks in that area. We picked Gregg up at noon and stopped for lunch at a nearby outdoor café. Gregg's first serious outing. Sina was a model of good behavior, and earned dog cookies from the café proprietor.

The next day Gregg went to church for the first time since his surgery. He admitted not wanting to go while wearing the catheter or drainage tube. At home, he'd started making coffee in the morning again, for which I was grateful. He even made pasta and a salad for dinner while I was out walking Sina. I cautioned him about doing too much too soon, but he assured me he was pacing himself and felt fine. I knew that he needed to do these things for his own sanity. Gregg isn't one to sit around!

Tuesday morning I woke feeling happy. Gregg made his first trip back to the Tuesday morning homeless breakfast, and I went to my shift at Sulphur Creek.

My training there continued with cleaning rodent cages and feeding the ever-hungry baby birds. I learned to care for a variety of animals—barnyard chickens and ducks, a pocket gopher, big resident birds—and to help with the coyotes, foxes, and opossums. The first time I picked up an opossum I didn't expect him to be so heavy! Two red-shouldered hawks in rehabilitation needed to be fed live food, which distressed us all. A coworker chanted Buddhist prayers over the selected mice, and I followed with a blessing prayer. Chaplaincy is where it calls, and teachers come in many forms. Coyote wasn't done with me, and the two tawny, gold-eyed coyotes at Sulphur Creek had lessons to teach me.

Gregg and I enjoyed grocery shopping together, and lunch afterward. Then he exploded because he couldn't find the letter opener. I responded in anger. Later, I gave myself a flunk for not honoring his frustration at change. The letter opener wasn't important to me, but I needed to recognize that, with so much major change in his life, it was important to Gregg that little things remained constant. I apologized for not acknowledging his feelings, and we talked it through. That in itself was a great step in a new kind of communication for us.

A few days later we had one of those days that made me grateful to be alive. Hawks called as they soared past. Crows, songbirds, flowers, gentle breezes. Even Tyson went outside, which was rare these days. I thought: Tyson might decide to live forever; he just keeps going.

Tyson continued to split his time between me and Gregg. I remembered that daughter Gwen had presented him to Gregg as a Father's Day gift. Tyson and I had grown so close that I sometimes forgot he had a strong relationship with Gregg too. Gregg was recovering well from his surgery, but wasn't up to climbing stairs yet and continuing to sleep downstairs. Tyson spent most of the time either under the bed or beside him, purring at full volume. The vibration of cat purr is healing. Tyson, Master Healer, was purring Gregg back to wholeness.

Sina did her work on Gregg too. I came downstairs one morning to a quiet house. Sina had climbed up on Gregg's bed and stretched out beside him. They looked so sweet together. I climbed in on the other side, and noted how every movement is magnified on an air mattress.

A couple of weeks later Gregg went to church by himself. I stayed home, feeling the need to be outside. I startled a fawn on my way down the hill. Settled under a big eucalyptus tree on the slope behind our house, I felt quiet and peaceful. Birdsong surrounded me. A red-tail hawk soared above, circling, gaining altitude. Warm sun, a gentle breeze, leaves falling in a slow rain. I felt Buki's presence. She said: *I'm here.*

"You're working with Tyson?"

Yes, he's almost ready to cross. Just be there for him. He knows, and he doesn't need all the tuna. It's something he can taste, though. You're doing fine; just let yourself be.

"Thank you, Buki."

After he came home from church, Gregg walked all the way to park with us for the first time. That evening we worked on the photos from our trip to Peru. We were invited to Alison's house for dinner, and had promised to give a slide show and tell about our journey. It showed us again that we work well side by side, and reminded us of what an incredible adventure that trip had been. Hard to believe only two months earlier we'd been in Peru.

Father's Day came, the eighteenth anniversary of Tyson coming to live with us. I remembered that little gray ball of fluff. Now he sat by my side, venerable sage that he had become. How many iterations of himself had there been! Coming to us, his hostile reception by Paddy Paws, Gregg going to Colorado, then all of us moving there. When we returned to this house, Tyson remembered the trailing mouse-tail piece of insulation on the front door. Then Buki came, and Paddy died. After a time Buki died, then Sina came. And Tyson had been with us through it all. I thought of the photos of him through the years, and wanted to add them to his book. He was thin and a little wobbly. His single gold eye now had a tinge of green. I gently stroked him with a warm washcloth, freshened his catnip mouse, and gave him salmon treats.

I felt more than heard that Tyson liked the rhythm Gregg and I had settled into. Tyson twitched in his dreams. He'd resumed his practice of stretching across my lap, head on my arm, to doze in morning sunlight while I sipped my coffee. In my arms, sleeping, he twitched all over—ears, whiskers, paws—in pursuit of dream prey, reliving his life in another dimension. How comfortable he was in my arms to give himself over to such a deep sleep. I knew that one of the strongest qualities of our relationship, although we'd not talked about it, was the deep trust we'd developed. We had walked, hand in paw, from one stage of life to another, deepening along the way. I sent him mental thanks.

Tyson said: *The angels will come.*

"Angels?"

That's Cathy's word. Spirit beings to help me across. Buki is near. My mom cat is too, and my sisters and brothers. I'm the last of my litter.

"Are you ready?"

I don't like feeling this way. Gregg is okay; my work is mostly done. There's always more to do. You still need help, and so does Sina. I'd like to see Sina settle into a real partnership with you in your ministry. We'll all still be here to help you, though. You need cat energy in your house. I'll send you a cat when the time is right.

On Father's Day I thought of my father. I missed him, and the relationship I would have liked to have had with him. That evening I found, tucked into a half-read book, a copy of Mother's funeral program. I read the poem she'd written, and felt tenderness for her.

When I told Gregg, he said, "I thought about Dad this morning too." His face reflected his growing acceptance that he had done what he could.

The next day was quiet and peaceful. Sun shone through leaves of the liquid-amber tree outside our front window. I sat on the couch with Tyson beside me. He said: *I'll go on until I can't go anymore. I want to experience the fullness of departure. Death is what it is.* He added: *The veil between the worlds—a lot of them have fallen. Other realms are more visible now. That will help us have a more enriched relation-*

ship. Keep it alive by going to the temple. Daydream; write poems. I'm proud of you. Tyson affirmed that he and I were together at Sacsayhuaman. He said it felt like coming home. He added that Sina was from that part of the world, too. All of us were going home on that trip.

The next evening I heard Sina in the backyard, agitated. I went out with a flashlight and saw Tyson on our slope. He struggled to climb it, but I sensed he didn't want help. He made it to the top. I picked grass burrs from his fur. He took a few steps toward the house, and then sat. He was dusty; a clump of feces stuck to his fur. I dampened a paper towel and cleaned him gently. He walked to his litterbox. There he fell over, the side of his face in the sand. It broke my heart to see him stuck like that, and I helped him up. Then, exhausted, he curled up in the bookshelf cubby where I'd put a soft towel for him. I patted him and told him, "It's okay, I love you."

Summer solstice came. Tyson stretched beside the chair where I spent so much time. I cleared a crystal and personalized it for his highest good—whether to ease his discomfort, to help him transition easily, or to give him strength to carry on—and placed it beside him. We had entered the final watch. Tyson could barely walk. It was a struggle for him to get to his food bowl. He hadn't used his litterbox or urinated anywhere that I could tell since the previous night. I stroked him softly, told him I loved him, and thanked him for being my jaguar-shaman cat.

Temperatures soared into the high nineties again the next day. Gregg said Tyson had urinated on the front entry tile. He'd made it that far. He lay on the cool kitchen floor. Tyson seemed to want to be alone. After a little while, we heard him give a little kitten sort of meow. His back legs had collapsed. I carried him to his water and food bowls and propped him up, but he wasn't interested in either.

Then to his litterbox. He was able to use and step out of the box by himself, and moved to his shelf cubby. I helped him curl up in his little cave and sat nearby, petting him softly and talking with him. He seemed to enjoy that. His tail twitched, very much still functioning. I sang him songs, and made up one just for him to the tune of "Twinkle, Twinkle Little Star":

> *Tyson, Tyson, Pirate Cat,*
> *Master Teacher, Poet, Sage.*
> *Fearless Warrior, Hunter Bold,*
> *gray of evening, eye of gold.*
> *Jaguar Shaman, healing purr,*
> *ageless friendship; we are one.*

I was still working on it. Tyson said: *Good so far.* He came out later to say hello, then went back into his cave. I gave him eyedroppers of water. We went to bed, not knowing if Tyson would be alive in the morning. It was comforting to know Buki was near. I prayed his passing would be smooth. "Protect him, please."

Tyson's Cat Tales

Day is done, night is near,
softness comes, there is no fear.
Love is all, united we.
So much I see with eye of gold.
— Tyson Cat

Eighteen years and three days after the fuzzy ball of Tyson came to live with us, he walked, slow and stately, if unsteady, down the long carpeted hallway to the open front door. Tyson's pewter-gray fur hung loose on his bony body as he gingerly stepped over the threshold and onto the sisal welcome mat. He took one step down to the rock-textured sidewalk.

Gregg came back into the house with the Sunday newspapers. "Tyson went outside. He's lying in the flowerbed by the front door."

The time had come. Tyson lay on his right side on the earth, below a mock-orange bush. The liquid-amber tree a few feet away cast shadow on him. He wasn't moving. It had taken all his energy to make this walk.

I lowered myself to the sidewalk beside him. His breathing was steady. His rapid heartbeat made ripples of reflected morning sunlight on his fur. *Waiting for the angels.* The time had come for Tyson to die, the way he wanted to— in his own way, his own time, and his own place.

Gregg called from inside. "Are you going to church?"

"No, I'm staying with Tyson."

The sun rose higher. Shade from the mock-orange bush and the green-leafed liquid-amber tree moved, and I felt Tyson grow uncomfortably warm. I went into the house and returned with an umbrella, a glass of water, and an eyedropper. The open umbrella, wedged between bushes and held in place with a rock, gave Tyson shade from the increasing heat of the June sun. It won't bother the angels when they come for him, I thought.

Tyson seemed glad for the water I dripped into his mouth. He didn't move, except for an occasional flip of the tip of his tail.

We sat together for another hour. I told him how much I loved him, how much I treasured his walking with me, hand in paw, through our years together. He had gently and not so gently guided me to my own path, even before I remembered how to communicate with animals. "Is there anything I can do for you, Tyson?"

Just stay with me.

I could do that.

I thought of the nearly ninety pages of "Tyson's Cat Tales" I'd scribed for him. I went back into the house, and returned with the binder of typed pages. Tyson lay on the earth and I sat near him, leaning against the rough stucco of the house, while I read his book out loud. I felt more than heard his pleasure that I'd been able to record so much. In one of his poems he had said:

> *When the leaving time has come,*
> *I will go with grace and dignity,*
> *welcoming the transition to light-filled spirit*
> *and new adventures, unfettered by body.*

He had shared wisdom, poetry, pointed one-liners, stories, and thoughts on living and dying. His words needed to go out into the world. It was the Wisdom of Tyson—Poet, Pirate Cat, and Master Teacher. Perhaps sharing his wisdom could be my gift to him. Later I would hear from him that my story, and our journey together, needed to be included too.

Gregg came home from church, hungry and needing coffee. I gave Tyson more water, and went inside to make sandwiches and start coffee while Gregg changed out of his suit. Gwen called. I answered her question and then said, "I have to go, Gwen. Tyson's dying, and I want to sit with him." I hadn't said the words *Tyson's dying* before.

I hurried back outside. I'd been inside for half an hour.

Tyson had moved so that he now rested on his left side, his head toward the house. He looked too still. I placed my hand on him, and felt no heartbeat. His long tail was limp. Then I saw the ants, already invading a body left behind when the angels came for his spirit.

Tyson was dead. His last words to me had been: *Stay with me.* I hadn't even done that. At the end, after all we'd been through together, I'd let him down. I hadn't been there for his final moments, I hadn't seen his brave heart beat its last, I didn't see him take his last breath or let it go; I didn't sense when his spirit left his frail body. Crushing regret folded around me, adding weight to the expanding blackness of loss and grief that enveloped me. "I'm so sorry, Tyson. Please forgive me for not staying with you."

I knelt on the rocks, my tears mixing with water from the glass as I cleaned him. I carried him inside and sat in the chair where I'd scribed so many of our conversations, cradling him in my arms as I cried into his fur for the last time.

Sina walked over, sniffed Tyson's body, and returned to her place on the rug.

Eyes glistening, Gregg wordlessly handed me Tyson's favorite baby blanket to wrap him in, and sat with me. I asked if he wanted to hold Tyson, and he did. Gregg carefully closed Tyson's eye.

Later, I called Cathy. She relayed that Tyson said it was okay that I hadn't been with him for his final moments. Buki's spirit was there, and I'd been there for the long haul. He told her to tell Gregg and me that he loves us very much, and thanked us for supporting him in dying as he wanted, on his own terms, lying outside on the earth as a true wild animal. Still, I couldn't forgive myself. I'd let him down.

That afternoon Gregg dug a grave on top of Buki's deep grave. We buried Tyson where his spirit could watch the passage of seasons and wildlife. Gifts buried with him honored his many selves: several toy mice, an open can of tuna as food for the afterlife, a sage bundle to honor his shaman-teacher self, a lit votive candle to light his way, and red roses. We read to him from his tales and prayed over him, steeped in sadness. We covered him with the dark earth and placed rocks over his grave to protect and mark it. The grave now grows wild grasses and holds a collection of special stones—including one from Tyson's creek in Boulder. Our valiant warrior had passed from this life into what comes next. The rest of his work will be done in spirit.

Gregg and I sat in silence by Tyson's and Buki's grave. My hand rested on the packed earth. Then I saw in my mind's eye a picture of Tyson as a kitten—feisty, exploring himself and his world, climbing the schefflera tree that first day, chasing the mouse-tail strip of insulation that had trailed the front door. Images of his life cascaded. Each time I focused on how Tyson looked at the end of his life, he sent me a picture of himself as a kitten, or in his prime. Always, though, the image had only one gold eye.

A Parting Glass

So much noise this two-footed makes,
walking on twigs and dry leaves.
I hear the birds laughing.
The patient trees stand quiet.
— N.S.

Gregg and I grieved the loss of Tyson's furry self and strong purr, even knowing he was present in spirit. We had buried Tyson's toys with him. We kept his collar, but I had nothing soft to hold in remembrance of him. He answered my need. I felt a nudge to look behind our dresser, and found a hidden fur-wrapped toy hamster he had chewed almost beyond recognition.

The day after Tyson's funeral I sat by his grave, said prayers, and gave thanks, and again asked his forgiveness for not being there in his last moments. I sensed his reassurance that he felt supported and knew I loved him. I still felt badly about it, though. Perhaps it was my need to be there, more than his. I felt a desolate aloneness, the shroud of grief blocking out the murmurs of my animal chorus. Birdsong sounded only like . . . birdsong.

Gwen had made me a bundle of sage with blossoms that was just right to burn for Tyson, since Gwen had brought him to us. For nearly two weeks, until it had all turned to smoke and ashes, I sat for an hour or two each day by his grave, holding the burning sage. Sometimes I sang to him and prayed, but mostly I just sat there. Some days I brought rose petals to scatter on his grave. I thought about all the elements present—earth of course, air in the bird feather I'd added and my breath blowing on the sage, fire in the smoldering sage, ether in Tyson's spirit and the rising smoke, and water beside me to pour over the embers. This daily ritual helped me slowly part the folds of the dark shroud and let in the beginnings of peace.

During a meditation in July, sitting in my rocking chair, I journeyed to Tyson's and my temple. He was there, changing into all his feline forms—one-eyed lion, puma, jaguar, housecat. We sat on the temple steps side by side, watching the sunset. I felt reassured that he was still with me. I remembered the poem I'd received in Boulder, the first time he'd given me words:

> Tyson, Tyson, gray as night,
> Eyes of lion, golden bright.

When Tyson said We are one, it was for real. He is part of me, and has been for a long time. He rode on my shoulder in Peru, and looked out of my eyes. I have walked in his paws. I wondered if that was partly why I seemed to be recovering from grief fairly quickly? I held my feelings close, and thought about him pretty much all the time. Spirit said yes to all of this.

When I passed the place where Tyson died, it pulled at my heart. That spot is now holy, having been blessed by his departing spirit, by Buki in spirit waiting there with him, and by the angels who came to take him away.

Sina needed reassurance, direction, and exercise. She kept us moving. One afternoon I trailed behind Gregg and Sina as we walked in the canyon. I reached out to connect with Buki, Tyson, Paddy, Hendrix, and Sina. Even though Hendrix hadn't known Buki or Tyson, he was part of my teaching group. It was his death that spurred Gwen to bring us Tyson. Hendrix was pleased to be included. For the first time since Tyson died, I was able to connect with the animals. I thanked them each for the gifts and lessons they taught me, and apologized for the times I didn't understand. Hendrix was love. Paddy, compassion. Buki, my wolf-bear shaman, and part of me. Tyson, Poet, Sage, Pirate Cat, Master Teacher, and also forever part of me. Sina and I talked about her stepping up to help in my ministry.

I'm not ready, she said.

"I'm not either," I replied. "We can get there together." She liked that.

A few days later when I called Sina into the house for the evening, I sensed Tyson coming through the sliding-glass door to the backyard as I closed it. I thought that at least now he could walk through doors. I heard him say: *I always could.* It gladdened my heart to hear him the way I used to. He reaffirmed that on a deep level I know he is with me. Thank you, Tyson, although I do miss your furry, purring self!

He said: *And I miss being held.*

I thought of all the lessons in caring and letting go that Tyson and my other animal companions had taught me. Tyson responded: *Don't make me more than I am.*

In September, sitting comfortably in the *between* place, I had conversations with Tyson and Buki. Sina wanted to be included too. It felt good to sit with these companions. They said I have the skills to do animal-communication readings but need to keep practicing. Tyson said to talk to the birds and trees and rocks. *Go deeper; get past surface impressions.*

In another meditation weeks later, I wrestled with uncertainty, unready to step forward on the path of animal chaplaincy and communication. I greeted White Buffalo as guardian of the North on the Medicine Wheel. He said: *You are strong on your path. Don't waver! We have accelerated you, as time is short. No one is ever ready. You will learn as you go. Call on us.*

Buki came forward. *You're doing well, my dear. Don't be afraid, I will watch over you. No negative thoughts—only positive ones and strength and moving forward.*

Then Tyson gave me the great blessing of showing me the moment of his death: His shimmering, pure-white translucent light body emerging from his fur body. Buki was nearby, also translucent, helping and welcoming, as were two bluish spirit beings with wings—Tyson's angels. All rose through the leaves of the liquid-amber tree into the sun. I wept with gratitude, knowing I couldn't have seen this vision with my earthly eyes.

Tyson said: *I'm proud of you; just keep going. I'm here. Get busy on my book!* I felt upheld, loved, guided, and protected as I gave thanks and brought the meditation to a close.

At Thanksgiving, our first major family holiday since Tyson's death, I thought of Tyson in his sanctuary and asked him to help me stay centered and grounded in the midst of the activity. He said yes, and reminded me that last year when everyone was here, he'd gone downstairs and stayed in the middle of it all, to say goodbye. I was glad I could again hear his one-liners.

Still weak from my intestinal bacterial infection and the resultant rapid weight loss, I didn't have the strength or energy to do more than dress the turkey and put it in the oven. The rest of the family took over—Gregg the gravy master, with Gwen and Allen, and Sean and Elizabeth, providing fresh bread and an array of vegetables and desserts. I spent most of the day sitting on the floor playing board games with a rotating set of grandchildren. The voices and sounds and scents from the kitchen brought joy to my heart. I didn't need to be in charge.

After our extended family had left, sitting quietly with my cup of tea, I sensed Tyson in my arms and snuggled him. Going into the kitchen later, I felt surrounded by furishness, and knew Tyson and my animal and spirit guides were all around me. I felt held and loved.

My commitment to myself was to draft the text for my new website before the end of the year—putting myself out into the world as an animal communicator and animal chaplain. But I was stuck. I asked for help. Tyson said the words were forming, and they would come when ready. A couple of weeks later, I received specific instructions.

Sina: *Say how much you love animals and regard us as beings with messages of our own. We have jobs to do and need to grow ourselves as well as help you.*

Buki: *Add a quote from one of the animals. People like that. Use fewer words.*

Tyson: *Explain what you do, and how it's the bridge between our worlds. You tend to think of us as wiser than people. Don't fall into that trap. The cycles of development apply to all life forms. It doesn't all need to be included, just enough to get the message across.*

Scrub jay: *Tell them our animal voices are talking to you all the time.*

White Buffalo: *We are all one. You worry too much. That blocks the flow. Just let it come.*

Mid-January, six months after Tyson's death, we received a special gift. I pulled the mail from the mailbox. On top was the Winter 2009 issue of *Species Link* magazine, a journal published by Penelope Smith for animal communicators, with three of Tyson's and my poems on the back cover! I wept tears of joy, and could feel Tyson's pleasure. It was solid validation for us. Congratulations, Tyson, and thanks to Cathy for sending our work to Penelope!

Tyson said: *I don't need validation the way you do; I just want to get the word out.*

Tyson continues to make his presence known. He particularly likes it when I study faith traditions and animal communication. Tyson said he will be with me until I get his book written. After that, he will come and go, but part of him will always live in my heart. I grow more accepting of the absence of his physical self, and more aware of his continuing presence in spirit as a guide and teacher.

A tough student I have been—reluctant, doubting and fearful, looking for answers from outside when they can come only from inside. Although I still tremble in insecurity at times, my feet are firm on this path that, like a labyrinth, asks only that I stay on it. I have chosen this path, and it has chosen me. Which came first doesn't matter.

Afterword:
Winter Solstice 2012

The first peace, which is the most important,
is that which comes within souls of people
when they realize their relationship, their oneness,
with the universe and all its powers, and . . .
that at the center of the universe dwells the Great
Spirit, and that this center is really everywhere,
it is within each of us.

— *Black Elk*

The four and a half years since Tyson left his furry body and emerged in spirit form have marked my journey through the void. The great bear of the West has nurtured and sheltered me during this turning of the wheel of my life, and the writing of Tyson's and my book—this book. Tyson in spirit has stayed by my side, prodding me to keep writing. We completed the first full draft of our book on Winter Solstice 2012, when the Winter Circle of stars was again in the sky.

I felt Tyson's presence beside me at a women's retreat when I introduced myself as an animal communicator and gave readings, describing the other women's animals and relaying the animals' messages to their people. Tyson, Buki, and my animal chorus encouraged my further studies in animal communication and animal Reiki. They cheered when I listened to the call to help others through their grief, and earned certification as a pet-loss bereavement counselor.

When questions and doubts plague me, I turn to the animals. In one such meditation, Tyson asked: *Why aren't you working on my book?*

"It's hard to settle."

Tyson sent me to talk with the dolphins. I heard their clicking, felt bubbles, and sensed the dolphins' joy. "I feel so off-track."

Oh no, they replied. *You're doing well. Vibration is what counts. You are vibrating our message. Your website is like a temple. You can minister from there. Just remember that we are always with you. Guiding you, swimming in your energy, whether you are aware of it or not.* The dolphins told me to ask Whale more about the fossil whale ear.

I called Whale, heard humpback-whale song, and repeated my questions and concerns.

Whale said: *The fossil carries ancient energy of our kind, memories, a record of life on earth. It has deep energy, from below the ocean. Your questions are in your heart. The better the question, the better the answer. Just focus and be. Decide each moment what is important in that moment. If it is sleep, do that. Don't let your reactions to others dictate your own actions. The life you have chosen is one that makes you strive for balance. You can't just isolate yourself and write, nor can you spend all your time at the beck and call of others. Create the balance!*

"Thank you. I was afraid that in being slow with the book I had let you down."

Let us down? That concept does not apply. To be let down requires expectation. There is no expectation! There is only journey and growth, giving and love. We journey together in wholeness. All that you do serves the whole. There is no timeline. What will be will be.

"Thank you." Thus guided, I was steeped in gratitude.

These four years have led me through deep work of the Tree of Life in Kabbalah, greater understanding of the Medicine Wheel, and how they apply to life every day. I've learned—slowly—to quiet my spinning mind, to sit and *just be.* My faith in the All That Is deepens, although the expression of it continues to evolve. Animals and beings in nature speak to me daily, often reminding me to be still and listen. The animals at Sulphur Creek Nature Center, where I continue to volunteer, urge me to finish this book so I can tell their stories. My ministry grows and expresses itself in ways both expected and unexpected, including writing.

Sina, more settled as a mature dog, still radiates Coyote spirit, fire and air energy, and a strong prey drive. She keeps us alert and ensures that no other cat will come to us on her watch. Family protection extended only to Tyson. Sina devotes herself to her mission—getting Gregg and me to lighten up, find joy in little things, and play, together and with her. Along the way, she has earned the Canine Good Citizen certificate—the first step to becoming a therapy dog. *Lighten up,* she says. *It's all only a game that you take too seriously.*

Gregg and I seesaw our way to balance. Each of us gives and receives, walking our individual and joint paths in an ongoing process.

That seesaw extends to our family. Each of our children has grown into a remarkable adult with his or her own talents, strengths, and challenges. Sean understands computer systems as a network of microscopic relationships not unlike those found in nature, and is a talented photographer. Gwen expresses her healing nature through teaching Pilates, yoga, and therapeutic exercise, and nurturing a flock of animals and children. Jeff speaks the language of computer databases and financial systems, and composes and plays bass-guitar music.

Each of our seven grandchildren is a unique individual. They show us different ways to approach life and steer us through the languages of youth. They help us learn when to speak and when to stay silent, when to act and when to stay out of the way.

The world shifts into a new era. Tyson beckons and pushes as I step into the next phase of my work. It's time to fulfill my promise to him to share his wisdom, messages shared by other animals, and some of what I've learned through this journey. I'm grateful for the love, support, and abundance that push and pull me ever forward on this journey.

As Tyson said, it's all about trust. Trust in Tyson, trust in Gregg, trust in the All That Is, trust in my internal truth. And so it is.

Acknowledgments

This book has come to life with the help of many teachers, guides and supporters, to whom I give thanks.

My writing teachers—Tania Casselle, Phaedra Greenwood, and Sean Murphy—encouraged while pointing out this or that would be stronger or clearer if I tweaked it thus. Their patience and skill are much appreciated.

Members of my online writing group—Peete Baer, Katherine Reynolds, and especially Christine Kalimurti—read sections and offered insightful comments.

Karen Baldwin, fellow Chaplaincy student and colleague, encouraged me through the years of writing this book with "Hey, you're making great progress!"

Special thanks to Alison Lewis and my daughter, Gwen Miller. Alison's insightful reading and commentary on the full first draft (all six hundred pages!) and later drafts helped me ferret out threads and weave them into a coherent story. Gwen's attention to detail caught inconsistencies and the things spell-check missed.

My editor, Nancy Carleton, helped chip away extraneous commentary to strengthen the story underneath and brought order to my punctuation and other inconsistencies. Her suggestion to move our poetry into chapter heading epigraphs was pure genius.

Thanks to Nikki Ragsdale and my son, Sean Schluntz. Nikki's creativity, technical ability, and patience resulted in a beautiful cover. Sean's photographic skill and generosity of time and talent produced a portfolio of author photos.

The intuitive insight and encouragement of my animal-communication teachers—principally Cathy Currea, Teresa

Wagner, and Marta Williams—helped quiet my doubts as I deepened into intuitive interspecies communication. Animal-communication buddies—Karen (Kay) Panico, Karen Burke, Renee Gallegos, and Barbara Martin—provided consistent affirmation that I do hear what I hear from the animals.

Gratitude to teachers and students of the Chaplaincy Institute. ChI provided the container for profound opening, gave me a framework and vocabulary for spiritual growth, and encouraged my path to animal chaplaincy.

Thanks to the teachers who have helped me dive deep and integrate the lessons from this period: Jane deCuir, Miriam Moussaioff, Megan Wagner, and Jim Larkin. Jane, with a twinkle in her eyes, kept the drumbeat as I made my way through the West of the Medicine Wheel. Miriam's insightful intuition and energy work coaching helped me clear cobwebs and put it all together. Megan and Jim, teachers and founders of the West Coast Kabbalah School, guided me through the Tree of Life as a workable model for personal and spiritual development.

The nonprofit human services agency where I worked provided a living laboratory for much of the internal growth described here. I've changed the name of the city and agency to protect the privacy of staff, volunteers, and clients. I'm privileged to have served there.

Special thanks to my family, especially my husband, Gregg, who sometimes questioned, sometimes poked, but who has been steadfast and strong, kept an even keel, and stood un-failingly by my side.

Deep gratitude to the animals who so freely shared insights about living and dying. "They sound bossy," one reader said. Yes, for this author often needs it! Thanks too to the animals who are and have been part of my life, especially Tyson, Buki, Paddy Paws, and Sina, who have gently and not so gently guided me along this path, and who are the real heroes of this book.

About the Author

Nancy Schluntz is an intuitive animal communicator, animal Reiki practitioner, and interfaith minister with certificates in spiritual psychology and pet-loss bereavement counseling. Nancy dedicates her practice to helping human and animal family members enrich their relationships, and provides spiritual guidance through life transitions. A teacher and public speaker, Nancy is author of numerous articles and essays. She lives in Northern California with her husband and dog, near their children and grandchildren. You can contact Nancy or read her blog, with wisdom from animals, nature, and world religions, at:

www.NancySchluntz.com.

The display type in *Hand in Paw* was set in Theano Didot.
The text is Bookman Old Style.

Made in the USA
San Bernardino, CA
10 August 2014